"Reading this book has been an invaluable opportunity to learn from Douglas Flemons. That opportunity is now yours."
—*Jeffrey Zeig, Ph.D., Director, The Milton H. Erickson Foundation*

"Flemons's wonderful book invites clients to 'think, feel, and act in poems that dissolve boundaries . . . .' Flemons's casework is interesting and effective. He is patient, modest, and inventive with people, or, as he would say, 'metaphorical and experimental.' The book includes clear concepts, apt and literate citations, and a keen knowledge of music, movement, and meditation. Essential reading for everyone utilizing hypnotic relatedness in therapy."
—*Eric Greenleaf, Ph.D., Director, The Milton H. Erickson Institute of the Bay Area, author of The Problem of Evil: Ancient Dilemmas and Modern Therapy*

"Douglas Flemons invites the reader to join him in a fascinating journey to explore the vast potential of the collaborative and synergistic hypnotist–participant relationship to create personal transformation. Along the way, he provides valuable instruction and insights regarding not only the nitty-gritty about how to conduct hypnotherapy, but also key facets of consciousness itself. I hope this engaging book, written with flair and verve, and chock-full of examples and case illustrations, scripts, and nuggets of clinical wisdom, finds the wide audience that it deserves."
—*Steven Jay Lynn, Ph.D., ABPP, Distinguished Professor, Binghamton University (SUNY), Director, Laboratory of Consciousness, Cognition, and Psychopathology*

THE HEART AND MIND OF HYPNOTHERAPY

THE HEART AND MIND OF HYPNOTHERAPY

Inviting Connection, Inventing Change

DOUGLAS FLEMONS

FOREWORD BY MICHAEL D. YAPKO

W. W. NORTON & COMPANY
Independent Publishers Since 1923

Excerpt(s) from KNOTS by R. D. Laing, copyright © 1970 by R. D. Laing. Used by permission of Pantheon Books, an imprint of the Knopf Doubleday Publishing Group, a division of Penguin Random House LLC. All rights reserved.

Knots, R. D. Laing, Copyright © 1970. Reproduced by permission of Taylor & Francis Group. Reproduced with permission of the Licensor through PLSclear.

Billy Collins, excerpt from "Introduction to Poetry" from *The Apple That Astonished Paris*. Copyright © 1988, 1996 by Billy Collins. Reprinted with the permission of The Permissions Company, LLC on behalf of the University of Arkansas Press, www.uapress.com.

For information about permission to reproduce selections from this book, write to Permissions, W. W. Norton & Company, Inc., 500 Fifth Avenue, New York, NY 10110

For information about special discounts for bulk purchases, please contact W. W. Norton Special Sales at specialsales@wwnorton.com or 800-233-4830

Manufacturing by Lake Book Manufacturing, Inc.
Production manager: Katelyn MacKenzie

ISBN: 978-0-393-71439-5

W. W. Norton & Company, Inc., 500 Fifth Avenue, New York, N.Y. 10110
www.wwnorton.com

W. W. Norton & Company Ltd., 15 Carlisle Street, London W1D 3BS

1 2 3 4 5 6 7 8 9 0

ALSO BY DOUGLAS FLEMONS

Completing Distinctions

Of One Mind: The Logic of Hypnosis, The Practice of Therapy

Writing Between the Lines

Relational Suicide Assessment (coauthor, with Leonard Gralnik)

Quickies: The Handbook of Brief Sex Therapy
(coeditor, with Shelley Green)

for

Shelley, Eric, Jenna, Amber, and Ward
Judy, Jane, Mog, Rachel, Isabel, Laurie, Herb, and Sandra—

transmuting absence into presence,
loss into beauty

I am doing it
the it I am doing is
the I that is doing it
the I that is doing it is
the it I am doing
it is doing the I that am doing it
I am being done by the it I am doing
it is doing it

—R. D. LAING (1970, p. 84)

The pronoun *I* is the name that most of us put to the sense that we are the thinkers of our thoughts and experiencers of our experience. It is the sense that we have of possessing (rather than of merely being) a continuum of experience.

—SAM HARRIS (2014, p. 91)

Le coeur a ses raisons que la raison ne connaît point.
The heart has its reasons of which the reason knows nothing.

—BLAISE PASCAL

I would like to talk about our zazen [sitting meditation] posture. When you sit in the full lotus position, your left foot is on your right thigh, and your right foot is on your left thigh. . . . They have become one. The position expresses the oneness of duality: not two, and not one. This is the most important teaching: not two, and not one.

—SHUNRYU SUZUKI (2006, p. 7)

The silence hissed in her ears and her vision was faintly distorted— her hands in her lap appeared unusually large and at the same time remote, as though viewed across an immense distance. She raised one hand and flexed its fingers and wondered, as she had sometimes before, how this thing, this machine for gripping, this fleshy spider on the end of her arm, came to be hers, entirely at her command. Or did it have some little life of its own? She bent her finger and straightened it. The mystery was in the instant before it moved, the dividing moment between not moving and moving, when her intention took effect. It was like a wave breaking. If she could only find herself at the crest, she thought, she might find the secret of herself, that part of her that was really in charge. . . . When she did crook it finally, the action seemed to start in the finger itself.

—IAN McEWAN (2001, pp. 33–34)

To understand how suggestions given in situations labeled as *hypnosis* can change bodily structures and functions, it is necessary to view hypnosis in a new way.

—T. X. BARBER (1984, p. 69)

CONTENTS

ACKNOWLEDGMENTS

Hypnosis is best understood as a shared-mind phenomenon, but so is writing about it. Working on this book afforded me the opportunity to share my mind with a broad assortment of remarkable people. I'm deeply grateful to all of them, and you should be, too, because they are stitched into every page, every sentence. You'll find in the reference list the writers who've most shaped my thinking and understanding, but then there are those people who not only shared their ideas but also offered love, friendship, knowledge, and support for me and my work:

My wife and co-adventurer, Shelley Green, read, encouraged, advised, and teased. Our kids, Eric and Jenna, have always kept me on my toes, always made me laugh. As adults, they inspire me with their knowledge, wisdom, and fearlessness. And now Amber has danced her way into our hearts. Eric also provided excellent guidance on Alexander the Great.

My brother Ward stood by and with me every step of the past few years. As Shelley is fond of saying, we are the same person. My brother Tom died just as I was about to start writing, so I didn't get the benefit of his eye, but his commitment to heretical inquiry and creative invention served as a North Star.

Nora Bateson not only told me the story, in Puebla, Mexico, of how she lost her desire for cigarettes but also gave me permission to tell it.

Sandra Roscoe brought her meditation and hypnosis expertise into her close reading of every chapter.

Steve Alford offered helpful comments on early drafts of Chapter 1, shared his own scribblings about related ideas, and sent me relevant articles and books. He also provided a German-translation consultation. Suzanne Ferriss helped me with a French coinage.

The first draft of the first chapter of the book was written during a six-month sabbatical from my teaching gig at Nova Southeastern University. Martha Marquez and Honggang Yang made it possible. My graduate assistant, Cindy Penalva, painstakingly transcribed talks and researched sources. Another graduate assistant, Fonda Mosal, scanned documents and facilitated and organized AI transcriptions of talks and lectures.

Students at the university and participants in my workshops challenged me to explain myself more clearly and to demonstrate and share—to embody—what I had in mind.

Jordan Harris interviewed me several times over the past few years; his probing questions helped me articulate ideas I didn't know I had. Eric Greenleaf and Maria Pia Allende offered me many opportunities to give idea-generating talks and courses in Latin America. Eric and his wife, Lori, also read early drafts of most chapters and offered incisive responses and warm friendship.

Judith Leemann brought her artist's eye and sensibility—and cultural sensitivity—to the reading of emerging drafts, as did Mog Hesthammer and Chris Welsby.

Many other wonderful people kept me on track with their support and/or comments on drafts: Robin Akdeniz, Alexandra Alfaro, Vanessa Bibliowitz, Erik and Trudy Bieck, Toni Bissonnette, Greg Blom, Art Bochner, Judy Brown, Cassie Cacace, Karon Carpenter, Jimena Castro, Laurie Charlés, Brittany Davis, Carolyn Ellis, Stefano Fanfoni, Yael Haklai, Mike and Cindy Jones, Valerie Judd, Martha Laughlin, Victoria Lazareva, Camillo Loriedo, Caitlin Lowry, Stuart McGeough, Rob McNeilly, Michael O'Neill, David Optekar, Emerson Optekar, Marsha Pierre, Michael Pirich, David Prentice, Carlos Ramos, Suzanne Rouleau, Dawn Shelton, Jennifer Sneeden, Kathee Todtman, Kate Warner, Kristin Wright, and Jeff Zeig.

Michael Yapko, from whom I've learned much, agreed to write the foreword long before I had anything to send him to read. I'm warmed by his confidence in me and inspired by his scholarship, clear thinking, and writing.

Deborah Malmud, my longtime editor at Norton, once again

found that magical balance between full-on trust and a discerning commitment to clarity. She and her wonderful team, including Kevin Olsen, Mariah Eppes, Kelly Auricchio, and Sara McBride Tuohy, helped in countless ways to get this book into your hands. Sarah Johnson, copyeditor extraordinaire, found and corrected my errors and cleared up my textual confusions.

My clients and demonstration volunteers shared their minds, their stories, and their hearts with me. I am honored and enlivened by their courage, creativity, and grace.

FOREWORD

When a panel of leading experts in the field of hypnosis was challenged to form a definition of hypnosis that would likely gain a large measure of consensus by knowledgeable colleagues, they ultimately settled on this definition: "A state of consciousness involving focused attention and reduced peripheral awareness characterized by an enhanced capacity for response to suggestion" (Elkins et al., 2015, p. 6). This definition conveys the unambiguous suggestion that hypnotic responsiveness is an entirely intrapersonal phenomenon, i.e., an indicator of some innate ability pre-existing within individuals that makes it possible for them to respond to suggestions given to them in this undefined "state of consciousness."

The panel's definition says nothing about the contextual factors that might influence one's responses, omitting any reference at all to something as foundational to successful hypnosis such as the quality of the relationship between the clinician and client. This is a glaring omission that is puzzling given that clinicians are typically heavily invested in co-creating a meaningful therapeutic relationship that can give rise to hypnotic responsiveness. *How* to do that, though, has received far too little attention in the literature— until now.

The Heart and Mind of Hypnotherapy is a most welcome and valuable contribution to the field of clinical hypnosis. It helps fill a large void in the hypnosis literature that has been perpetuated by the obsolete view that hypnosis is something that only occurs within the individual. Douglas Flemons is a highly respected hypnosis expert recognized for his depth of knowledge and multidimensional considerations of applied hypnosis. Through this wonderful book, Flemons offers clinicians a far more comprehensive and realistic array of invaluable insights into the essence of the hypnotic relationship. By carefully and convincingly defining hypnosis as an interpersonal phenomenon and providing ways to integrate that essential perspective, he elevates hypnosis to a higher level, allowing it to become something much richer and far more meaningful than mere technique.

Flemons is clear and articulate in describing the "shared-mind attunement" or "connected knowing" that he describes as core elements of successful hypnosis. His emphasis on the quality of the relationship between clinician and client is unwavering throughout the book and is most compelling. When he insightfully says, "hypnosis unfolds in the mutuality, the synergy, of the relationship between hypnotist and client," he draws our attention to the importance of that vital relationship. What makes for particularly inspiring reading, though, is how Flemons is able to provide both the perspectives and the language to make the "shared mind" a practical reality in clinical practice.

Flemons takes care in the early sections to highlight the complex relationships between mind, brain, and body and how hypnosis can serve to bridge the gaps between them. His articulation of "embodied minds and mindful bodies" literally demands readers to think and *act* in multidimensional yet integrative terms. Throughout the book, Flemons offers numerous engaging personal and professional anecdotes that illustrate well the points he makes, particularly about the ways people get into self-limiting "knots" that require novel interventions that can be provided both in and out of hypnosis.

When discussing the overlaps of hypnosis and mindfulness and when sharing case details, Flemons goes a step further and invites the reader to *experience* some of what he's describing. His emphasis on *inviting* the client into hypnosis rather than merely performing an induction is not only modeled in his many case examples, but also in his treatment of the reader. *You're invited, too!* Flemons thus creates the possibility of a meaningful relationship with you, offering ideas for good hypnotherapy with respect and a gentle touch. There's a lot to be learned from studying his case examples, his samples of the language he uses even when not using hypnosis in a formal or direct way, and even from the way he invites the reader to be an active collaborator in the process of "inventing change."

A recurring theme throughout the book is the emphasis Flemons places on the value of curiosity. While Socrates is credited with the maxim, "Curiosity is the beginning of wisdom," Flemons makes this observation clinically relevant. He describes empathy as "a commitment to proactive and projective curiosity," a unique and insightful perspective that is wonderfully rich with therapeutic possibilities.

Curiosity is a catalyst for explorations, whether in the world around you or the one within you, and curiosity gives rise to the extraordinary discoveries these explorations often yield. Curiosity drives people past their fear into the greater desire to know the unknown, and it is a pathway for finding the unexpected. When the unexpected discoveries clients make are of personal strengths and resources that had previously been either entirely unknown to them or simply dormant within them, the context of hypnosis can be dramatically empowering for them. When Flemons shares his ways of actively and curiously wondering aloud to his clients about their experience and where the boundaries of their distress are that can be self-adjusted, he defines his clients as most worthy of his careful attention. He further provides a powerful reminder that some of the greatest strengths of hypnosis are found in its redefining experiences of all sorts as malleable. His emphases on connection and malleability represent both the heart and the mind of hypnotically based psychotherapy. In the process, Flemons' own heart and mind are shared openly and are offered as gifts to the reader. His benevolent and generous invitation to form a meaningful collaboration and explore malleability is simply too good to refuse.

Where Flemons particularly excels is in the many ways he amplifies the familiar notion of "utilization" in hypnosis and stretches it in directions previously underexplored. He describes the parallels with meditation by characterizing the therapeutic gains to be made when *en*countering one's stressors rather than the all-too-common strategy of trying to counter them. His case examples are truly inspiring in this regard and will no doubt resonate with readers who recognize the importance of acceptance as a vital precursor to therapeutic change. Effective utilization is an art and Flemons shares his artistic talents generously.

The Heart and Mind of Hypnotherapy is a wonderfully original contribution that builds on the work of some of the most important theorists and practitioners the field of hypnosis has produced. With this important book, Flemons takes his place alongside them, having given us a whole new way of reaffirming the value of applied hypnosis and, especially, the value of the hypnotic relationship.

Michael D. Yapko, Ph.D.
www.yapko.com

REFERENCE

Elkins, G. R., Barabasz, A. F., Council, J. R., & Spiegel, D. (2015). Advancing research and practice: The revised APA Division 30 definition of hypnosis. *International Journal of Clinical and Experimental Hypnosis, 63,* 1–9. doi:10.10 80/00207144.2014.961870

PREFACE

The word *hypnosis* (from the Greek *hypno*, "sleep") is something of a misnomer, given that "hypnosis is *not* sleep" (Yapko, 2019, p. 31). James Braid had second thoughts about the coinage soon after coming up with it in the 1840s, but his do-over suggestion, *monoideism*, never caught on. Although it captures nicely the concentrated nature of hypnotic experience (from the Latin *mono*, "one" + *idea*, "idea": one idea), the word doesn't exactly roll off the tongue: too many syllables, perhaps, for a word meant to evoke a singularity of focus.

Braid would have had more success in capturing the flavor of what happens in hypnosis (and perhaps would have managed to head off some of the subsequent theoretical muddle in the field) had he maintained the pronunciation of the word but changed its spelling to *hipgnosis*.[*] Of course, he could only have come up with this rendering by anachronistically channeling Kerouac and other Beat writers of the 1950s and grafting their word *hip*[†] ("in the know, cool, sophisticated") onto *gnosis* (from the Greek *gnōsis*, "knowledge"), which Plato used to refer specifically to sensory-derived know-how (Jim Smeal, personal communication, April 29, 2008). The result would have been a term imbued with overtones of "sophisticated embodied knowing" or "cool experiential awareness": definitely an upgrade from the current *hypno*-inspired undertones of "sleepy-time knowing" or "nodding-off awareness."

Adopting *hipgnosis* for use throughout the book would allow for

---

[*] I originally wrote about this in *Family Therapy Magazine* (Flemons, 2008, p. 17).
[†] Beat writers popularized the word but didn't invent it. Its first use predates them by half a century.

the happy coupling of an evocative etymology and accurate phe-
nomenology; however, I suspect that bumping into it again and
again would quickly become annoying. Committed to intriguing,
not irritating, you, I will also not, mercifully enough, repeatedly
subject you to the word *hipgnotherapy*. You're welcome. But I have a
favor to ask in return. Well, more of a suggestion, really. Each time
you encounter the term *hypnosis* or *hypnotherapy* in the forthcoming
pages, automatically hallucinate—for purposes of epistemological
clarity—its Kerouac-and-Plato-inspired doppelgänger.

Even my use of the conventionally spelled term *hypnotherapy* is
bound to get on the nerves—perhaps even hit a raw one—of some
readers. Shortly after the publication in 2002 of my first book on
hypnosis and therapy, *Of One Mind*, I was invited to give a public
talk about it at a local bookstore. One of the people in the audience
criticized me for talking about hypnotherapy; he argued that the
word misleadingly implies there is something inherently therapeutic about hypnosis. Curiously, he didn't have a problem with the
term *psychotherapy*, even though there is nothing inherently therapeutic about the psyche. Nevertheless, the man was not alone in
his reservations. Considering hypnosis "an adjunct to emerging and
well-established psychotherapies" (Green et al., 2014, p. 203), not a
stand-alone treatment, many experts in the field frown on its use
(e.g., Frischholz, 1997). As Orne et al. (1995) opined, "Hypnosis is
a technique, not a psychotherapy" (p. 1812). Weitzenhoffer (1957)
said something similar: "The main role of hypnosis in psychotherapy is to facilitate and enhance the therapeutic process, while at the
same time remaining within the bounds of the particular therapeutic setting in question."

This dividing line between psychotherapeutic approach and
technique seems clear and straightforward, but it isn't as distinct
or simple as it first appears. Kirsch noted that "hypnosis can be
thought of as an analogue of psychotherapy" (2017, p. 683) or as
"psychotherapy in miniature" (1990, p. 181). For example, hypnosis

> begins with the establishment of rapport, proceeds to an assess-
> ment of the individual's beliefs and expectations, continues with
> the presentation of a rationale that corrects misconceptions, and

utilizes individually tailored and flexibly administered rituals for producing changes in experience and behavior. (Kirsch,
1990, p. 181)

The correspondence between hypnosis and psychotherapy is not
just a coincidence. Those who conceptualize hypnosis simply as
an add-on technique, to be accessed as needed, miss the degree to
which the history and current practices of psychotherapy are thoroughly entangled with the phenomenon and logic of hypnosis.

After studying hypnosis with two prominent neurologists and
hypnosis researchers in France—Jean-Martin Charcot and Hip-
polyte Bernheim—Freud originally accorded it a central role in his
psychotherapeutic method (Pintar & Lynn, 2008, p. 87). Indeed,
"hypnotherapy and psychotherapy at that historical moment were
virtually synonymous" (Pintar, 2010, p. 36). Freud later officially
distanced himself from hypnosis, but he, "we know, derived the
concepts of resistance and transference from his hypnotic experiences" (Greenleaf, 2001, p. 93), and his focus on catharsis was "not
so removed from the crisis invoked by Mesmer more than a century
before" (Pintar & Lynn, 2008, p. 87). These hypnosis-informed elements from Freud's work continue to shape the therapeutic assumptions and choices of contemporary clinicians.

More recently, Milton Erickson, notable for his research and clinical explorations of hypnosis, developed an approach to psychotherapy (Geary & Zeig, 2001; Haley, 1973; Short et al., 2005) that
sometimes, but not always, involved hypnosis. He "used formal
hypnosis in only a fifth of the cases he treated (Beahrs, 1971), but he
consistently used hypnotic technique even when he was not 'doing
hypnosis'" (Zeig, 1985, p. 5). Indeed, he "embedded hypnosis so
deeply into his psychotherapeutic techniques that it is possible in
looking at Ericksonian psychotherapy to forget it is there at all"
(Pintar & Lynn, 2008, p. 115).

The approach to hypnotherapy I develop in this book does not
lean on or draw from an established psychotherapeutic school or
model. Rather, it derives from an understanding of how minds
and bodies interact, learn, and change, as well as from how practices and rituals of connection, such as meditation and hypnosis,

facilitate the fluidity and present-moment availability necessary for a change in experience, and thus a change in problems, to unfold.

I'd been meditating for a few years—both sitting and moving (tai chi) varieties—when, early on in a master's program in counseling psychology, I took my first workshop in hypnotherapy. I found the overlap between meditation and hypnosis intriguing, if confusing, and as I've continued practicing all three approaches to bridging the mind-body gap, I've used each to probe and deepen my appreciation and understanding of the other two. This book reflects the results of an inter-tradition dialogue that I've been stirring and swirling inside of for 40 years.

In Chapter 1, I introduce ideas and research findings that help make sense of how brains, bodies, and minds think and communicate. An understanding of the inner workings of perception and language makes it possible to question commonly held assumptions about the circumscribed nature of the self and to explore what happens to our self-conscious awareness when we become creatively absorbed in the flow of meaningful activity. Hypnosis is often misunderstood as a state of consciousness unilaterally imposed by the therapist. This chapter makes clear that it is, in fact, a collaboratively composed relationship, an instance of shared-mind attunement.

Chapter 2 takes a close look at the practices of meditation and self-hypnosis, highlighting similarities and divergences. Both share a commitment to engaging with, rather than fighting against, afflictions that confound and trouble us. Rather than attempting to *counter* disturbances, which can unintentionally create spiraling patterns of suffering, practitioners in both traditions find ways to *en*counter them instead. To give you an experiential grasp of how to nondivisively respond to disruptions, I walk you through the logic of, and a few methods for, inviting a generative mind-body connection.

Hypnotherapy is a method for dissolving or dissipating problems, made possible by the close connection between therapist and client. In Chapter 3, I explore how empathy forges this connection. I clarify that empathy isn't a receptive emotion like sympathy but, rather, a commitment to proactive and projective curiosity. Empathically communicating with clients helps you to shift from being scrutinized as an outside expert to being accepted as an inside con-sultant. What you say and how you say it helps clients to trust that you aren't just claiming to understand what they're going through. Through empathic communication, you earn their trust, allowing them to relax the boundaries keeping them distinct from you and from their own experience. In so doing, you establish the necessary interpersonal connection for the invitation of hypnosis.

Chapter 4 poses and answers the question, "When does hyp-nosis transition into hypno*therapy*?" It isn't incorrect to mark the shift as the point at which the therapist begins to make therapeutic use of clients' hypnotic responsiveness. However, a more complete answer comes into focus when you recognize that you begin formu-lating hypnotherapeutic possibilities right from the outset of your contact with clients. Long before you formally invite hypnosis and initiate some kind of shift in a problem, you are establishing the context for this to happen, taking into account clients' commitment; their understandings and expectations; their fears, reluctance, and desires; and their anticipations and expectations. And you're also scoping out clients' skills and resources that can be applied to the process. Often this entails operating at the experiential level of symptomatic description rather than the abstract level of labels and diagnoses, orienting to change not as a phenomenon of curing but, rather, as one of learning.

In Chapter 5, I focus on the *invitation* of hypnosis. I prefer this term to the more standard *induction*, as it underscores the collab-orative nature of the process. You don't *hypnotize* your clients; you and they cooperate in getting in sync and in exploring possibilities for avolitional—nonpurposive, effortless—shifts in their experi-ence. You support and enhance this cooperation through what Mil-ton Erickson called *utilization*—an orientation to practice that takes potential or actual distractions from, or threats to, the process and reconstitutes them as contributions.

As I make clear in Chapter 6, hypnotherapy takes the shared-mind, flow-based experience of hypnosis and directs it toward the altering of clients' afflictions. You invite clients to let go of their exhausting and often fearful efforts to ignore, evade, contain, con-trol, or obliterate their problem, and, together, you get curious about it instead. This curiosity doesn't take the form of an exasperated "Why?!" but, rather, an immersed wondering and extemporaneous tracing of when and how the problem appears and becomes accentuated, when and how it shape-shifts, and when and how it goes missing or becomes attenuated. Curiosity is only the beginning of a reorientation toward connecting with the problem, which, within the context of that changed relationship, offers opportunities for inventing—both discovering and creating—ways for the problem to alter its patterned expression.

This book goes to the heart of hypnotherapy, in both senses of the word. It illuminates core principles and practices of hypnosis and their application to therapeutic change, *and* it does its best to convey the *beating* heart of this way of working—the use of empathy, the *invitation* of hypnosis, and the *facilitation* of therapeutic change. Woven throughout is a deep respect for and appreciation of the mindfulness of the body and the embodiment of mind, both intra- and interpersonally. This sensibility informs not just the explication but also several experiential demonstrations of the approach. I hope you're able to *incorporate* (from the Latin *in-*, "into" + *corpus*, "body": to unite into one body) a feel for and grasp of hypnosis into your practice and into your bones.

AUTHOR'S NOTE

In the stories depicted in the following chapters, I have changed names and identifying details. I have also, at times, created client descriptions and presented case transcripts that are composites of different people and different conversations. Nevertheless, I have not surgically enhanced any of the depictions or therapeutic results.

THE HEART AND
MIND OF
HYPNOTHERAPY

MIND, BODY, SELF*

*The royal road to solving the mind-body problem involve[s]
unraveling the mystery of hypnosis.*

—T. X. Barber (1984, p. 77)

*All distinctions are mind, by mind, in mind, of mind
No distinctions no mind to distinguish*

—R. D. Laing (1970, p. 82)

*Consciousness is nothing more than the splitting of Reality into
this and that. Consciousness is making distinctions and drawing
lines. That is set off "over there," and you're set off "over here."
Consciousness divides what is otherwise the direct experience of a
seamless Whole into the world of multiplicity.*

—Steve Hagen (1997, p. 140)

My friend Nora started smoking cigarettes when she was a teenager, typically a pack a day, and she continued the habit through her
20s, up until the moment she found out she was pregnant. Committed to protecting the health of her developing baby, she immediately quit cold turkey, but the withdrawal effects and the desire to
smoke didn't abate. She *craved* a smoke. Agitated and exhausted by
her battle with the nagging urge that accompanied her everywhere,
she met her mother, Lois, for lunch and told her of her struggles and
waning willpower.

Nora expected to hear commiseration and perhaps a pep talk

---

* This chapter is derived in part from Flemons (2020).

from a woman who herself was a smoker. But that's not what happened. Instead, Lois cheerfully said, "Nora, don't be so hard on yourself! Go ahead and smoke! You've got enough to deal with! I continued smoking *all through* my pregnancy with you, and you turned out okay, didn't you? Five fingers, five toes? God knows you *deserve* a cigarette!"

Nora was shocked and deeply offended by her mother's encouragement. This was the first she had heard not only that Lois had not stopped smoking during her pregnancy with Nora but also that she had not even cared to try! Nonplussed, Nora got up to leave. Her craving didn't accompany her. From that moment on, she was relieved of any desire, any urge, to smoke, and it never returned, not even after her daughter was born. Nora told me this story 16 years after it happened, and she was still effortlessly smoke- and nicotine-free.

Lois wasn't a hypnotist, and her response to her daughter wasn't intentionally offered as a therapeutically strategic or paradoxical intervention (Loriedo & Vella, 1992). Nevertheless, Nora's transformative experience shares the hallmarks of hypnotherapeutic change, as well as some of the conditions of a hypnotic relationship. This is *not* to say that Nora lost her desire to smoke because Lois somehow "naturalistically hypnotized" her. Such an invocation of hypnosis as a theoretical deus ex machina would offer nothing but conceptual muddle. Committed to clarity, I'd like to develop some ideas that will help make sense of what went on in the relationship between Lois and Nora, as well as between Nora's mind and body, that made it possible for Nora's craving to effortlessly—avolitionally—dissolve.

The key notions I'll be developing draw from the work of Nora's dad, actually, the transdisciplinary systems theorist Gregory Bateson (1991, 2000, 2002; Bateson & Bateson, 2005). He died a decade or so before his wife and daughter had the conversation I just recounted,* so he never weighed in on what transpired. Bateson is perhaps best described as an epistemologist, not within the field

---

* His ideas live on and continue to influence the fields of cybernetics, ecology, family therapy, brief therapy, communication, organizational development, and qualitative research.

of philosophy but, rather, biology (1991, p. 231). He defined episte-mology as a meta-science "whose subject matter is . . . mind in the widest sense of the word" (2002, pp. 81–82). And because the epis-temological investigation of mind is also itself within the realm of mind, epistemology can also be understood as "that science whose subject matter is itself" (1991, p. 231). Dizzy yet? Hang on. Or bet-ter yet, spin along with me. Bateson devoted much of his career to researching and theorizing about the self-referential and multilevel nature of mind, focusing on phenomena and ideas such as play, learning, difference, paradox, addiction, adaptation, information, classification, and metacommunication. All have significantly con-tributed to and enhanced my understanding and practice of hypno-sis and hypnotherapy.[*]

Bateson's ideas have particular relevance to the field of hypnosis, in part because of his various associations with the psychiatrist and hypnotherapy innovator Milton Erickson,[†] who will also be hov-ering in the background, and sometimes the foreground, of these pages. But mostly they're relevant because they beautifully explicate the nature of mind, and you can't grasp how hypnosis and hypno-therapy work without having in hand a sense of how minds and bodies perceive, conceive, learn, communicate, and change.

A heads-up: Like everything having to do with hypnosis, the tra-jectory of this chapter will demonstrate that sometimes the most efficient way of moving forward is to take a step or two sideways.

---

[*] I'm not the first hypnosis theorist or clinician to draw on Bateson's ideas (e.g., see Fourie, 1991; Gilligan, 1987; Haley, 1968; Lankton, 2004; Matthews, 1985; Wilk, 1985), and this isn't the first time I've relied on them when writing about therapy (e.g., Flemons, 1991) and hypnosis (e.g., Flemons, 2002).

[†] In 1942, Bateson, Erickson, and Margaret Mead (Bateson's wife at the time) were active participants in the first Macy Conference on "Cerebral Inhibition," which was devoted to exploring the topic of hypnosis. Bateson and Mead later reached out to Erick-son and his wife, Betty, to help them analyze ritual trance behavior among the Balinese dancers they had filmed in the 1930s (see "Trance and Dance in Bali," available on YouTube). Also, from 1952 to 1962, Bateson led a small team of researchers—Jay Haley, John Weakland, Don Jackson, and William Fry—in an investigation of paradox and associated peculiarities of communication, including play, learning, humor, schizo-phrenia, and hypnosis. Haley proposed that they examine the work of Milton Erick-son, one result of which was Haley's "interactional explanation" of hypnosis (Haley, 1968). Bateson himself made only passing reference to hypnosis in his writings (e.g., in Bateson et al., 1956).

Juxtaposition is better suited than linear exposition to the challenge of charting the recursive, layered nature of mind and phenomena such as hypnosis. Depth of understanding can emerge from side-by-side consideration of contrasting sources of information, whether ideas, practices, stories, art forms, disciplines, or traditions. What follows is a weaving together of relevant scientific, clinical, artistic, contemplative, and philosophical insights about brains, bodies, and minds (e.g., Barrett, 2020; Bateson, 2000; Siegel, 2012). Let's start by taking a look at the notion of difference.

DIFFERENCE

Difference, according to Bateson, is the fundamental unit of information. Indeed, he defined information as "news of difference" (2002, p. 64). A difference is a *relationship* between two some-things (say, between a foreground object and the wall behind it, or between a good idea and a bad idea), or between the same something at two different times (for example, between you at ages 8 and 18). Contrary to what we commonly believe, we don't perceive things. What a "sensory end organ responds to is a *difference* or a *change*" (p. 89), and this "perception of difference is limited by threshold. Differences that are too slight or too slowly presented are not perceivable" (p. 27). If a difference is to become information, if it is to be known and acted upon, it has to be both discernible and notable. In other words, it has to be a "difference that makes a difference" (p. 212).

For Bateson, "the word 'idea,' in its most elementary sense, is synonymous with 'difference' " (1991, p. 459). We presume that we perceive and think and talk in terms of "things," but, actually, things are abstracted from differences or distinctions. Mind is woven of *relationships*: "Objects are unobservable. Only relationships among objects are observable" (McLuhan, 1967, p. 260).

If everything exists (from the Latin *ex-*, "out of, from" + *sistere*, "cause to stand": to stand out) only in relationship, then difference itself needs to be understood in relation to what *it* isn't. This brings us to *in*difference.

INDIFFERENCE

When my son, Eric, was 3, my in-laws, visiting from Texas, looked after him for several days while my wife (and Eric's mother), Shelley, and I were at work. One afternoon when we got home, Eric excitedly told us that he'd gone to Wendy's for a Frosty. We asked his grandparents how far they'd had to drive to find the place. They looked at us like we'd lost our minds. "We drove to the top of your street, turned right, and there it was." We'd been living in our neighborhood since before Eric was born, and neither of us knew about the fast-food burger joint just around the corner. We passed by it every day, but, as vegetarians, we'd had no interest in it, so it didn't make it onto our radar.

Something may be potentially discernible—say, a stand-alone building with a big picture of a red-headed girl out front—but if you're indifferent to it, it won't emerge from the background and thus won't carry news of difference. It won't become information, and you'll remain oblivious. The same thing happens to you if you wear glasses: The vast majority of the time, you don't feel them on your face and don't notice the rims in your peripheral vision.

Sometimes, indifference develops in a relationship or activity that has previously meant something to you. You fall out of touch with a friend, lose interest in a book or television show, neglect to renew your gym membership. Someone or something stops mattering to you. This movement, from differences that make a difference to differences that no longer make a difference, is of particular relevance to the practice of hypnotherapy. But before getting there, let's consider a few non-therapy examples of this sort of shift.

Only upon moving into that first house of ours did Shelley and I realize that we'd failed to account for how close we would be living to a railroad crossing. Nor had we realized the round-the-clock frequency of the trains or the fact that every one of them would be loudly broadcasting a warning that it was approaching the crossing. Our ignorance and naivete were blasted to smithereens every few hours the first night, and again, right on schedule, the second. But by the third, the regularity, the predictability, of the warning blasts was working in our favor. We were pleasantly surprised to discover that we had started accommodating to them, and before long, no longer carrying news of difference, they stopped disturbing our sleep.

In "Ali Baba and the Forty Thieves," one of the stories in the Middle Eastern folktale collection *One Thousand and One Nights*, a thief discreetly marks the door to Ali Baba's house with chalk so that he can return to the neighborhood later that night with his compatriots, locate the designated house in the dark, and kill the inhabitants in their sleep. A creatively resourceful young woman, Morgiana, sees the thief make his mark. Suspecting trouble, she puts the same chalk symbol on the doors of two or three houses on either side of Ali Baba's. When the thieves return, they can't determine which house belongs to their desired victim, so their plans are foiled (Lang, 2013). A real-life version of this story happened during WWII when the Nazis issued an order in Denmark

> to the effect that all Jews had to wear the yellow Star of David armband. . . . The king [announced] that there were no differences between one Dane and another, that the German decree therefore applied to all Danes, and that he would be the first to wear the Star of David. The population overwhelmingly followed the king's example, and the Germans were forced to cancel their order. (Watzlawick et al., 1974, p. 107)

All these examples have in common the *indifferentiation* of differences, which results in the imperception of boundaries, the absence or loss of information, and/or the dissolution of meaning.

Psychotherapists and hypnotherapists are often tasked with helping people to similarly become indifferent to something disturbing that has been making too much of a difference—a source of pain, a substance or activity to which they're addicted, an object or setting that triggers panic, a thought or dream that haunts them, a person they can't leave or can't not remember. Clients end up in our offices because they have discovered how impossible it is to purposefully engineer indifference. Efforts to ignore, to forget, to not care: All ironically serve to further inscribe the defining borders of whatever people try to reject. A different approach is required, one that makes it possible for problems to dissolve or slip away. This is where hypnosis comes in.

To recognize the relational knots that bind people, and to invent hypnotherapeutic ways to release them (see Chapter 6), it helps to understand something about paradox, which in turn requires a grasp of communication and context.

PARADOX, COMMUNICATION, AND CONTEXT

Paradox has a way of inevitably—and often, invisibly—infiltrating experience and communication (e.g., Bateson, 2000, p. 193). Let's say you and I are in a relationship and you get sick of my being so passively agreeable, so damn compliant. You insist that I stop doing what I'm told and think for myself: If I accede to your directive to stop being obedient, then any defiance I muster will be tainted by my doing what I was told. I'll be able to truly defy you only by refusing your demand that I do so, which will require me to defiantly remain obedient. I can either obediently defy you or be defiantly obedient. Either way, we remain caught in a paradoxical tangle that Watzlawick et al. (1967) called a *Be spontaneous!* paradox. Let's look at a real-world example.

My daughter, Jenna, attended a Catholic high school with a strict honor code. Swearing was prohibited, deference to teachers and administrators was required, and so on. In 10th grade she took social studies from a firebrand teacher named Mr. Hanson. I don't know whether he was wanting to make a point or was simply attempting to jolt the class out of its early-morning slumber, but one day he singled out Jenna, probably the most respectful student in the school, and, apropos of nothing, demanded that she call him a "douchebag." She refused.

MR. HANSON: I insist. Call me a douchebag.
JENNA: I'm not going to do that.
H: I demand you call me a douchebag.

J: The school says I'm not allowed to swear.

H: And the school says you must respect your teachers.

J: Exactly.

Jenna was caught in what Bateson called a *double bind*, a communicational paradox. If she were to follow the school's honor code by complying with her teacher's demand, she would be breaking the code by hurling an insult at him. But if she adhered to the code's insistence that she not swear at anyone, especially a teacher, she would be breaking it by defying her teacher's assigned task. Either response put her in the wrong.

The complexity of Jenna's dilemma can be further appreciated by taking into account the competing contexts within which she was caught. Her teacher was claiming that the rules of his classroom, set by him, overrode the rules of the school, set down in the honor code, even though he and his classroom were part of the school and even though he was referencing the honor code to establish his authority for requiring her compliance.

H: I'm your teacher, and I'm telling you to call me a douchebag. If you refuse, you're being disobedient and thus disrespectful.

J: It would be disrespectful to call you that.

Often when people find themselves in such binds, they freeze up or twist and turn, trying to extricate themselves.

H: Call me what?

J: What you're insisting I call you.

H: A douchebag?

J: Yes.

But there is no easy escape from a double bind. It is structured rather like a Möbius strip, so the way out takes you back in. Release from the defining rules (expectations, demands, requirements) of the context required a response that shifted the tone from tortured deference to delighted defiance.

H: Call me that!

J: Okay! {said with gusto and humor} You're such a fucking douchebag! {Mr. Hanson laughs; the class, now very much awake, cheers}

Fed up with her teacher's needling, Jenna's exclamation extricated her from the constraints of Mr. Hanson's demand for compliance and her own failed attempts not to break any rules. She catapulted herself out of her no-win efforts by embracing the freedom of enlivened self-expression. Fuck the fucking honor code!

Jenna's liberation was generated by way of what Bateson called *metacommunication*—communication *about* communication. The humor in her eyes and the animation in her voice were metamessages that classified the words she uttered, making it possible for her to clearly convey that she was not merely doing what she was told. Her metacommunication transported her from a helpless victim to a self-defining contributor in the interaction.

Metacommunication contextualizes communication, thereby determining its meaning. Information always only makes sense in context. Imagine a wife saying to her husband, "I love you." The husband's understanding of her statement—the meaning he makes of it—will be tempered or modified by any number of metamessages accompanying it—a sigh, an accusing or pleading tone, a tear or furrowed brow. And its meaning will be further shaped by the complexities of the couple's historical, situational, and interactive context—whether they've just enjoyed making love or just had an argument; whether he's just announced that he wants a divorce or he's asked if she hates him; whether she's just told him that she's pregnant or she's revealed that she's having an affair; whether this is the first time she's ever said this to him or she's only ever murmured it when drunk. And so on.

Bateson offered the metaphor of a picture frame as a way of characterizing this defining nature of context (e.g., 2000, pp. 177–193): "The picture frame is an instruction to the viewer that he should not extend the premises which obtain between the figures within the picture to the wallpaper behind it" (p. 189). The framing of a communicational interaction works similarly. You foreground and group together certain information, and you attribute a particular meaning to what you discern to be a pattern. For example, a client, alert to her racing heart, nausea, and tight chest, will likely group these sensations together, framing them as a harbinger of a fast-approaching panic attack. Later, in a hypnosis session with you, noticing that her arms feel too heavy to move, that she can't feel her hands, and that the room is starting to spin, she might similarly frame these perceptions as concerning symptoms of anxiety, rather than reassuring indicators of hypnotic experience.

The client, of course, wouldn't say she is actively engaged in *framing*; from her perspective, she is merely passively perceiving and *recognizing* what is tangible and seemingly true about her experience. Like most of us most of the time, she commits what Bateson would describe as an error of logical typing or what Whitehead (1925/1953) would call an instance of "misplaced concreteness": mistaking a categorical grouping of body responses—a framing of them—as if it were itself one of the items within the frame, that is, as if it were itself a body response: "My heart was racing, I thought I was going to throw up, I couldn't catch a breath, and I was all pan-icky." In Chapter 4, I talk about how, for hypnotherapy, it works best most of the time to work with the items within a frame—the partic-ularities and sensory details of experience—rather than the catego-rization (that is, a diagnosis or a label) of them. And then in Chapter 6, I address how the meaning of an experience can be altered by reframing it, by recontextualizing it (Watzlawick et al., 1974).

Bateson (2000) recognized that the use of the metaphor of a pic-ture frame for talking about context is problematic, as it "is exces-sively concrete" (p. 187). It obscures the degree to which context is woven of the same fabric as whatever it is contextualizing. It too is information, just at a more abstract or encompassing level—a dif-ferentiated pattern of differences, a whole that is inclusive of the parts that combine to compose it. Thus, information *about* context—the naming of and thus the meaning given to it, for example—gets reintroduced into the communicational flow, contributing to the experience of whatever is unfolding.

When your client contextualizes her body sensations as signifiers of a coming panic attack, the sensations become what Bateson called *context markers* (2000, pp. 289–290); that is, they point to the context the client is using to define them, to give them meaning. This meaning gets caught up in the spiraling that produces the anticipated panic and crystallizes for the client what seems to be objective evidence that she was right all along: Just as she feared, the panic, once started, had a mind of its own. She fearfully and hopelessly concludes that it couldn't have been controlled or stopped. In Chapters 4 and 6, I explain in greater detail the cycling involved in situations such as this, and I describe what can be done to facilitate its slowing down, dissipating, or reversing direction. Such changes inevitably involve a shift in context markers, in what they signify, and/or in how they enter the self-referential cycling that gives rise to what happens. And in Chapter 5, I illuminate the various important ways context marking comes into play in classifying hypnotic experience *as* hypnosis.

We're continually contextualizing our experience. We react, adapt to, and make sense of our experience by framing it, by categorizing it. Hypnotherapy can be helpful precisely because meaning is so implicated in perception—really, to a startling degree.

PERCEPTION AND THOUGHT

The process of perception seems so straightforward, doesn't it? Some physical stimulus tickles this or that sense organ, which translates it into an electrical signal that heads to the brain, where it is then recognized for what it is. Right? Yeah, not so much. As the cybernetician Heinz von Foerster said, "There are no 'pure facts.' A fact is interpreted from the moment of its observation" (Segal, 2001, p. 22). This recognition is echoed in Dowling's (2018) observation that

> our visual system constructs images based not only on incoming sensory information but also on experience. What we see depends very much on our expectations—what we have seen

before—as well as on the information coming from our reti-
nas. . . . Visual perception is reconstructive and creative. (p. 261)

Such full-press participation in the active formation of what we
take to be passive perception is true beyond our visual system.
According to the neuroscientist Lisa Feldman Barrett (2020), "your
day-to-day experience is a carefully controlled hallucination" (p. 71).

Scientists are now fairly certain that your brain actually begins
to sense the moment-to-moment changes in the world around
you *before* those light waves, chemicals, and other sense data hit
your brain. The same is true for moment-to-moment changes in
your body—your brain begins to sense them before the relevant
data arrives from your organs, hormones, and various bodily
systems. (p. 71)

Our brains are continually fleshing things out, filling in gaps, finding patterns in noise, predicting what will come next:

Your brain issues predictions and checks them against the
sense data coming from the world and your body. . . . If your
brain has predicted well, then your neurons are *already firing*
in a pattern that matches the incoming sense data. This means
[that] . . . sense data itself has no further use beyond confirming
your brain's predictions. What you see, hear, smell, and taste in
the world and feel in your body in that moment are *completely
constructed*. (pp. 74–75)

Ted Kaptchuk would concur: "Our bodies are not only receptors
of information. . . . We *create* the information" (my italics; quoted in
Marchant, 2016, p. 254). A recognition of this proclivity for the creative construction of perception helps to account for the effects of
placebos—"substances that are administered in the guise of active
drugs but that do not in fact have the pharmacological properties
attributed to them" (Kirsch, 1985, p. 1189). Placebo effects are those
changes in a person's physical and/or psychological functioning
that correspond not to the "active ingredient" in a treatment but,

rather, to the person's expectations of and beliefs about the treatment. Moerman (2002), considering the degree to which "meaning can activate biological processes" (p. 151), believes that the best explanation for the "placebo effect" is what he calls the "meaning response." Barrett (2020) offers an explanation for why "mere words" can influence body processes so profoundly:

> Why do the words you encounter have such wide-ranging effects inside you? Because many brain regions that process language also control the insides of your body, including major organs and systems. . . . These brain regions, which are contained in what scientists call the "language network," guide your heart rate up and down. They adjust the glucose entering your bloodstream to fuel your cells. They change the flow of chemicals that support your immune system. The power of words is not a metaphor. It's in your brain wiring. (p. 89)

Bateson and Bateson (2005) explain the phenomenon in terms of the mindfulness of the body:

> The efficacy of placebos is a proof that human life, human healing and suffering, belong to the world of mental process, in which differences—ideas, information, even absences—can be causes. . . . The most conspicuous techniques of healing by visualization now being developed . . . invite the patient to invent his or her own placebo. (pp. 65–66)

Clearly, experiencing, thinking, and language are inextricably interwoven, connecting mind and body. If this weren't the case, hypnosis and hypnotherapeutic change wouldn't exist.

EMBODIED MINDS AND MINDFUL BODIES

Descartes is famous for his dualistic formulations. He was the inventor of Cartesian graphs, with their perpendicular x and y axes, and he proclaimed that mind is fundamentally separate from the body—that the body does not think and that mental operations have no need for it. He says in "Meditation VI," written in 1641,

> Because . . . I have a clear and distinct idea of myself . . . as . . . a thinking and unextended thing, and . . . I possess a distinct idea of body, inasmuch as it is only an extended and unthinking thing, it is certain that this I . . . is entirely and absolutely distinct from my body, and can exist without it. (1641/1911, p. 28)

Descartes's contributions to mathematics were enormously helpful; his contributions to epistemology, misguided and misguiding. We now know how wrong he was. Kittens have to physically move through their environment to develop normal perceptual skills (Held & Hein, 1963), and physical engagement and movement are integral to humans' cognitive development. "Babies learn about the world by physically exploring it" (Beilock, 2015, p. 232), and

> physical activities can help children learn to read and solve problems. Printing letters helps jump-start areas of the brain needed for reading. Piano practice can enhance finger dexterity, counting competence, and math skills. . . . How we move can aid how we think. (Beilock, 2015, p. 233)

Brain and body are, in fact, interdependent:

> Body-brain communication goes both ways, from body to brain and in reverse. . . . The body-to-brain signals, neural and chemical, permit the brain to create and maintain a multimedia documentary on the body, and allow the body to alert the brain to important changes occurring in its structure and state. . . . The brain-to-body signals, on the other hand, neural as well as chemical, consist of commands to change the body. The body tells the brain: this is how I am built and this is how you should see me now. The brain tells the body what to do to maintain its even keel. (Damasio, 2010, pp. 100–101)

For the body to send and act on signals to and from the brain, it must itself be able to think. Siegel (2017) pointed out that

> there are neural networks . . . in the intrinsic nervous system of our heart and intestines. We're seeing that we have a head-brain, heart-brain, and gut-brain, which, at a minimum would make the mind in both energy and information flow fully embodied, not just enskulled. (p. 153)

You have more neurons in your digestive system than in your spinal cord or peripheral nervous system (Hadhazy, 2010), and your immune system contains the same mood-altering endorphins found in the brain—"not just the chemicals, but the receptors as well" (Moyers, 1993, p. 180). This finding inclines in the same direction as Varela's (1994) argument that the immune system should primarily be considered a "cognitive entity":

> Even to fulfill a defensive role, the immune system must exhibit properties that are typically cognitive. To start with, it must have some capacity for the recognition of molecular profiles: the shapes of the intruding agents (or antigens), the "foreign-ness" capable of endangering the bodily integrity of the subject. Next, the system must have a learning ability, to recognize and defend itself against new antigens. Then, it must have a memory, in order to retain information about the antigens it has encountered, for future comparison with new antigens. (Varela & Coutinho, 1991, pp. 240–241)

Such findings and theorizing establish how various systems of the body are equipped with the necessary neural and chemical resources to receive, process, respond to, and send signals within and between themselves and the brain.

Mind, then, can be characterized in terms of the communication circuits within and between body-brain interactions: "There is no mind distinct from the body and . . . no body distinct from the mind" (Bateson & Bateson, 2005, p. 181). Shunryu Suzuki (2006), the founder of the San Francisco Zen Center, made the same point slightly differently:

> Our body and mind are not two and not one. If you think your body and mind are two, that is wrong; if you think that they are one, that is also wrong. Our body and mind are both two *and* one. (p. 7)

When you're out of sorts—when you're in pain or you're trying and failing to control some chunk of your experience—you tend to feel at odds with yourself, divided from your body. At such times, mind and body definitely feel "as two." And when you're not in pain and/or you're absorbed in a meaningful activity, it's much easier to feel more a sense of inclusivity, to recognize mind and body "as one." Hypnosis is a means for establishing a comfortable, inclusive mind-body connection that can, in turn, facilitate the hypnotherapeutic alteration of problems. But I shouldn't get ahead of myself. Before saying more about hypnotic experience, I need to talk about variations in the experience of being a self.

MY MIND, MY BODY, MY SELF

Bodily experience is the primal basis for everything we can mean, think, know, and communicate.
—George Lakoff and Mark Johnson (1999, p. xi)

Your senses orient you in space, helping to define where the environment ends and you begin. The boundaries of your self come into more stark relief when you feel too cold, when the light is too bright, when a sound is too loud or shrill, when something smells too strong or tastes too hot. At such times, you shield yourself from the source of the perception—protecting yourself from the elements, shading your eyes, covering your ears, plugging your nose, spitting.

Language gets into the act of self-definition, too. Your descriptions of who and what you are *not* help underscore the boundaries that define who and what you *are*: "I'm nothing like my mother." "I didn't grow up here, so I wouldn't know." "No, I would never have said that." "What am I, chopped liver?"

And then there's what happens when you feel at odds with your situation or surroundings—when you're bored, awkward, afraid, impatient, disgusted, uncomfortable, inadequate, dissatisfied.

Notice the degree to which discomfort, displeasure, and other forms of contrast—edges, juxtapositions—contribute to your experience of feeling, of being, separate and distinct. Uniquely you. This is true not only of your relationship to what's outside and around you but also of your relationship to yourself. You dislike the sound of your voice on a recording. You chide yourself for something you did or said. You gird yourself against pain or nausea or anxiety.

Through the perceptions, sensations, emotions, and thoughts that compose and define the parameters of your awareness, you orient yourself in contradistinction to your surroundings, other people, and your own experience. This is what allows you to be conscious: the ability to mark boundaries that define perceptions of, ideas about, and attitudes toward what's happening outside and inside. This self-referentially circles back to circumscribe consciousness itself: You are conscious of being conscious and, in so doing, conscious of being a self. However, the boundaries defining this self are not fixed in place; they shift according to circumstance and relationship, according to where the difference between "me" and "not-me" is located.

The identification of self with body can be heard when you caution another person, "Be careful not to bump into me," or you explain, "I'm feeling tired" or "I'm excited." The self you're defining at such times is inclusive of your body, inclusive of your emotions, inclusive, it seems, of *all* of you.

Something subtly shifts in what is included in and excluded from this self, though, when you think or say, "My stomach feels so much better"; "I can't contain my excitement"; or "My idea is a little different from yours." Through the assertion of ownership—"*my* stomach," "*my* excitement," "*my* idea"—you bring your body, feeling, and thought within the domain of what you experience as "myself," but such assertions reveal the fault line of an implicit division: the gap between owner and owned. By virtue of defining elements of your experience as *a part of* you, you simultaneously distinguish them as *apart from* a more circumscribed sense of self.

The assumed reality of this ownership dynamic is heightened, in part, by your feeling that this circumscribed self is in charge. You think, "I'm going to get up now," and your legs swing off the bed. You decide to look *there* and then *over there*, and your eyes follow suit. You choose to take another sip of coffee before getting into the shower, and your hand, arm, and lips fall in line. But this "impression of agency" (S. Harris, 2014, p. 90) is just that: "The sense of self—the sense that there is a thinker behind one's thoughts, an experiencer amid the flow of experience—is an illusion. The feeling that we call 'I' is itself the product of thought" (S. Harris, 2014, p. 102). This "I," this circumscribed self, isn't just a product of thought; it's literally an *after*thought:

> Your brain is wired to initiate your actions before you're aware of them. . . . In everyday life, you do many things by choice, right? At least it seems that way. . . . But the brain is a predicting organ. It launches your next set of actions based on your past experience and current situation, and it does so outside of your awareness. (Barrett, 2020, p. 76)

When your circumscribed self experiences itself making and implementing a decision, it is actually playing catch-up, making note of an implementation that is already underway (Bear & Bloom, 2016). Contrary to what you feel to be true, "all actions, mundane or novel, planned or unplanned, hypnotic or otherwise, are at the moment of activation initiated automatically, rather than by a conscious intention" (Lynn et al., 2008, p. 126). As the novelist Michael Crichton (2008) wryly put it, this artifact of the reflexive nature of consciousness, this "human sense of self-control and purposefulness, is a user illusion. We don't have conscious control over ourselves at all. We just think we do" (p. 135).

Now reflect on what happens when you, the seeming owner and controller of your body, emotions, and ideas, become their helpless, hapless victim: "My stomach is on fire"; "My thoughts are torturing me"; "My brain keeps replaying that damn song, over and over and over"; "I'm terrified I'll have a panic attack!" The pain, thoughts, song, and fear are all "yours," but because they all feel so decidedly *other*, they throw the seeming insularity of your embattled circumscribed self into still sharper relief.

Otherness and *selfhood* are cleaved; they mutually define each other. The experience of being or having a self is reflexively spun into existence by virtue of the recognition of differences, of thresholds. "You" are foregrounded against a background context—sometimes your surroundings, sometimes another person, sometimes intrapersonal experience. The boundaries are inscribed more clearly when you feel out of sorts or out of place or when there is a need for you to stand up to, defend against, or retreat from some external or internal threat.

The boundaries become much less defined—indifferentiated— when, rather than *standing out*, you are *fitting in*; rather than *counter*acting, you are *inter*acting and intermingling; and rather than *contending with*, you are *engaging in*. Berman (1989) notes that in "situations of intense relatedness—romantic love, psychosis, mystical experience— . . . it is impossible to distinguish where Self ends and Other begins" (p. 38). Mind and body feel connected as one when the necessity or significance of the self-other boundary dissolves, and the outline—the sense of being a reified, insular self— dissolves along with it.

This is what happens when you're actively absorbed in an activity that closely pairs compatible levels of skill and challenge. A feeling of separation gives way to one of effortless connection. You enter what Mihaly Csikszentmihalyi (1990) calls *flow*: "Concentration is so intense that there is no attention left over to think about anything irrelevant, or to worry about problems. Self-consciousness disappears, and the sense of time becomes distorted" (p. 71). Athletes who are "in the zone" are experiencing flow, as are medical teams performing surgery:

> It's a form of hypervigilance, a single-pointed concentration almost like meditation. . . . There's an amazing rhythm and flow when you have a good team—everyone is in sync. Our minds

and bodies work together as one coordinated intelligence. (Doty, 2016, p. 6)

The poet Jane Hirshfield also speaks of concentration, an awareness that is "penetrating, unified, and focused, yet also permeable and open" (1997, p. 3). Having described different rituals for writers to enter into it, she underscores that

however it is brought into being, true concentration appears—paradoxically—at the moment willed effort drops away. . . . At such moments, there may be some strong emotion present—a feeling of joy, or even grief—but as often, in deep concentration, the self disappears. We seem to fall utterly into the object of our attention, or else vanish into attentiveness itself. (p. 4)

The dropping away of willed effort: This would also serve as a good description of the movement into hypnosis. Absorption into the flow of the process is accompanied by various sorts of avolitional—unwilled, effortless, nonpurposive—changes, some arising spontaneously; others, in response to the therapist's suggestion(s). A sensation intensifies or fades, transforms or moves; an image takes form and develops; a hand lifts seemingly on its own; eyelids find themselves inexorably closing, unable to open; a dream or hallucination unfolds; time fast-forwards or stretches out; automatic workings of the body (e.g., blood flow or heart rate) make self-corrective adjustments to themselves; awareness seems to float above or beside the body; and so on. All such instances of hypnotic experience usher in, accompany, and/or are preceded by the dissipation of the boundaries of the circumscribed self.

Musicians jamming onstage undergo a similar transformation. As the guitarist Leo Kottke put it, "Once you're out there, you disappear. . . . I don't know anything else I've tried that eliminates me so readily as performance does" (Schaefer, 2007). Bruce Springsteen describes it similarly:

Playing . . . is a moment of both incredible self-realization and self-erasure at the same time. You disappear and blend into all the other people that are out there and into the notes and the chords and the music that you've written. You kind of rise up and vanish into it. (Remnick, 2017)

People who meditate know something about this, as well.

Mindfulness Meditation

When practicing mindfulness meditation, you typically sit in a relaxed, self-supporting, upright posture, and you bring your awareness to the automatic rhythm of your breathing. Unlike with yoga, you don't direct your breath; you coordinate with it. Along the way, inside and outside happenings present themselves as potential interruptions—an itch, a text-message ping, a worry, a memory, a barking dog, a story line. Whatever makes it onto your screen of awareness as a distraction grabs and keeps hold of you until you realize that it has carried your focus away, at which point you acknowledge, without self-recrimination or frustration, whatever it is that caught your attention, and you return to the breath. You do this with equanimity so that any emotional reaction to the necessity of refocusing doesn't itself become a distraction.

This self-correcting repair process continues throughout the meditation. "If you have to let go of distractions and begin again thousands of times, fine. That's not a roadblock to the practice— that *is* the practice" (Salzberg, 2011, p. 50). Like other flow experiences, meditation has an interesting effect on your sense of self:

Normally you think, "*I* am seeing." Yet in the ultimate sense, the seeing that happens isn't anyone's. Although hearing occurs, there's no self who hears. Rather than a homogenous entity, we find a collection of parts. Unless observed closely, what we regard as the self appears to be a solid, personal identity that perceives things. But in truth there is no metabeing who unifies the parts. All our actions happen without an agent, or self, performing them. There is no seer, just the seeing; no hearer, just the hearing. (Thatcher, 2009, pp. 33–34)

Suzuki (2006) offered a circular explanation: "If you are concentrated on your breathing you will forget yourself, and if you forget yourself you will be concentrated on your breathing" (p. 139). The best way I know to make sense of how this happens is to talk about soup. Well, two soups, actually.

Separately prepare two creamy soups that are the same thickness but different colors, perhaps one made with red peppers and the other with yellow (e.g., the Online Culinary School's video "Red and Yellow Bell Pepper Cream Soup Recipe—How to Serve 2 Soups Side by Side," https://www.youtube.com/watch?v=pr5L_3t0zeI). To serve, ladle the soups into separate measuring cups and pour them simultaneously into opposite sides of a bowl. As it fills, the two soups remain separate; the juxtaposition of their respective colors creates a clearly distinguished boundary down the middle.

And now prepare a second serving. Rinse out the measuring cups and fill them again, but this time, ladle the *same*-colored soup into each one. Take a clean bowl and, repeating the procedure you followed before, fill it by pouring the two identical liquids simultaneously from opposite sides. The result will again be a bowl that juxtaposes two separate soups, but because each is the same color and consistency as the other, the juxtaposition, the boundary, is imperceptible—an indifferentiated difference. The two soups are perceived, experienced, as one.

Let's bring this sensibility back to the experience of devoting yourself to following your breath. Your attention moves in sync with the filling and emptying of your lungs, the rise and fall of your chest, the airflow in your nostrils. Awareness and breath move in the same direction at the same rate, until they reverse and, still in sync, head in the opposite direction, simultaneously reaching the threshold that begins the cycle again. When interruptions present themselves, you bring your focused attention to them, too, regardless of whether they originate from inside or outside, so again there is a pairing: the experience of a thought or memory or anticipation, and the noting of it, in sync with the breath; the experience of a sound or a feeling or a sensation, and the noting of it, in sync with the breath. The result is rather like two separate ladles of the same soup in the same bowl: "not two and not one" (Suzuki, 2006, p. 7).

Your unfolding embodied experience and your unfolding awareness of your unfolding embodied experience are rhythmically aligned; in the unfolding, the difference between them is indifferentiated, and the boundary demarcating a discrete sense of self dissipates:

> The air comes in and goes out like someone passing through a swinging door. If you think, "I breathe," the "I" is extra. There is no you to say "I." What we call "I" is just a swinging door which moves when we inhale and when we exhale. It just moves; that is all. When your mind is pure and calm enough to follow this movement, there is nothing: no "I," no world, no mind nor body; just a swinging door. (Suzuki, 2006, p. 13)

The practice of meditation, attended-to breath by attended-to breath, challenges self-other dualities by dissolving the boundary between them. We could call this a commitment to *connected knowing*.

Connected Knowing

The Buddhist practice of *maitri*, usually translated as "loving-kindness," can be understood as unconditional friendliness (Chödrön, 2013). A way of extending compassion (from the Latin *com-*, "with, together" + *pati*, "to suffer": to suffer together) both internally and externally, *maitri* is a practice of *connected knowing*, an antidote for dualistic thinking: "Focusing our attention on inclusion and caring creates powerful connections that challenge the idea of an 'us/them' world by offering a way to see everyone as 'us'" (Salzberg, 2011, pp. 146–147). Extending feelings of warm inclusivity to whatever or whomever you identify as *other* is a way of bridging the gap between you, indifferentiating the boundaries that substantiate your sense of being a circumscribed self.[*] As Suzuki (2006) put it, "When our mind is compassionate, it is boundless" (p. 3). *Maitri* is a border-crossing transportation device, a way of transcending (from

---

[*] You help disperse the self-defining boundaries of your clients through the connected knowing of empathy, which I'll be discussing at length in Chapter 3.

the Latin *trans-*, "across, beyond" + *scandere,* "to climb") the usual divisions of conventional, conscious awareness.

As meditators know, judgment, whether of another person or of your own experience, circumscribes and thus separates you from whatever or whomever you're judging. *Maitri* is a corrective, a radiating attitude of acceptance that extends outward to the whole of the self (e.g., thoughts, body) and then beyond to other people. In so doing, it generates the compassion that Suzuki (2006) mentioned—a commitment to caring that renders unnecessary and irrelevant the protected borders of the circumscribed self.

A similar crossing can happen when a person encounters a work of art, say a poem:

> The poem dissolves loneliness, by bringing the confirmation of shared experience. This happens, I think, in reading almost any good poem, though it's only noticed, or needed, when the poem has to do with pain. . . . In reading [the] poem, the ache of an elemental longing is slipped from hand to hand between writer and reader, a coin and token of recognition, and by that transaction, is changed. What was carried alone is suddenly carried by two, by many. (Hirshfield, 2015, pp. 276–277)

In receiving confirmation of your experience in the words of another, the boundaries of the self are redrawn, becoming inclusive, in some sense, of both of you. Bateson (2000) believed that the recognition of beauty is the recognition of pattern that connects you to it:

> It is when we recognize the operations of [mind] in the external world that we are aware of "beauty" or "ugliness." The "primrose by the river's brim" is beautiful because we are aware that the combination of differences which constitutes its appearance could only be achieved by information processing, *i.e.,* by *thought.* We recognize another mind within our own external mind. (pp. 470–471)

Art in general can be conceived of as a mode of connected knowing. But as Billy Collins, former U.S. poet laureate, sees it, poetry is

unique in its ability to get inside the phenomenological experience
of the self:

> I have an image that distinguishes writers . . . of poetry. . . .
> People who write fiction and plays are standing outside people's
> houses and spying on them, like Peeping Toms. They're inter-
> ested in the domestic lives of strangers, of other people, and
> even their erotic and psychological business. The poet, how-
> ever, is inside that house, looking out the window and telling
> his readers, or her readers, what he [or she] sees. (2019b)

Poetry is a mode of connected knowing, but not only because
of the boundary-crossing perspective-taking of the poets. It also is
in the thrall of metaphor, and metaphor is, itself, nothing but pure,
gleeful connection:

> Metaphor systematically disorganizes the common sense of
> things—jumbling together the abstract with the concrete, the
> physical with the psychological, the like with the unlike—and
> reorganizes it into uncommon combinations. . . .
> Metaphorical thinking—our instinct not just for describing
> but for *comprehending* one thing in terms of another . . . —shapes
> our view of the world, and is essential to how we communicate,
> learn, discover, and invent. (Geary, 2011, pp. 2–3)

As Hirshfield (1997) pointed out, "Both the reading and the writing
of poems explore one thing by means of another; each draws on
a fundamentally metaphorical mind in order to reach toward the
new" (p. 35).

Hypnotherapists also reach toward the new by drawing on the
fundamentally metaphorical nature of mind. The process begins
when you first meet clients and begin empathically exploring their
world. By reliably communicating what you grasp of your clients'
experience, you make it possible for them to hear, to take in, a care-
filled articulation of what they've been feeling, thinking, and perhaps expressing. The dynamic of the process changes the self-other
boundary between you and them, which in turn changes how they

hear and respond to your subsequent suggestions for hypnotic and hypnotherapeutic experience, both of which rely to a significant degree on the logic of metaphor. Hypnosis is a form of connected knowing, and we hypnotherapists, like Billy Collins and his fellow poets, work from inside the house. I'll have much more to say about this in Chapters 3 and 5.

If practices of connected knowing can alter the perceived boundaries of the self, what does this tell us about the boundaries of the mind? The neuroscientists and epistemologists have been waiting patiently for us to get here, and they have an answer at the ready.

SHARED MIND

We've already established that "mind is [not] simply brain activity" (Siegel, 2012, p. xix), that it "extends beyond the physical cortex of the brain's flesh" (Beilock, 2015, p. 210). But it is essential to recognize that mind is also not just an intrapersonal phenomenon. According to Barrett (2020), "a mind is something that emerges from a transaction between your brain and your body while they are surrounded by other brains-in-bodies that are immersed in a physical world and constructing a social world" (p. 100). Siegel put it like this:

> The mind is both embodied and relational. . . . [This] means that to know our minds we need to know about the body, including the nervous system that is distributed throughout, and interacts with, the entire body. . . . The mind is also a relational process, . . . influenced by, indeed fundamentally created in part by, our social interactions as well as our relationships with entities beyond our bodily selves. . . . The mind is . . . embodied and it is embedded in our relational worlds. (2012, ch. 1, p. 5)

In keeping with both Siegel and Barrett, Bateson (2000) conceived of mind relationally. He tracked it not only in the networks within brain and body but also in the systemic interactions between person and environment:

We may say that "mind" is immanent in those circuits of the
brain which are complete within the brain. Or that mind is
immanent in circuits which are complete within the system,
brain *plus* body. Or, finally, that mind is immanent in the larger
system—man *plus* environment. (p. 317)

This more encompassing sense of mind includes the communicational interactions between self and other:

My mind is not something confined inside me. A good deal of it
is inside me. But a good deal of it is outside. . . . With that view
of self, . . . [w]hat happens when you and I talk? . . . Obviously
all the things that I do, which are picked up by your perceptions,
are a part of you. And things that you do, which are picked up
by my perceptions, are a part of me. And there's an enormous
overlap in our two minds. So that it is not unreasonable to speak
of a "shared mind." This is not a miraculous phenomenon; it is a
commonsense phenomenon. (Bateson, 1997, p. 144)

A shared mind emerges in any regular conversation; however, if
the participants in a dialogue are arguing or even just disagreeing,
they won't experience it that way. The marked contrast between
their positions will define and entrench the boundary distinguishing them, circumscribing each person's sense of being a separate
self. Contention feeds dualistic—self-versus-other—thinking.
It follows, then, that whatever diminishes such contrast, allowing it to become insignificant, will contribute to connected—non-
dualistic—conversing and knowing, dissipating the boundaries of
the circumscribed self.

David Bohm (1996) designed a method for doing just that. He
was interested in the creative potential of intensely meaningful
dialogues:

When people are in really close contact, talking about something which is very important to them, their whole bodies are
involved—their hearts, their adrenalin, all the neurochemicals,
everything. They are in far closer contact with each other than

with some parts of their own bodies, such as their toes. So in some sense, there is established in that contact "one body." (p. 31)

Barrett (2020) similarly documented the embodied expressions of close connections, describing them as a shared dance, as what in Chapter 5 I refer to as a process of *entrainment*.

When you're with someone you care about, your breathing can synchronize, as can the beating of your hearts, whether you're in casual conversation or a heated argument. . . . We often mirror each other's movements in a dance that neither of us is aware of and that is choreographed by our brains. One of us leads, the other follows, and sometimes we switch. (p. 84)

Bohm was particularly interested in what could happen when partners in a dialogue take care to alter those habits of thought and interaction that inadvertently serve to underscore the differences between them. He encouraged conversation participants to suspend assumptions and judgment and to explore possibilities for change without trying to convince or persuade the other person(s) to shift position:

If [they] can . . . listen to each other's opinions, and suspend them without judging them, . . . then [they] . . . have "one mind" because [they] have the *same content*—all the opinions, all the assumptions. At that moment, the difference is secondary. . . . [They] have in some sense *one body, one mind*. (my italics; Bohm, 1996, pp. 31–32)

Bohm wasn't talking about therapeutic encounters, but he could have been. When you remain nonjudgmental with your clients, you relieve them of the need to defend themselves against you. And when you make empathic comments—the logic and process of which I'll be discussing at some length in Chapter 3—your clients hear a reflected version (Bateson, 2002, would say a *transform*) of what they've been telling you, along with your best sense of their emotional relationship to it. To the degree that what you say and how you say it accords with what they're feeling, thinking, and describing, the differences that separate you from them become indifferentiated. For the time being, the self-other boundary becomes secondary—insignificant—and with that shift, you and your clients' *shared* mind approaches a sense of being of *one* mind (Flemons, 2002), or, in Suzuki's (2006) terminology, *not-one-not-two* mind. Siegel (2010) described it as a process of *attunement*:

> When we attune to others we allow our own internal state to shift, to come to resonate with the inner world of another. This resonance is at the heart of the important sense of "feeling felt" that emerges in close relationships. (p. 27; cited in Yapko, 2019, p. 75)

This brings us to hypnosis.

HYPNOSIS

How you think about hypnosis significantly determines how you practice it. In both the popular imagination and the research literature, hypnosis has characteristically been understood, described, and undertaken as something that's done *to* people (Yapko, 2005/2006). Many researchers retain at least an implicit embrace of the idea that the hypnotist *hypnotizes* the subject by way of a standardized *induction*, and that the hypnotist then employs various *deepening* techniques to prepare the subject to experience more elaborate hypnotic phenomena, such as hallucination and pain alteration (e.g., Barabasz & Barabasz, 2017). Meanwhile, the *hypnotized* subject is tested, measured, and classified in terms of their level of *hypnotizability*[*] (Hilgard, 1965; Spiegel & Spiegel, 2004), measurable via one or more of the standard hypnosis scales.[†]

---

[*] This is only one of many different terms that researchers and theorists have proposed for characterizing individual variations in the ability to experience hypnosis.
[†] For example, the Stanford Hypnotic Susceptibility Scale: Form C (Weitzenhoffer & Hilgard, 1962); the Harvard Group Scale (Shor & Orne, 1962); or the Hypnotic Induction Profile (Spiegel & Spiegel, 2004). Interestingly and problematically, most of the

The linear, particulate underpinnings of this conception of hypnosis can be found in dualistic descriptions of "the influence of the *mind over the body*" (my italics; Christensen & Gwozdziewycz, 2015, p. 449). Such characterizations are in keeping with Descartes's (1641/1911) assertion that the mind is "lodged in [the] body as a pilot in a vessel" ("Meditation VI," p. 29). The trouble is, one part of the self can't and doesn't have unilateral control over some other part, despite what the circumscribed self assumes: "We do not live in the sort of universe in which simple lineal control is possible. Life is not like that" (Bateson, 2000, p. 444).

To accurately map the mind, the process, the communicational complexity of hypnosis, you need to think recursively—in circles—and contextually, taking into account the interpersonal interactions through which it occurs (cf. Bányai, 1991). As Shor (1959) put it, "The flesh and blood of hypnosis—its multidimensional clinical richness and variation—only appears when hypnosis is viewed in terms of the dynamic interrelationships between real people" (p. 594; cited in Diamond, 1987, p. 95).

If you conceive of hypnosis linearly, then you'll tend to think that this or that scripted induction or deepening technique or hypnotherapeutic intervention, worded in just this way, is a self-contained determining factor in the hypnosis and thus is best invariably delivered through monologic recitation, either by reading or memory[*] (e.g., Barabasz & Barabasz, 2017, p. 75; Hammond, 1990).

But hypnosis unfolds in the mutuality, the synergy, of the relationship between hypnotist and client. The whole circuit of the relationship develops—sometimes more slowly, sometimes more quickly—a sense of *coherence*, altering the boundaries of the self for both participants: "The essence of the relationship of hypnotist to subject consists of [a] blurring of the boundaries between the two,

---

scales are not highly correlated with each other (Sutcher, 2008), which suggests that they aren't measuring the same thing. An exception is the Elkins Hypnotizability Scale, which is highly correlated with the Stanford Hypnotic Susceptibility Scale: Form C (Kekecs et al., 2016).

[*] Or, for research purposes, prerecorded and played so that all subjects in all groups are subjected to the same experience.

which occurs regularly during the process of induction" (Kubie, 1972, p. 215).

What you say and how you say it facilitates a process of syncing up: Your clients get in sync with you, you get in sync with them (see Bányai, 1991, p. 569), and they get in sync with the whole of themselves, with those parts that the circumscribed self construes as other. Hypnosis is a process of attunement (Bányai, 1991; Siegel, 2010, 2012) or resonance. As the attunement develops, the differences defining the clients' circumscribed self—separating them from you and from their body and their experience—are indifferentiated. Stephen Nachmanovitch (1990) describes an analogous process that unfolds when encountering art:

> We find ourselves weeping at certain moments in movies or plays . . . when something in them has "struck a chord." This metaphor is exact, because it refers to the phenomenon of resonance or sympathetic vibration. If you stroke a violin string, and there is another violin in the room, the second will resonate, will sing out on the same tone as the first. When we feel resonance it is the sure symptom of identity with the thing that sings. (pp. 174–175)

Utilization and Permissiveness

If the sense-making and experiencing of hypnosis depends on the indifferentiation of the boundaries defining your clients' circumscribed self—a process that begins with the empathic connection you make and maintain with them—then whatever facilitates that indifferentiation will contribute to their being in sync with you and themselves and thus will contribute to avolitional experience. This has traditionally been accomplished by the hypnotist—

- **entreating clients to follow directives:**
  "Now, if you wish to relax, imagine and feel all of my suggestions. Do not try too hard. Just try to concentrate on my suggestions to the best of your ability. Don't press, just relax! . . .

The better you relax, the better you will concentrate on what I am saying." (Kroger, 2008, p. 63)

- **defining what currently is or shortly will be happening:**
  "Notice now that your eyes are getting very, very *heavy*; your *lids* are getting very, very, very *tired*. Your lids are getting *heavier* and *heavier*." (p. 65)

- **telling clients what to do:**
  "If you really wish to go into a deeper state of relaxation, all you have to do is to let your lids close *tightly*. . . . Now, *close your eyes tight* and let your eyeballs roll up into the back of your head." (p. 66)
  and

- **specifying what clients will want or feel:**
  "You will close your eyes not because you have to, but because you really wish to go deeper and deeper relaxed. . . . As your eyeballs roll up into the back of your head, notice how your lids are sticking tighter and tighter together. You feel the tightness, do you not?" (p. 66)

To the degree that clients follow such directives and experience on cue what is predicted and what they expect, their self-circumscribing boundaries will successfully indifferentiate and they, inter- and intrapersonally in sync, will likely experience hypnotic responsiveness. However, if they don't follow along, whether because they are distracted, circumspect, or disinterested, then the divisions defining their ordinary conscious awareness will tend to remain in place or become even more clearly inscribed, and the hypnotist, and perhaps they themselves, will likely conclude that they are resistant and/or not hypnotizable.

Milton Erickson reversed this conventional way of thinking and working. Rather than putting the onus on his patients to cooperate with *him*, to follow along with whatever he was telling them to do, he strove to cooperate with *them*. He took responsibility for entering the experiential world of his patients, getting in sync with whatever was keeping them out of sync with him. Erickson (2008a) treated "the subjects' own attitudes, thinking, feeling, and behavior, and aspects of the reality situation . . . as the essential components of the trance induction procedure" (p. 301). He termed this approach, this way of working "inside the house" (Collins, 2019b) of other people, "Techniques of Utilization":

> These techniques are in essence no more than a simple reversal of the usual procedure of inducing hypnosis. Ordinarily trance induction is based upon securing from the patients some form of initial acceptance and cooperation with the operator. In Techniques of Utilization, the usual procedure is reversed to an initial acceptance of the patients' presenting behaviors and a ready cooperation by the operator however seemingly adverse the presenting behaviors may appear to be in the clinical situation. (Erickson, 2008a, p. 272)

Utilization involves accounting for potential disruptions to the developing flow of your clients' hypnotic experience and incorporating them in what you say, whether they originate from distractions in the physical environment—

> If you were driving that emergency vehicle out there, your siren would be a reassuring *signal to* the other drivers to just *slow down* and to *safely open up space* so that *you can move freely and safely down* the street. *All you need to do* if you are one of the other drivers, *in response to hearing the siren, is to relax, knowing* you have done what's necessary *to open the way* for anyone seeking safe and timely passage *to proceed effortlessly and smoothly to wherever* they're going.

—or arise from the clients' expectations, worries, efforts, reluctance, or behaviors. In the following interchange, Erickson's statements are in italics; his patient's, in regular font:

> *You really can't conceive of what a trance is*—no, I can't, what is it?—*yes, what is it?*—a psychological state, I suppose—*a psychological state you suppose, what else?*—I don't know—*you really don't know*—no, I don't—*you don't, you wonder, you think*—think what—*yes, what do you think, feel, sense?*—(pause)—I don't know—*but*

you can wonder—do you go to sleep?—*no, tired, relaxed, sleepy*—
really tired—*so very tired and relaxed, what else?*—I'm puzzled—
puzzles you, you wonder, you think, you feel, what do you feel?—my
eyes—*yes, your eyes, how?*—they seem blurred—*blurred, closing*—
(pause)—they are closing—*closing, breathing deeper*—(pause)—
tired and relaxed, what else?—(pause)— . . . I feel funny—*funny, so
comfortable, really learning.* (Erickson, 2008a, p. 277)

Rather than trying to stop, control, or dispense with distractions
or disruptions, you *connect* with them, getting in sync with whatever
is keeping your clients out of sync. Erickson accomplished this also
by offering permissively worded suggestions (O'Hanlon & Martin,
1992). If you *claim* something will happen and it doesn't, a sharp
difference is established between you and your clients, as well as
between the clients and their experience. However, if you *suggest*
that something *might* happen and a point is reached where it still
hasn't, then the suggestion wasn't wrong. The difference between
what currently *is* and what *could be* is less defined (and thus more
easily dissolvable) than the difference between what *is* and what
is not. Thus, rather than telling clients that something *will* happen,
you can permissively suggest that it *may*, or that something equally
as valid *might* occur, instead:

> As I continue to talk, you *may* begin to feel your eyelids getting
> heavy, or you *might find them* closing even before you notice any
> heaviness. People experiencing hypnosis often find themselves
> *able to* hear everything going on around them, while others
> become so absorbed in what starts happening on the inside that
> they lose track of the outside. I *don't know* if any part of you will
> stay even somewhat oriented to anything out there, or *whether* it
> will just become background support as you're exploring inside
> discoveries.

Your use of utilization and permissiveness contributes to the
indifferentiation of your clients' self-defining boundaries by making it easier for them to get in sync with you and with however they

are responding to what you're saying. In Chapters 5 and 6, I will return to and further elaborate on utilization as an encompassing orientation to practice.

A Working Definition of Hypnosis

Three times over the past 25 years, Division 30 of the APA has attempted to offer theoretically neutral, empirically based definitions of hypnosis, composed by committees to be accessible, acceptable, and useful to clinicians, researchers, and the lay public (Elkins et al., 2015; Green et al., 2005; Kirsch, 1994). I endorse the idea of fashioning a definition that can serve as an organizing inspiration for setting research directions and making clinical choices. But I find the goal of theoretical neutrality problematic. As the biologist Humberto Maturana once pointed out, "everything that can be said is said by an observer to another observer" (quoted in Segal, 2001, p. 8), and all observers hold at least tacit assumptions informing their observations. So, rather than aiming for unattainable neutrality, I'm going after theoretical consistency. I'd like to offer a working definition of hypnosis (open to revision) that distills the ideas I've presented thus far and anticipates where I'm headed over the next five chapters:

> Hypnosis can be understood as a mode of connected knowing, a context and method for facilitating avolitional experience and learning. The hypnotist facilitates the indifferentiation of both interpersonal and intrapersonal differences, making it safe for the everyday boundaries of the client's self-conscious awareness—a circumscribed self—to become temporarily unessential. This frees up the client to leave off scrutinizing and judging the hypnotist's communications and to let go of assuming responsibility for and attempting control over mind-body communications—thoughts, emotions, sensations, and imaginings. With effortless absorption, the client is able to entertain, explore, and creatively engage with the hypnotist's invitations to experience hypnotic phenomena.

This relational understanding of hypnosis resonates with Csiksz-entmihalyi's (1996) conception of creativity, which, he points out, "does not happen inside people's heads, but in the interaction between a person's thoughts and a sociocultural context. It is a systemic rather than an individual phenomenon" (p. 23). The systemic nature of creativity, like the systemic nature of hypnosis, can be recognized, in part, by the dissolution of the boundaries defining a circumscribed self and the questioning of and playing with the boundaries defining conventional ways of perceiving, choosing, and experiencing:

> For art to appear, we have to *disappear*. . . . When we "disappear" in this way, everything around us becomes a surprise, new and fresh. Self and environment unite. Attention and intention fuse. . . . This lively and vigorous state of mind is the most favorable to the germination of original work of any kind. (Nachmanovitch, 1990, p. 51)

It's not surprising, then, that interesting parallels have been found between hypnosis and creativity, including focused but effortless associative processing (Bowers, 1979). I'll return to the issue of creativity within hypnotherapeutic contexts in Chapter 6, where I'll explore the importance of improvisation and a sense of playfulness (cf. Nachmanovitch, 1990).

With hypnosis, you facilitate the indifferentiation of the boundaries that have been keeping the client's circumscribed self distinct from you, from the surroundings, and from the rest of the self, and you invite avolitional shifts in perception (hallucination), sensation (e.g., analgesia or anesthesia), and action (e.g., hand levitation). Such hypnotic experiences feel dissociative to the client (cf. Hilgard, 1991), as if parts of them are operating independently, with a "mind of their own." But, of course, they are made possible by the *associative* quality of the attunement between you and the client and between the client and their experience. If, as a result of this attunement, there is no self-consciously inscribed "I" to assume ownership of and responsibility for the instances of avolitional responsiveness, then the shifts in experience will *feel* dissociated. However, they are more properly understood as instances of *associated dissociation* or, as I've described elsewhere, *connected separation* (Flemons, 1991, 2002). The hypnotic context is a context of connection, of varying degrees of resonance.

As this chapter has, I hope, made clear, an understanding of hypnosis is a window into the relational complexities of interpersonal and intrapersonal communication, into the layered and self-referential nuances of how minds and bodies work and communicate (cf. Barber, 1984). Knowing this, as well as knowing the role of suggestions, expectancy, and meaning in the shaping of experience, is critical to developing any approach to helping minds and bodies to change.

As you venture into the rest of the book, you will find a panoply of ideas and suggestions for helping you to orient therapeutically and hypnotically in your practice. But before you head off, let's return to the story of Nora and Lois. I'd like to offer a hypnotherapy-informed take on what transpired.

As you may remember, Nora, newly pregnant and committed to fighting her addiction to cigarettes, met with her mother, Lois, to share with her the unrelenting urges to smoke she was battling all day and every day. She expected her mother to empathize with her and to encourage her to keep fighting. Instead, she was gobsmacked and offended when Lois warmly encouraged her not to worry so much about smoking while pregnant, given that she, Lois, had enjoyed cigarettes all through her pregnancy with Nora. Immediately, unexpectedly, and, as it turned out, permanently, Nora's craving went up in smoke.

Had Lois been a strategic therapist and Nora her client, Lois might have, with therapeutic intent, encouraged her to smoke, anticipating that she would recoil from the suggestion. But as I said earlier, Lois's message was offered earnestly, not paradoxically, and the setting was a mother-daughter lunch, not a therapy session. Nevertheless, it shared some critical qualities with a hypnotherapeutic context, qualities that make sense given what we know about minds, bodies, and relationships.

My clients talk all the time about partners and family members who know how to "push their buttons." I take that to mean that the shared mind of intimate relationships is often characterized by the kinds of indifferentiated boundaries that we strive to make possible with our clients through our empathic comments and hypnotic invitations. The words of loved ones can feel like they are coming from inside, rather than outside, the person's sense of self, and this makes them less likely to be critically scrutinized before they are deeply felt.

Nora and Lois obviously enjoyed this sort of close relationship, which made it more likely that Nora wouldn't—couldn't—evaluate her mother's statement at arm's length. Add to that the fact that Nora was caught so completely off guard by her mother's generous, inviting, surprising advice, and it is easy to see that she swallowed it whole—or inhaled it—*before* reacting to it. This meant that the rejection that followed wasn't intellectual, it was *visceral*: She didn't *think critically* about the idea; she *felt revolted* by it. Her avolitional response involved *all* body-and-mind of her, galvanizing a clarified sense of self—her now fully formed identity as a protective mother. With that conviction seared in place, cigarettes became as irrelevant for her as a neighborhood burger joint would be for a vegetarian. Craving? What craving?

Such changes happen outside the controlling efforts of the circumscribed self. You can't convince yourself not to desire something, you can't talk yourself out of it, you can't logically contain it, and you can't admonish yourself enough to get rid of it. But given the right conditions, such patterns of experience—habits, urges, thoughts, sensations, and so on—can, in the blink of an idea, image, or feeling, find themselves avolitionally transforming. Welcome to hypnotherapy.

MEDITATION AND SELF-HYPNOSIS

*The body isn't a machine run by the mind. The body and the mind
is one phenomenon, body-mind. And understanding this as an idea
means nothing; the body-mind has to know it. Doing zazen
[meditation] enacts this in us.*

　　　—Norman Fischer (Fischer & Moon, 2016, pp. 172–173)

*You do your best work when you're not conscious of yourself. That's
what's so exhilarating about it—you're out of your self.*

　　　　　　—Peter Matthiessen (Krementz, 1996, p. 52)

*It is curious that both meditation and dancing are ways to
"disappear." The world's cultures are full of very specific and
technical means for getting to this state of emptiness. . . . These
traditions and the practices they prescribe take us out of ordinary
time. Slowing body/mind activity down to nothing, as in meditation,
or involving us in a highly skilled and exhausting activity, as in
dancing or playing a Bach partita, the ordinary boundaries of our
identity disappear, and ordinary clock-time stops.*

　　　　　—Stephen Nachmanovitch (1990, p. 53)

From the outside, meditation can appear so passive and inconsequential. It can even seem ludicrous: "Don't just do something, sit
there" (Boorstein, 2011). But from inside the practice of it, you discover, in its quiet, unassuming way, just how fundamentally radical it is. Meditation is a 180-degree shift in business as usual, a
reversal of the common reactions we rely on when our well-being
is disrupted—trying to ignore annoyances or irritations, recoiling

from what frightens us, shielding ourselves from and/or confronting what offends us, or striving to control or banish what imperils our safety or identity. All such reactions rally attempts to *counter* whatever is disturbing us, and, in so doing, they establish a position—inscribe a sense of self—in opposition to it. A strategy of countering maintains the dualistic thinking I mentioned in Chapter 1—a way of seeing and acting predicated on the deeply held belief that it is possible to insulate ourselves from, and impose our will on, what disturbs us.

Certainly, sometimes we can successfully manage for a short period of time to purposefully ignore, say, an annoying sound. But it is dangerous to ignore a cancer diagnosis, and in early 2020, governments that ignored the threat of COVID-19 gave it a chance to uncontrollably spread. Recoiling from a snake can help you avoid getting bitten, but if you recoil from everything that resembles a snake, your life will become unmanageable.

Whenever we mount some form of opposition to what we deem *other*, we undertake the exhausting effort to control or eradicate it. In so doing, we are simultaneously inscribing and reinforcing the boundaries of our insular sense of self. There are times when this is important and necessary, such as when dealing with a bully, abuser, or oppressor. The ability and willingness to say no is essential to identity development, and by standing up to injustice, it is sometimes possible to get persecutors removed from positions of destructive influence. However, if the threat you face is part of you (pain, intrusive thoughts, emotional upheaval) or you are a part of it (marital strife, addiction, global warming), then any countering strategies you employ will maintain and perhaps intensify the oppositional dynamic of an ongoing alienated relationship that is itself contributing to your distress. The achievement of well-being—a dissolution of suffering—then requires a fundamental reorientation of your efforts. That's where meditation comes in.

The meditative alternative to these countering strategies is to *en*counter what you find disturbing. Instead of turning your back to it and ignoring it, or getting your back up and confronting it, you *turn toward* it, acknowledge its presence, and skillfully engage with it: instead of shunning, inquiring; instead of opposing, attending:

> Meditation practice is how we stop fighting with ourselves, how we stop struggling with circumstances, emotions, or moods. . . . This is the primary method for working with painful situations—global pain, domestic pain, any pain at all. We can stop struggling with what occurs and see its true face without calling it the enemy. . . . It's like inviting what scares us to introduce itself and hang around for a while. (Chödrön, 2016, pp. 156–157)

The ramifications of this shift in approach are significant, and they are true not just of meditation but also of hypnotherapy. Stitched into both practices is the recognition that it is easy to get caught in the illusory belief that we have a circumscribed self that is separate from and thus capable of effectively shutting up or shutting down problematic experience. Release from the knots of this illusion is delivered through methods of connective engagement.

> In meditation we become the breath, not simply to regain the fragrance of really being alive, but to let the boundaries between "me" and "my breath" break down and fall away. . . . To become breathing is to become more boundless, seamless, and indivisible; for breathing belongs fully to the universe and has no mind of separation at all. (Murphy, 2006, pp. 5–6)

During meditation, the indifferentiation of the circumscribed self entails noticing and acknowledging whatever interrupts the following of the breath. Instead of attempting to separate from it, trying to push it down or away, you approach and connect with it, which, ironically enough, sets the stage for letting it go.

An analogous process unfolds in hypnotherapy. Once you and the client, and the client's mind and body, are in sync, you, through hypnotic suggestions for avolitional responsiveness, facilitate a connection between the client and their symptomatic experience. This establishes the necessary conditions for the knotted hold of the symptom to begin unraveling, for the spiraling inherent in suffering to peter out (see Chapter 6). I think of it as dissolution-focused therapy.

Some approaches to meditation, such as yoga, tai chi, and chi kung, involve intentionally concentrating, directing, deepening, and/or extending the breath. Other approaches, such as TM, structure attention through the chanting of a mantra. All are ways of managing distractibility, as is the hypnotist's practice of offering a compelling point of foreground focus, perhaps an object on which to rest the gaze and/or a set of instructions to follow. Limiting distractibility facilitates and protects absorption, which "is a key feature of the hypnotic experience as well as an integral part of advanced concentration meditation" (Markovic & Thompson, 2016, p. 79). Both meditation and hypnosis techniques are means of transforming hurdles or threats to a mind-body connection into background noise or, more creatively, into special effects that contribute to, rather than detract from, the experience of melding, of inclusivity.

And yet hypnosis is not a form of meditation, just as "meditation is not a form of hypnosis" (Gunaratana, 2011, p. 13).* People listening to a guided meditation are offered directions for focusing attention—on the breath, or perhaps on body sensations or a mantra—and for exploring, say, mindfulness or loving-kindness. Clients being invited into hypnosis are, in contrast, offered directions for the letting go of intentionality and for the development of avolitional hypnotic phenomena—shifts in sensation, perception, imagination, or the experience of time. Meditators dismiss such effects as epiphenomena, diversions from their experiential investigation of present-moment mind, whereas hypnotherapists utilize them as stepping-stones toward the altering of symptoms.

Meditators strive to sit consistently, a daily ritual for coming into and developing concentrated, clear-eyed awareness, but most clients don't undertake hypnosis as an ongoing practice; rather, they view it as a means to an end. They anticipate time-limited involvement in a therapeutic process organized to reach a specific goal—relief from or change in a problem. Some people do maintain a self-hypnosis practice to keep a symptom in check or to access a flow-based

---

* Gunaratana was correct in asserting this; however, in his otherwise excellent book on mindfulness, he mischaracterized what hypnosis is and what the experience of it is like.

relationship with themselves for accomplishing challenging tasks, but unlike meditators, they don't normally consider their practice as an organizing principle for conducting their life.

People who meditate, like those undertaking hypnotherapeutic change, seek relief from suffering; however, they don't anticipate quick resolution.* They commit to sitting consistently, knowing that over the long term, the results can be transformative. However, they take care to avoid a foreground focus on changing themselves, lest they get ensnared by the dualistic distinction between a present-day unsatisfactory self and a future-day desired self. They aren't goal directed so much as discovery oriented, bringing their curiosity and compassion into play as they empirically investigate an approach to experiencing that relieves them from habits of thought and action that inevitably incur suffering (cf. Gunaratana, 2011).

Still, both meditative and hypnotic traditions involve a bridging of the mind-body gap, the development of flow experience, and a concomitant shift in the perceived boundaries of the self. And they each typically produce a feeling of stillness, relaxation, calm.

> Clinical hypnosis and GMM [guided mindfulness meditation] are highly similar in the way they focus attention, each giving rise to similar qualities of experience that people describe as different from usual consciousness. These qualities include a sense of detachment, a sense of timelessness, and absorption in the experience. Not surprisingly, the neurophysiology of hypnosis and meditation is also similar. (Yapko, 2011, p. 121)

Given such similarities, an embodied understanding of meditation can provide a useful port of entry into the nature of hypnotherapeutic change as well as the processes of hypnosis and self-hypnosis.

When appropriate with clients, I'll suggest they incorporate meditation into their daily lives. Those who grab hold and run with it (okay, sit with it) tell me about significant benefits they notice in

---

* Zen Buddhism, particularly the Rinzai school, would seem an exception to this assertion, given that it understands "awakening" or enlightenment "to be a sudden flash of insight rather than a gradual revelation" (Buswell & Lopez, 2014). However, such flashes happen within a tradition of practice and learning suffused with expectancy.

their well-being, which accords with studies that demonstrate that regular meditation helps with stress and anxiety, depression, addiction, and PTSD (see Elkins & Olendzki, 2019, p. 17). I'm always looking for ways of promoting client independence from me and from therapy in general, and meditation can help facilitate that. It isn't a panacea, nor is it a substitute for therapy, but it can help clients stay fresh and resilient in their changed relationship to a problem.

There are a number of excellent meditation phone apps—Ten Percent Happier, Calm, Headspace, Smiling Mind—that can help people get started with meditation, and there is one—Mindset—devoted to self-hypnosis; however, I don't outsource the responsibility for introducing clients to the process of creating a mind-body connection. I take it upon myself to introduce them to a meditation approach to which self-hypnotic elements can be inserted or appended as needed. As I talk about and demonstrate how they can meditate when I'm not around, I simultaneously invite them to experience, in the moment, what I'm describing. The process thus can double as a hypnotic induction or, as I prefer to think about and call it, a hypnotic *invitation* (see Chapter 5).

The meditation practice to which I introduce my clients is a variation of the breath-based technique of mindfulness meditation, as it best fits with the avolitional heart of hypnosis. I diverge somewhat from standard mindfulness-based practice, and my way of making sense of what's going on is also a little idiosyncratic. In what follows, I'm not going to just talk about meditation; rather, I'll give you some opportunities to test-drive it, interspersing guidance and orienting explanations.

> *In a moment I'm going to invite your eyes to close. If you accept the invitation, your visual field will be limited to internally produced perceptions: perhaps colors, shapes, patterns, movements, or images, or perhaps the perception of just peaceful darkness, of nothing at all. That's an interesting possibility, eh?—the perception of the absence of perception?*
>
> *This delimited inner focus can make it easier for you to notice your breathing, to shift from the visual to the visceral. The sensations that*

accompany and mark your breathing are always available, but you don't usually register them consciously. So when you get to the end of this paragraph, take a break from reading for a minute or two and, as your eyes close, tune in to your breathing. How and where in your body do you notice it? After you explore a bit, come back to the page and continue reading.

. . . . .

You may have located the rhythm of your breathing in the filling and emptying of your lungs, in the movement of the muscles in your back, in the expansion and relaxing of your belly, in the feeling and/or sound of the movement of air in your nostrils, or in the temperature shift of the air heading in and then heading out.

Now, take another short break from reading and absorb yourself in syncing up your awareness and your breath. Align your exhale and your awareness-of-the-exhale, and then do the same with the inhale: As you breathe in, your awareness of the fact of the inhale can be right there, right with the inhale itself.

. . . . .

As the awareness-of-breath and the rhythm-of-breath become synchronized, the information on each side of the mind-body divide corresponds closely with the information on the other: Breathing-in aligns with awareness-of-breathing-in; breathing-out aligns with awareness-of-breathing-out. Breath and awareness-of-breath aren't identical, but they rhyme, and this rhyming serves to indifferentiate some of the differences between them, thereby establishing something of a mind-body bridge. Josho Pat Phelan (1996) explains how this comes about:

In Zen meditation, our intention is to join our breath, to become one with our breath; rather than trying to observe or watch our breath the way you might watch TV or watch something separate from yourself. In mindfulness practice, there is no objective observer in the sense of objectifying your experience or separating yourself from your experience in order to observe it. Although we use the terms "to follow your breathing" and "watching the breath," we do this from the inside. Thich Nhat

Hanh teaches that the way we are to observe something in meditation is to become the thing we are observing by removing the boundary between subject and object. He says, "Nonduality is the key word. . . . The body and mind are one entity, and the subject and object of meditation are one entity also."

Chödrön (2013) characterizes the shift this way: "As you work with the breath as your object of meditation, you will begin to feel your body and mind becoming synchronized. You are no longer divided" (p. 39).

Let your eyes close again and further discover what happens as you explore this mind-body alignment a little longer.

. . . . .

At some point, to varying degrees, for varying amounts of time, this rhyming will be interrupted. Your attention will drift, will be disrupted. A thought, and then another one, will intrude; you'll recall an errand you need to run later; some nearby sound will startle or intrigue you; or some physical or emotional discomfort or irritation or pleasure will become foreground. Take another few minutes to watch the disruptions come and go. Notice what grabs your attention.

. . . . .

Clients sometimes tell me that they are not good candidates for meditation because their minds are too busy, too distractible. They are misled by the not uncommon belief that the quieting or slowing of the mind is a precondition for, rather than the developed result of, meditative experience. They try, and inevitably fail, to block out interruptions or to steel themselves to stay focused. But meditation does not involve the posting of a sentry to prevent sources of disruption, nor does it require effortful avoidance of some quality of distractibility; rather, it engages you in a continual process of recovery, of losing and then regaining a syncing up of mind and body. As I mentioned in Chapter 1, meditation *always* involves ongoing corrective recalibration, a continual process of nonjudgmentally coming back from distraction. You might as well, then, embrace it as a core part of the process (Salzberg, 2011).

Ready yourself for the next interruption. No need to be on high alert or to tense up in anticipation. Just recognize that your connection with your breathing will be disrupted by something, whether a perception of something outside or inside, and when you notice it, make note of it—acknowledge the fact of its presence. You can do this by slightly nodding to it, as you would when greeting an acquaintance from some distance away; or you might just gently, barely, move the tip of an index finger as if silently tapping, offering a discreet, quiet greeting. Experiment with one or both forms of acknowledgment— nodding and tapping—for a few minutes.

. . . . .

The acknowledgment of interruptions serves the same purpose as the following of your breath—it bridges the gap between awareness and experience by indifferentiating the differences between them. When you turn toward and acknowledge disruptions, you fold them into the scope of your present-moment attention. Like a stand-up comic who extemporaneously riffs off of hecklers' provocations, making them an essential part of the routine, your acknowledgment transforms interruptions into contributions. This is also the logic of Ericksonian utilization, to which I'll return in Chapters 5 and 6. Rather than trying to prevent disruptions, and rather than getting disgruntled by them, you greet them as guests, allowing them the opportunity to contribute to your experience—honing your focus, drifting through or fading from your awareness, or nuancing or augmenting your mind-body connection.

This approach to distractions makes it possible for you not to gird yourself against them and also to let go of any judgment regarding your having lost your focus to them. You return to your breath with patience, without irritation or frustration.

You're best-off eschewing not only negative but also positive judgment. Meditation can, at times, feel exhilarating—relieving, freeing, trippy—and this can incline you toward giving it your stamp of approval: "Wow, this feels fantastic!" The problem is, anytime you judge, you distinguish yourself as separate from whatever you're deeming either bad or good. Jay Haley (1981, p. 241) tells the story of a student who said to a Zen master, " 'Isn't the mountain beautiful?' The Master replied, 'Yes, but isn't it a pity to say so.' " Even positive judgment sets you apart from what you are appraising, which undermines the mind-body connection you are developing.

Another way to effectively respond to distractions in meditation is to classify them, succinctly and silently naming them as they appear (e.g., "pressure," "thought," "memory," "tightness," "color," "worry," "anticipation," "traffic," "itch"). Such language-based acknowledgment is not neutral; how you do the naming, at what level of specificity, will shape in part how you experience the intrusions. For example, if you categorize a stab of pain as "sensation," it may help you not gird against it; however, the vagueness of the classification may inadvertently increase the gap you're attempting to close. As I'll address in my discussion of empathy (see Chapter 3), expressing the qualities of an experience in nuanced language improves the resolution of the description, thereby indifferentiating some of the inevitable differences between map and territory.

Take a few minutes and experiment with different levels of classification. First, use general categories in your acknowledgments ("sound," "feeling," "thought," "sensation," "color").

. . . . .

Now, again make note of what you're noticing, but this time, bring some degree of specificity into your naming ("traffic," "unsettled," "concern," "discomfort," "red").

. . . . .

And now, one last time, bring even more granularity into your descriptions of whatever makes it onto your screen of awareness ("engines and tires," "uncertainty," "second-guessing," "muscle cramp," "crimson").

. . . . .

In Chapter 1, I mentioned that because the conveyance of information fundamentally depends on the perception and communication of contrast and context, mind can be understood in terms of differences that make a difference (Bateson, 2000). If verbal language is in play, referentiality and negation become possible: You are able to point to something not immediately present ("Andre went to the store"; "Remember Paris?"; "I graduate in May"), and you can indicate opposition to, for example, assertions of intent ("I won't do that"), of desire ("I don't want to do that"), or of belief ("That is not true").

For negation to make its case, it must point to what it is opposing ("I'm not racist"; "That's not important"; "Don't even think that"). If I tell you, "I don't hate you," the negation doesn't exist as a stand-alone entity but, rather, as part of a polarity: It only makes sense, only carries meaning, in relation to its opposite, "I hate you," which hovers as a background (and thus often unnoticed or unconscious) orienting referent. This is why when you attempt to negate—reject, cast out—troubling thoughts, emotions, or urges, they lurk on the outskirts of your awareness, plotting a comeback. A friend of Dan Harris's (2014) once said to him: "Your demons may have been ejected from the building, but they're out in the parking lot, doing push-ups" (p. 52).

This relational quality of negation accounts for a large proportion of failed solution attempts (see Flemons, 2002), but a recognition of how polarities mutually define each other also informs the logic and practice of hypnotherapy and mindfulness meditation. For example, if I am inviting you to get in sync with yourself and I tell you, "Don't relax too quickly," then the use of negation in my suggestion spritzes relaxation into the air.

Similarly, Sharon Salzberg (2011, p. 55) suggests categorizing all distractions you notice as "not breath." This is an inspired way of using negation to orient you back to the breath in the very act of acknowledging that you have drifted away from it. In a similar vein, I suggest to my clients struggling with their sleep to meditate in bed, classifying all distracting thoughts, sounds, emotions, perceptions, and sensations as "not sleep" or, for reasons that will make more sense a little further along in the book, "not yet sleep."

Let's use Salzberg's suggestion to experiment with using negation in a positive way.

In a moment, you'll again develop your visceral awareness by closing your eyes and finding and following your breath. This time when

your focus is interrupted, acknowledge whatever occurs to you as
not-breath.

. . . . .

Did the negation make it easier to get back aligned with your
breath?

You've no doubt noticed differences in your mind-body syncing
up across these various methods of acknowledgment. Let's explore
how you can further enhance the rhythmic support of the mind-
body connection you're developing.

At the end of this paragraph, go ahead and close your eyes and find and
follow your breath. Just like before, you will notice and make note of
what interrupts your present-moment attending to the rhythm of your
breathing. However, this time when you acknowledge the disruption,
whether physically (with a slight nod or slight lift of your index finger)
or in language—categorizing it broadly ("sound," "thought," "sensa-
tion"), with specificity ("dogs barking," "judging," "prickly pain"), or
via negation ("not peaceful," "not accepting," "not yet comfortable")—
I suggest you time your noting so it coincides with your next exhale. In
doing so, you'll already be back attending to your breath in your syn-
chronized acknowledgment of what took you away from it.

. . . . .

Okay, let's do one last, related exploration.

This time, when you close your eyes and begin following your breath,
find a place of discomfort—say, tightness—somewhere in your
body. Maintain a double focus, attending to both the rhythm of your
breath and the tightness of this place in your body. And now, as you
exhale, acknowledge the fact of the tension by classifying it as not-yet-
relaxed. Don't try to relax it, just follow your breath, and make note
of this not-yet-relaxed place.

. . . . .

With this last experiment, we've ventured into territory jointly
shared by meditation and self-hypnosis. Both practices are

characterized by a commitment to indifferentiating the mind-body gap; however, with self-hypnosis, you make use of this relationship-to-self to facilitate avolitional changes in some kind of problematic experience.

Some clinicians (e.g., Kohen & Olness, 2011, p. 102) consider all hypnosis to be self-hypnosis. Recognizing that hypnosis is a cooperative venture in which clients freely choose to participate, they reason that if clients can't be hypnotized against their will, then they must be in charge—they must be hypnotizing themselves. Such a characterization correctly acknowledges the limitations of the therapist's influence; however, it doesn't account for the shared-mind nature of the hypnotic relationship. As detailed in Chapter 1, I consider hypnosis a collaborative relationship that dissipates the boundaries defining the client's everyday sense of identity. I thus reserve the term *self-hypnosis* for those occasions when people use hypnotic methods on their own to bridge the mind-body gap and invite avolitional change.

Such invitations can easily go awry. An impossible problem appears the moment you start dictating to yourself a description of—or a prescription for—what you want to happen: relaxation, sleepiness, relief from pain, or whatever. For something hypnotic to unfold, there needs to be an element of spontaneous responsiveness to proffered possibilities. But whether you silently intone suggestions to yourself or prerecord them so you can play them back later, it is still you yourself doing the proffering. This catches you in the same reflexive predicament as when you try tickling yourself. It is a form of the *Be spontaneous!* paradox I mentioned in Chapter 1. It

> enters into the pragmatics of human communication . . . through an injunction demanding specific behavior . . . [that] by its very nature can only be spontaneous. . . . Anybody confronted with this injunction is in an untenable position, for to comply [would mean having] . . . to be spontaneous within a frame of compliance, of nonspontaneity. (Watzlawick et al., 1967, p. 180)

This paradox also lies in wait for people who meditate, for stymied artists in search of their creative spark, for athletes trying to climb out of a slump, and for lovers fearful of performance anxiety. All discover how easy it is to get tripped up trying not to try. All find that they can't order freedom off a menu.

But whereas the *specifics* of freedom can't be detailed, the *conditions* for it can be arranged: The setting can be set. Your intentionality won't undermine you if you limit it to shaping an expectation or readiness for spontaneity to occur. As with artists, athletes, and sexual partners, your success with self-hypnosis involves the *creation of a context* for avolitional responsiveness, at which point you invite your intentionality to clock out. In other words, the solution to the *Be spontaneous!* conundrum is achieved by reversing the formulation of the problem. To keep intentionality from unintentionally blundering into the middle of your spontaneous creation, you intentionally facilitate unintentionality running the show: "The jazz great Charlie Parker is said to have advised aspiring musicians, 'Don't play the saxophone. Let it play you'" (Slingerland, 2014, p. 1). Sonny Rollins, another jazz great, said in an interview that when improvising in a performance, "the optimum condition is not to think. I just want the music to play itself. . . . If I have to think about what I'm doing, then the moment is already gone" (Gross, 1994). And the novelist Ursula K. LeGuin (1996) said something similar about writing:

> When I'm trying to control the story and make it do something, it doesn't work. When I quit trying, when I let the story tell me what it is, I get to a whole deeper level. . . . It's not passive; it's actively passive, passively active.

Milton Erickson (2014) brought an analogous sensibility to the practice of facilitating self-hypnotic (or, as he called it, autohypnotic) experience:

> The insomniac lies in bed and says: "Now I've got to go to sleep—I've got to go to sleep—I've got to get some rest. . . . And what happens? He stays wide awake . . . because he is constantly telling himself what he's *got* to do. But the smart person

who wants a good night's sleep . . . just lets sleep happen to him. . . .

If you want to learn autohypnosis you sit down quietly in the chair, you arrange yourself comfortably, and then you say to yourself: "Well, here I am. I have at least two hours, and I wonder how long it will be before I drop into an autohypnotic trance. It ought to be interesting." And then you wait passively, quietly, and comfortably. . . . You do not do what the insomniac does. You do not attempt to compel yourself into a state of unconscious behavior from the conscious level. (pp. 252–253)

Intentionality messes things up, in part, because it maintains the dualistic structuring of everyday awareness—you have your circumscribed self, ostensibly in charge, assigning tasks or offering encouragement to some other part of the self ("Thoughts slowing down, slower and slower"; "Time for sleep—becoming sleepier and sleepier"; "Calm down, just relax, letting go of that tension, heart slowing down"; "Pain diminishing, pain lessening"). Such injunctions inadvertently underscore the boundary between the source (the conscious awareness of your circumscribed self) and the recipient (your body) of the suggestions, which precludes the mind-body connection necessary for any hypnotic effect. Erickson (2014) again:

So many people who attempt to go into an autohypnotic trance say to themselves: "Now I am going to go into an autohypnotic trance, and I am going to produce an anesthesia of my leg because I've got pain there. And I am going into the autohypnotic trance, and I am developing anesthesia." No, that is completely wrong. First you develop the autohypnotic trance, and having developed it, then take over the proper utilization of it. Do not attempt to do both things at once. (p. 252)

Prioritizing the non-willful attunement of mind and body (or of awareness and experience), you establish an expectation for something spontaneous to unfold: *"[In] contemplative practice, . . . we balance two seemingly opposite movements: acting without hesitation and remaining still long enough for perception to dilate and take in the unknown"* (Nachmanovitch, 2019, p. 51). For an artist, this orientation to discovery requires you to be "very, very attentive, alert, but patient. Slow." (LeGuin, 2012, p. 189):

> First you have to be able to wait. To wait in silence. Wait in silence, and listen. Listen for the tune, the vision, the story. Not grabbing, not pushing, just waiting, listening, being ready for it when it comes. This is an act of trust. (p. 217)

The same is true for the practice of self-hypnosis. You get ready for the possibility of something happening and then, with this orientation in place, you patiently protect the time and the space for it to creatively emerge.

One way to define a context for spontaneous discovery and change is to float a question for yourself and then actively avoid searching for an answer, allowing instead the speculation to hover, orienting your curiosity. To illustrate what this might look like, I'd like to talk for a minute about running.

It isn't uncommon for runners to try to push beyond the limits of their exhaustion by urging themselves to try harder. Some blast themselves with self-talk that resembles the rantings of a critical coach ("And you call yourself an athlete?! Go! Faster, damn you!"), while others take a more positive approach ("You can do this!" "Keep going!" "You're doing great!"). Research has indicated that positive encouragement, particularly when posed in second, rather than first, person (i.e., "*You* can do this," not "*I* can do this"), improves race times (Douglas, 2019).

I've been running for 30 years, and I've developed an orientation to performance enhancement that involves neither negative nor positive urgings. Before I describe it, I should hasten to add that I'm far from fast (just ask my daughter), and I've never distinguished myself in any of the hundred or so 5K races I've run for fun, so know that this is not a pro tip from an elite athlete. Nevertheless, I have on occasion relayed this approach to clients who are high-level competitors, and I offer it here as illustration of the logic of self-hypnosis.

Rather than *push* myself to run faster, I *invite* myself to discover that I can, and I do this by intermittently posing questions and then staying alert to how my body finds itself answering them: "I wonder how much you can pick up your pace?" or "What would it be like if heading up this hill felt like running down it?" or "I wonder whether it would be possible to go all-out between the stop sign and that blue car up there?" More often than not, my body finds itself effortlessly responding to such questions by accelerating or at least persevering.

Posing a question that invites a to-be-discovered, rather than a to-be-worked-out, response is a way of facilitating and maintaining the kind of mind-body connection characteristic of self-hypnotic experience. Instead of your circumscribed self issuing directives to some part of or all the rest of you, you pose a question or a possibility, or you acknowledge a task or a conundrum that needs to be addressed, and then you let it float. This sets the conditions or establishes the parameters for a spontaneous avolitional response, eschewing the circumscribed self's proclivity for impatient micromanagement. In so doing, you protect the possibility of flow-based invention or discovery. Erickson and Rossi (2008a) put it this way:

> We go into autohypnosis in order to achieve certain conscious goals, yet the conscious mind cannot tell the unconscious what to do. The conscious mind can structure a general framework or ask questions, but it must be left to the autonomy of the unconscious as to how and when the desired activity will be carried out. (p. 201)

Let's put this understanding into practice by way of an experiment. As a preliminary to beginning, bring to mind some shift in your experience, some change that would perhaps mark a beginning, a welcome development, or a completion of something. If you were a novelist, you might hold in mind the need for a turn or resolution within or at the end of the story you were working on. If you were in pain, you'd be looking for some measure of relief; if suffering from insomnia, the ability to sleep.

Find a comfortable position you can maintain for a period of time, so your head and neck and back are well supported, either through an upright meditative posture or by way of a cushioned chair. Then close your eyes and pose a question that simply and in positive terms introduces the possibility of an unspecified but welcome shift in your experience. Your question will be constructed somewhat along these lines: "I wonder how my encompassing self (or my body, my unconscious, my mind-body) will creatively arrange, find, inspire, or synergize this change?" In posing such a question, you are giving shape to your curiosity, which is also aided by your introducing an element of expectancy into the process. Take a few minutes with your eyes closed to form a well-constructed question. When you're ready, come back to reading.

. . . . .

Now, with a question articulated, you're going to take your conscious awareness offline. You aren't going to actively search for an answer—no racking your brain, no wondering why you haven't been able to do this in the past, no making a list of options, no thinking through possibilities, no yearning, no fretting. Instead, you're going to disengage all such usual efforts of your circumscribed self and patiently wait, allowing the question you've posed to contextually define the outer limits, the defining boundaries, of your open-ended curiosity. You're creating the space for musing:

> No accident, that word used to describe the ways in which thought's more fluid transformations occur. "To muse" implies entering a condition of idleness, outside the responsibilities of the fully adult: a playfulness marks the self-amusing, musing mind. It lifts a thing, turns it over, licks it, sees if it moves; explores in a way that leaves behind both simple preconception and the directionality of strict purpose. "Muse" derives from the Latin *mussare*, meaning first "to carry in silence," then "to brood over in silence and uncertainty." . . . Musing, it seems, is a thing that happens best in the circumstances of quiet. (Hirshfield, 2015, pp. 26–27)

Just like meditation, self-hypnosis involves getting in sync with yourself, indifferentiating the boundary between your circumscribed

*self and the rest of you. So if you like, you can start by posing the
question silently to yourself, allowing your eyes to close, and following your breath. As with meditation, when that focus is interrupted,
you'll just acknowledge whatever it is and go back to the breath. Don't
bother going back to the question. It is orienting the process, so you
needn't revisit it. You're already inside it. Take a few minutes to try
this out.*

　　. . . . .

There are other ways of inviting a mind-body connection. One
is to keep your eyes open, locate an object in your line of vision,
and rest your gaze on it. Just keep your focus there and notice and
acknowledge the perceptual changes that start happening. Erickson
described how to employ a version of this approach when needing
to efficiently accomplish a demanding task:

> Autohypnosis is when the subject sits down quietly in the room
> and says, "I am going to stare at that object until I fall into a
> hypnotic trance and after I get into the trance I'm going to dic-
> tate so many case histories." He then stares, and all of a sudden
> he starts dictating case histories into the dictaphone. When he
> finishes the given number [of case histories], he wakes up star-
> ing at [the object]. Now it's dinner time! (Rossi et al., 2015, p. 33)

Let's try this method out.

*Positioned comfortably, float your question and then, with your eyes
open, hold an object in your line of sight. Allow your awareness to
narrow in on this one object, freeing up anything in your peripheral
vision or peripheral awareness to blur or fade or otherwise dissolve
into insignificance.*

　　. . . . .

Visualization offers still another way of providing nonintru-
sive orienting direction for self-hypnotic experience. When you
visualize, you are conjuring up a virtual version of a "real world"
perceptual experience, which then prompts the same or a similar

body response. This happens all the time when you're watching a movie—your body vicariously experiences what the protagonist is living through.

A client of mine used to chase sleep. She now uses a very effective self-hypnotic approach to invite sleep to come to her. When she lies down at night, she takes a very slow, elongated breath in through her nose, and as this happens, she sees a wave receding from a beach, the water draining from the sand back into the ocean. And then, as she slowly breathes out through her nose, she watches as a new wave curls up and over, breaking onto the sand, with rivulets of water extending still further up the beach. She watches the sparkling light playing off the water and is captivated by the movement of the wave, all the way up, until the inexorable flow of the water back out to sea coincides with the next inexorable flow of air back into her lungs. Within half a dozen of such animated breaths, she is typically effortlessly drifting off, and this happens without her consciously thinking about sleep or giving herself any direct sleep-related or relaxation suggestions.

The connection between the imagery and the desired effect—between waves and sleep—doesn't need to be explicitly stated or urged. The context, already established by the setting and the time, orients the process by virtue of implication, not direction. This keeps intentionality at bay and allows the self-hypnotic process to facilitate avolitional drifting off.

> *Time for another experiment. Get comfortable, close your eyes, and instead of posing a question to yourself, visualize the realization of some desired effect. When your attention drifts, gently bring it back to what you're imagining. You might, like my client, entwine some rhythmic aspect of what you're noticing with the rhythm of your breath. Become a fascinated observer—rather than trying to actively conjure up something happening, wait with patience and passively discover what develops and emerges, getting a feel for nuances, qualities, textures, colors, scents, sounds, and so on. No need for concern if your imaginings are not in technicolor; accept whatever level of resolution and specificity comes to you.*
>
> . . . . .

Once you can self-hypnotically activate an avolitional response, it is possible to reliably evoke it through a combination of visualization and body feeling. Another of my clients learned through self-hypnotic visualization to significantly lower his blood pressure. He told me that, as a practical joke, he once facilitated a drop in his pressure just before the nurse at his regular check-up put a cuff on his arm. His reading alarmed her until he laughed and explained what he'd done.

Another practical joker, Milton Erickson's daughter Betty Alice, learned via self-hypnosis how to independently alter the size of her pupils. "She would get the question, *I wonder if I can change the pupils of my eyes*, and then she set herself the task" (Erickson, 2015, p. 140). However, she didn't just pose the question and wait; she also employed visualization and attended carefully to the body-based feeling associated with the changes:

> Betty Alice started . . . by thinking to herself: I've got my eyes shut. . . . Now, if I open one eye and look right at the sun, I would feel it in my eye, but the other eye wouldn't feel it so much; then if I shut this eye and opened this eye and looked at the sun [the reverse would happen]. And she practiced that over and over again until she began to get feelings of a certain sort in her eyes. . . . The contracted pupil gave one sensation and the dilated pupil gave another sensation. (p. 142)

She brought this skill with her the next time she needed to get her eyes checked:

> The ophthalmologist was examining her eyes: he looked in her right eye and measured the pupil—it was widely dilated, and he recorded it. He examined the retina, and then he shifted over to the left eye. He was utterly astonished: the left pupil was contracted way down. So he looked back at the right pupil, and now that was contracted way down! He checked on his measurements, and looked back at the left one and that was dilated! Betty Alice was just entertaining herself. (p. 141)

Your clients, of course, will more likely be interested in the therapeutic, rather than entertainment, value of the practice. I taught self-hypnosis to a man who suffered from debilitating headaches. He learned in our sessions how to greet, meet, and let pass by an approaching headache, and he then learned how to do this on his own. He got good at identifying the visceral premonition that a headache was developing, at which point he would stop whatever he was doing, close his eyes, and adopt an idiosyncratic posture that he had discovered could activate his self-hypnotic responsiveness. He told me that he didn't know what he did after that point in the process but that the majority of the time he could take care of a headache just before it arrived. Such not-knowing, not trying to know, and not trying to determine, are all essential for protecting avolitional spontaneity—the active passivity, the passive activity, of hypnotherapeutic change.

By introducing your clients to meditation and self-hypnosis practices, you offer them non-countering agency—the means to resourcefully respond on their own to what plagues them so they no longer feel victimized by it. Instead of trying to counteract what troubles them, they discover they can *en*counteract it.

By introducing *yourself* to the practice of meditation and self-hypnosis, you'll gain, in addition to any personal benefits, an insider's body-based appreciation and knowledge of flow experience, which is invaluable for learning how to facilitate hypnotherapeutic change. With a feel for the territory of meditative and hypnotic experience, you'll have a firsthand grasp of what's possible and what can get in the way. And learning how to get in sync with yourself will help you connect with your clients and with whatever unfolds for them in hypnosis. That's where we go next—the art of inviting and making use of connections.

CONNECTING WITH CLIENTS

I have been told, both in approval and in accusation, that I seem to love all my characters. What I do in writing of any character is to try to enter into the mind, heart, and skin of a human being who is not myself. . . . The primary challenge lies in making the jump itself. It is the act of a writer's imagination that I set most high.
—Eudora Welty (1980, p. xi)

The Germans must have a term for it. Doppelgedanken, *perhaps: the sensation, when reading, that your own mind is giving birth to the words as they appear on the page. Such is the ego that in these rare instances you wonder, "How could the author have known what I was thinking?" Of course, what has happened isn't this at all, though it's no less astonishing. Rather, you've been drawn so deftly into another world that you're breathing with someone else's rhythms, seeing someone else's visions as your own.*
—Leah Hager Cohen (2009)

The preparation for hypnotherapy presents you with three challenges or responsibilities. You need to gather pertinent details regarding your clients' experience, helping to refine or adapt their characterization of their problem so that you and they agree on what a resolution would look like and how to proceed toward it; you need to orient them to the hypnotic process, clearing up misunderstandings and shaping their expectations; and you need to connect with them, to become of one mind with them. Throughout your initial session(s), you're taking care of all three of these responsibilities simultaneously, but I'm going to address them separately, starting, in this chapter, with the third: connecting. I'll circle back to the first two in Chapter 4.

Prior to meeting and talking with you, your clients might have learned a little about you—from an ad, from googling, from a friend or another professional—but you are still essentially an unknown entity: a stranger, an outsider. In their first appointment(s) with you, as you're doing your best to learn about them, they are scoping you out, deciding whether and how much to trust you and how much to divulge. They are weighing the possibility of allowing you privileged access to their sense of self, of allowing you to move from outsider to insider.

Hypnosis is out of the question unless and until you can ensure that your clients feel safe and comfortable granting you privileged access to their sense of self. After all, they are faced with sharing with you not only information but also their mind. Contrary to common (mis)understanding, this sharing does not entail their relinquishing control to you; however, it can certainly feel that way to them, given that their participation in the process involves a letting go of the controlling aspirations of their conscious awareness. But this is what happens in any flow experience—the usual boundaries of the circumscribed self dissolve into the engagement in the activity itself. When we read a novel or watch a movie, we agree to have our experience shaped by what is unfolding on the page or screen, but we always have the option of pulling ourselves away, of retreating from the shared-mind experience by reasserting the distinctiveness of our identity, separate from whatever we've been absorbed in. We put a bookmark in, we press Pause, we reorient to our immediate surroundings.

The same is true of hypnosis. As your clients relax the scrutinizing and evaluating efforts of their conscious awareness, they make it possible for their sense of self to become inclusive of, rather than separate from, both you and their body. But, all the while, they have a bookmark or a pause button available, should they at any time need or choose to distinguish themselves—to remove themselves—from the flow experience of a shared mind.

This is what Milton Erickson's daughter Betty Alice did one day when she was a teenager. She had for some time traveled on the weekends with her father to professional meetings, serving as a demonstration subject for his hypnosis lectures. But on this particular occasion, Betty Alice wasn't having it. When Erickson went to demonstrate various phenomena, such as a hand levitation, nothing happened. Nothing. The most accomplished and renowned medical hypnotist in the world couldn't get that 15-year-old's hand to budge (Eric Greenleaf, personal communication, December 12, 2019).

Betty Alice's act of adolescent defiance underscores that hypnosis is fundamentally a collaborative, not controlling, venture, from which engagement can be withdrawn anytime. This brings us back to the *Be spontaneous!* paradox introduced in Chapter 1—you can't determine or demand avolitional responsiveness; the most you or any hypnotist can do is establish the parameters and conditions within which hypnotic phenomena can emerge. Such context setting begins with your clients trusting you enough to relax the boundaries of their circumscribed self as they venture into mind sharing. You earn that trust and facilitate the sharing through the medium of empathy.

EMPATHY

Definitions and understandings of empathy vary considerably. Carl Rogers viewed accurate empathic understanding as one of three core conditions necessary for therapeutic change, along with acceptance and "unconditional positive regard," or "non-possessive warmth" (Truax & Lister, 1970, p. 229). Jay Haley (1981) warned against the pairing of empathy and warmth, at least when that style of engagement doesn't match the client's way of being:

> If a therapist is warm and empathic with a patient who is a cold fish, there is something wrong with that therapist and he should be more considerate. To be cold in that situation would be more appropriate and human. . . . . The [patient] will feel that yet another person does not understand her. The therapist must join that [patient's] universe and from within that universe bring about change. (p. 239)

Haley recognized that connecting closely with clients requires not only a demonstrated understanding of what they say but also a fitting in with how they are. Rogers agreed with the importance of the therapist working within the client's worldview. Empathy, he said, is "the therapist's sensitive ability and willingness to understand the client's thoughts, feelings and struggles from the client's point of view. [Empathy is] this ability to see completely through the client's eyes, to adopt his frame of reference" (Rogers, 1980, p. 85). It involves not only the development of an understanding, but also the "endeavor . . . to communicate this experience to the client" (Rogers, 1957, p. 96). Haley's point was that in this communication, it matters not only what you say but also how you say it, how you engage. You connect more thoroughly if your demeanor matches in some way that of your client. He learned this from Milton Erickson.

According to Zeig, Erickson would establish "a high degree of empathic rapport" with his patients, but he did so implicitly, using a style of indirection to demonstrate it (Erickson & Zeig, 2008, p. 286). He sometimes spoke with his patients in ways that, from the outside, would have sounded harsh and deeply critical, yet his patients heard what he was saying as an accurate reflection of them and their circumstances. For example, he once worked with an obese young woman whose family members had all died. She believed that she, too, was destined to soon die, and she was certain that because of her appearance, Erickson would refuse to work with her. Erickson concluded

> that the only possible understanding this girl had of intercommunication was that of unkindness and brutality. Hence, brutality would be used to convince her of [my] sincerity. Any other possible approach, any kindness, would be misinterpreted. She could not possibly believe courteous language. I realized that rapport would have to be established—and established very quickly. She would have to be convinced, beyond a doubt, that I understood and recognized her and her problem and was not afraid to speak openly, freely, unemotionally, but truthfully. (Erickson, 2008b, p. 75)

Erickson delivered his "brutal truth" in the form of stinging criticisms of the client's appearance. This established a ground of agreement and trust between them that he subsequently built on to help her alter her relationship to herself and to other people. Years later, when she was happily married with two adolescent children, the client said to Erickson, "When you said those awful things about me, you were so truthful. I knew that you were telling me the truth, that I could trust you. I am so glad you told me the truth" (2008b, p. 79). The intensity, attitude, and manner of speaking that Erickson adopted when conversing with his client was familiar territory for her and was the empathic foundation of the hypnotic work they did together.

Clearly, then, empathy does not necessarily involve kindness or warmth. It has much more to do with developing a shared sensibility. To illuminate its connective capabilities, I'll begin by distinguishing it from sympathy and compassion.

Sympathy, Compassion, and Empathy

In popular culture, *sympathy*, *compassion*, and *empathy* are often used interchangeably. This makes sense for the first two, given their etymologies. The Latin roots of *compassion* (*com-*, "with, together" + *pati*, "feeling" or "suffering") are virtually identical to the Greek roots of *sympathy* (*syn-*, "with, together" + *pathos*, "feeling" or "suffering"). Both speak to the emotional capacity to share another's burden— the willingness and ability not just to recognize but to emotionally register the suffering you are witnessing or contemplating. At least with compassion, this "feeling with" can transport you outside the isolation of your circumscribed self and into a way of relating that indifferentiates the division between "us" and "them." It is no surprise, then, that it plays such an important role in mindfulness practice, which involves not just unencumbered attention but also *maitri*-infused awareness.

Sympathy as it is used today more often describes a kind of "feeling for" or "feeling about," rather than a "feeling with." As a result, it tends to maintain, rather than dissolve, the everyday division between you and the person(s) to whose suffering you are emotionally responding. There is a certain safe distance involved in sympathy, which is more starkly recognizable in the feeling of pity.

A person feeling compassion recognizes the shared humanity of those who are suffering, reaches out to console, and offers concrete help; a person feeling sympathy acknowledges the pain of those who are suffering and offers heartfelt condolences; a person feeling pity sees the helplessness of those who are suffering and, unmoved and removed, communicates implicit condescension.

And then there's empathy. The word has a fascinating history. It was introduced into English in 1909 by the psychologist Edward Titchener, rendering the German word *Einfühlung* (*ein-*, "in" + *fühlung*, "feeling": feeling into), which was coined in 1873 by a German philosopher of aesthetics, Robert Vischer. *Einfühlung* helped Vischer explain how certain works of art move those who view them.

Another German philosopher, Theodor Lipps, adopted and further developed Vischer's notion of Einfühlung to describe "the emotional 'knowing' of a work of art from within, by feeling an emotional resonance with [it]" (Riess, 2017, p. 75). Lipps said that "the moment a viewer recognizes a painting as beautiful, it transforms from an object into a work of art. The act of looking, then, becomes a creative process, and the viewer becomes the artist" (Corbett, 2016, p. 21).

Lipps was a renowned teacher who inspired and influenced many artists and intellectuals, among them Wassily Kandinsky, Rainer Maria Rilke, and, most notably for our purposes, Sigmund Freud, who took the concept of Einfühlung from the realm of aesthetics and applied it to the practice of psychoanalysis, viewing it

> as a tool for understanding patients. He urged his students to observe their patients not from a place of judgment, but of empathy. They ought to . . . strive toward the "putting of oneself in the other person's place," he said. (Corbett, 2016, p. 23)

"Empathy" is a good translation of *Einfühlung*, in that it draws from the same Greek word that first inspired Vischer: *empatheia* (*en-*, "in" + *páthos*, "feeling" or "suffering": feeling into). The etymology is important: It distinguishes empathy as what we might call a pro-active emotion. In contrast to the receptive willingness of both sym-pathy and compassion to "feel with" the other, empathy involves a projective curiosity, a desire to develop a body-based understand-ing of the other from within their world. You empathize with your clients in order to develop a *sense* of—to get a *feel* for—what it must be like to be them.

Cameron et al. (2015) note that "empathy is a choice that we make whether to extend ourselves to others." When the choice is acted upon, it produces what Buber called an I-Thou relationship (Riess, 2017, p. 75). To empathize is to imagine yourself inside the other's context, immersed in their historical and current experience. As such, it can be considered a mode of metaphoric knowing, a means of going in search of a body-informed, fleshed-out answer to the multifaceted question, "If I were you, what would I be thinking, feeling, doing, wanting, hoping, demanding, protecting, remem-bering, anticipating?" Rogers underscored the importance of hold-ing on to the subjunctive quality of this projected curiosity:

> The state of empathy, or being empathic, is to perceive the inter-nal frame of reference of another with accuracy and with the emotional components and meanings which pertain thereto as if one were the person, but without ever losing the "as if" condition. Thus, it means to sense the hurt or the pleasure of another as he senses it and to perceive the causes thereof as he perceives them, but without ever losing the recognition that it is as if I were hurt or pleased and so forth. If this "as if" quality is lost, then the state is one of identification. (Rogers, 1980, pp. 140–141)

The goal is not to passively lose yourself in the other's world but, rather, to purposefully explore it, making your way around inside it, taking in the details and significance of their experience. You proj-ect yourself into it as if it were a work of art. Where *maitri* radiates, empathy probes. As you get your bearings, you offer up what you're noticing:

To sense the client's anger, fear, or confusion as if it were your own, yet without your own anger, fear, or confusion getting bound up in it, is the condition we are endeavoring to describe. When the client's world is this clear to the therapist, and he moves about in it freely, then he can both communicate his understanding of what is clearly known to the client and can also voice meanings in the client's experience of which the client is scarcely aware. (Rogers, 1957, p. 99)

As a form of connected knowing, empathy reflects a commitment to developing an insider's grasp of the perspective, story, and emotional realities of another person. It isn't so much a feeling that arises within you as it is an intersubjective sensitivity and contextual sensibility you can learn and hone as a skill. Like Eudora Welty (1980), you "enter into the mind, heart, and skin of a human being who is not [your]self. . . . The primary challenge lies in making the jump itself" (p. xi).

At the heart of empathy lies a willingness and ability to let go of the comfortable security of removed judgment, striving instead for embodied understanding and respect, engendered by engaged curiosity. To arrive at such an understanding, you can't just gather facts and impressions. To ensure the accuracy of what you're coming to appreciate, you need to communicate your impressions and then listen to and watch how your clients respond.

Empathic Communication

It is best to develop your empathic sensibility of your clients in collaboration with them, frequently sharing what you're grasping and surmising so you can get the real-time feedback necessary to correct, expand, or refine what you're coming to understand. Your clients rely on the specifics of what you say to determine whether your characterization of their experience is accurate and adequately comprehensive and nuanced. And you, in turn, rely on their responses to what you're saying as you calibrate and recalibrate your empathic depictions. Most clients will respond affirmatively when you're on the right track ("right," "yes," "exactly") and will correct you when you're not ("no," "not quite," "not really"). They are, in effect, remotely steering you, helping your sense of them to come into alignment with their sense of themselves. As the accuracy of your comments improves, clients are given the opportunity to witness a high-resolution witnessing of their experience.

When I've recommended to my students that they frequently insert empathic comments into their clients' descriptions, explanations, and stories, some have worried about how their clients will respond to such "interruptions." They've told me about wanting to show their respect by sitting quietly and listening attentively, politely waiting for an appropriate pause before offering a reflection or a question.

Respect is critical, but deference precludes the kind of collaborative interaction essential for the development of an empathic sensibility. If you silently nod while loquacious clients delve into their history, you will be indicating that you're following along with what they're saying, but you'll also be encouraging them to continue expounding. You may be gleaning a lot from what they are saying, but they won't know that you actually have a grasp of what they are describing, thinking, or feeling until you give voice to your impressions.

It is much easier to talk about empathy than to put it into practice. One of the best ways to develop the involved skills is to record a session (with your client's permission, of course), play it back later, and find sections where the client is providing a description, explanation, or example of something that happened:

> c: I had a panic attack last week while I was driving. I was on the highway, and I had the steering wheel in this, like, death grip. My heart was pounding—I could hear it, I swear—and I was afraid I was going to pass out. I have no idea how I got over to the shoulder without killing myself or someone else. Cars were whizzing by me on both sides and I had to get over, I had to stop, but I couldn't stop, not in the middle of the frickin' highway. I was crying and shaking like a leaf.

Press Pause and practice formulating empathic comments or hunches that convey something of what you've heard. Be succinct, take into account key details or turning points, and capture something of the person's emotional engagement in the experience:

> T: Your heart was pounding in your ears, and your body was screaming for you to get over and stop, but you had no way to do that, what with the cars screaming past you. What an impossible situation!

or

> T: You were trying like crazy to keep from passing out or losing control of your car. Nothing felt safe. No wonder you were shaking!

or

> T: Somehow that death grip delivered you to safety. You kept it together so you could get off the damn highway, alive, but it took everything you had not to faint or give up.

But you needn't wait so long to insert a comment. If you replay the clip from the beginning, you can pause and construct an empathic response at the end of each of the client's statements:

> C: I had a panic attack last week while I was driving. I was on the highway, and I had the steering wheel in this, like, death grip.
> T: White-knuckling it.

> C: My heart was pounding—I could hear it, I swear—and I was afraid I was going to pass out.
> T: Light-headed with a pounding heart: You were in emergency mode.

C: I have no idea how I got over to the shoulder without killing myself or someone else.

T: Sounds impossibly dangerous.

C: Cars were whizzing by me on both sides and I had to get over, I had to stop, but I couldn't stop, not in the middle of the frickin' highway.

T: A desperate need to stop and a desperate need to keep going.

C: I was crying and shaking like a leaf.

T: So afraid and so determined.

Effective empathic communication does not involve the passive cataloging of what your clients tell you and then offering back a digested version. Rather, you're collecting details of what they recount to help you recreate in your projected imagination what it must be like to *be* them, reliving the reality they are relaying to you. You're expressing what you conceive to be your clients' experience, in terms of not only the details they're providing but also the emotional effects these details have been having on them.

I don't consider—and more importantly, clients don't generally experience—interspersed empathic comments as interruptions (from the Latin *inter-*, "between" + *rumpere*, "to break": to break into, to break in upon).* Rather than *rupturing* the flow of your clients' stories, you are simply *interlacing* (from the Anglo-Norman *entre-*, "between" + *lacer*, "to weave": to interweave) your empathic

---

* For her dissertation research with me, one of my former doctoral students, Victoria Lazareva, studied the use of empathy in medical settings. Part of the project involved my video-recording a series of 15-minute consultations with five standardized patients (actors who help train medical students by simulating the symptoms and behaviors of real patients). All came to their unscripted interviews with a supplied backstory and diagnosis, as well as an etched-out medical history that involved some difficulty in relating to their medical doctor. I interlaced empathic comments throughout all the conversations. After we finished recording the interviews, Victoria asked the actors, now out of role, to reflect on what the experience had been like for them. None were irritated by the frequency of my empathic comments; in fact, they all commented on feeling good about what had transpired during our conversations. Two of the actors reported being personally moved by their participation in the recorded demonstrations.

statements throughout them, transforming client soliloquies into interactive, contrapuntal conversations. You turn this:

C: I have this licensing exam coming up, and I've failed it twice before, so I've gotten myself pretty worked up over it. It's hard to explain because I don't have typical test anxiety—I can take regular tests. It has something to do with how important this one is. I don't think I was even anxious the first time, and I thought I'd passed it, so that tells you something. I was so upset when I got the results 'cause I scored three points shy of the cutoff. And then when it came to the second time, I got really nervous because now I knew I didn't know what they wanted. So all the way through it, I kept reading through the questions and then the answers, and then back to the questions—losing my focus. And sure enough, I blew it that time, too. Did even worse than the first time. And now this is the third time, and it is my last chance. I'm really scared I'm going to fail again.

into this:

C: I have this licensing exam coming up, and I've failed it twice before, so I've gotten myself pretty worked up over it.
T: You're facing a big hurdle.
C: More like a wall. A high one.
T: A wall you can't just hop over—you've got to scale it.
C: Yeah, and I guess I don't know how to do it. Or *if* I can do it.
T: That makes it doubly hard, if you're wondering what you need to do to pass the exam but then also whether you have what it takes.
C: I thought I knew the first time. I don't think I was even anxious. When I walked out of the exam center, I was sure I'd passed.
T: Your heart must have sunk when you got the results.
C: I was stunned. So then the second time, I was a nervous wreck.
T: Leading up to it?
C: For sure, but also during it. I could barely concentrate.
T: Your confidence had been shaken.
C: Totally.

T: It's so hard to stay focused in a situation like that—when you're second-guessing yourself.

C: The whole time! I ran out of time! I kept going back, changing my answers and then changing them back again.

T: You wanted so badly to get it right, it slowed you down.

C: So ridiculous! I know the material! And now I'm having to take it a third time?!

T: You sound both incredulous and exasperated. Like you can't believe it happened to you.

C: I am! Exactly! What the hell?

T: Because you know the material.

C: I do!

T: So now you just need to be able to *demonstrate* that on the exam.

C: Exactly!

You may recall from the discussion of meditation that the mindful following of the breath affords a dissolution of the everyday intrapersonal boundary between awareness and experience. The rhythm of the breath and the absorbed awareness of the rhythm of the breath closely align, allowing the difference between them to become indifferentiated. Conscious mind and body process connect.

Something analogous happens in the interpersonal sphere when you respond empathically to your clients. The interactive process of generating empathic understanding is itself a boundary-dissolving process. As the content and expression of your descriptions of your clients' experience come into alignment with what they themselves are thinking and experiencing, the differences between the two sources of information can become, for the clients, inconsequential or even irrelevant. This makes it possible for them to become indifferent about any of the myriad differences between you and them. As self and other connect, as your clients' sense of self, rather than excluding you, *encompasses* you, then you and your clients become of one mind.

Empathy can thus be conceived of as a transportation device, delivering you from outsider to insider status. When your ideas and suggestions are offered from this position, they will be less likely experienced as impositions to be guarded against than as invitations to be entertained and explored. This is why empathy is such an essential stepping-stone into hypnotic engagement.

For your empathic offerings to result in a boundary-altering connection with your clients, what you say needs to convey both the head and heart of their descriptions, explanations, and stories. This requires you to listen for and reflect back the details they offer, or perhaps a summation or distillation of the details. But also, when you can and when appropriate, you'll want to accompany this content with a characterization of their emotional engagement, which sometimes they'll convey in words ("Yeah, I'm . . . scared and pissed") but which often you'll be inferring from their tone, facial expressions, gestures, and/or posture. As you offer your empathic reflections, your word choices, the paralinguistic elements of your voice, and the nonverbal positioning and movements of your body should match or at least resonate with those of the client. Here is an example from a case with a client who had, for a long time, felt shut down by a demanding and demeaning boss:

> C: I just couldn't take his sarcasm anymore. I *refused*. I was scared to death, but for the first time, I stood up to him.
> T: You were determined,

I inferred this from what she said and how she said it.

> C: Yes!
> T: despite being frightened.

This is an empathic rendering of what she said, but I muted the intensity of her description. I should have said, "despite being *terrified*."

Your clients' emotional engagement with you gives you a feel for how they were making sense of themselves as the protagonist of the story they are telling.

> C: I was roiling inside.
> T: Ready to blow?

This hunch came from my imagining what I might have felt in her position. As it turned out, I was wrong.

    C: No. . . . I wasn't so much angry. . . . More just fed up.

Her correction helped me improve the resolution of my projected imaginings.

    T: {clipped and louder} You'd had enough.

In my tone and pace, I attempted to capture something of the emotional tenor of her fed-up determination.

    C: Absolutely.
    T: But with enough roiling in the mix to get you ready for what you needed to do.
    C: {laughing} That's for sure.

You can use empathic statements to shift the focus from the nature of your clients' involvement in the story they are telling, to what is happening for them now in your office, as they're narrating the story:

    T: Which even now seems a little surprising.

I surmised this from the wonder in her voice as she talked about what she did.

    C: {laughing} I still can't quite believe it.
    T: A discovery.
    C: Oh, I'm pretty pumped. I finally did it.
    T: Now you realize you're capable of it and can feel—I don't know—rightfully proud? But when you stood up to him, you were discovering that potential in the moment. I imagine it was a kind of revelation.
    C: Right. I didn't know I was going to do it till I was doing it.

Empathic communication involves *demonstrating*, not *claiming* that you understand. If you make assertions such as "I get it," "Yes, I understand," or "I know what you mean," you will inspire the person with whom you're communicating to reassure you that no, actually, you don't have a clue.

A client told me about his "impossible son," a teenager who consistently rebuffed my client's efforts to ease some of his pain. I asked for an example of what would happen. He said that earlier in the week, his son had come home from school complaining about how horrible his day had been. The dad asked him what had happened, and the son began telling him about these guys in the next grade up who had been making his life miserable. Soon into the relaying of what these older kids had done, the father, in a sincere effort to be helpful, had said, "I know what that's like. When I was your age, I remember one time when . . ."—at which point his son blew up at him and stormed out of the room. The father, now in my office, was still angry, believing that his son wanted only to complain, that he wouldn't even listen to some wise counsel. No wonder he was having such a hard time at school, given that he wasn't interested in hearing from someone who could help!

But, of course, what the father hadn't recognized was that his claim to understand, followed immediately by a story from his past, was demonstrating to his son that he absolutely didn't get what the son was going through and, furthermore, was inadvertently signaling that he wanted only to talk about himself, that he didn't have the patience or interest to listen.

When communicated effectively, an empathic statement doesn't feel like an *im*position but, rather, a *juxta*position: What you say is juxtaposed with—placed next to—what your clients are experiencing. You float it alongside. And when the two align, the difference between them becomes inconsequential. This, as I mentioned earlier, sets the shared-mind ground for the later offering of suggestions. When you and your clients are of one mind, the hypnotic suggestions you introduce don't feel to your client *im*posed but, rather, *com*posed—collaboratively created and experienced possibilities that can unfold avolitionally.

Empathic Enclosure

If you use empathy to connect closely with your clients, it becomes necessary for you to practice what might best be called *empathic enclosure*. I quoted Rogers a few pages back saying that the "as if" quality of empathic understanding must be held on to, lest you begin identifying with your clients. This happened to a psychologist who came to see me because, as she put it, she had become infected by some of her patients' symptoms.* In keeping with the people she'd been seeing, she'd recently begun washing her hands compulsively, having panic attacks, and perseverating on troubling thoughts. She'd become so distraught at taking on the burdens of her patients, she was considering closing her practice.

It helps that empathic curiosity is not a feeling that comes over you but, instead, a choice to engage, a purposeful approach to relating and exploring client experience. This means that you can hone your ability to proactively set time- and context-limiting boundaries for it. Just as you choose to enter into your clients' reality, you can choose to exit it, to come back into your own distinct sense of self. All you need is a means for doing it, a method or even a ritual for collecting yourself, for leaving behind this hour's client and coming back into yourself before starting your next appointment. Writing your session case note might be all it takes, or perhaps a few mindful breaths, or the adopting of some physical posture and/or movement that grounds or centers you. If, as with my client, still more is needed, a short ritual of some kind could be in order—something that transforms the context.

Given that the psychologist was feeling infected by her patients, I suggested that her urge to wash her hands was an inspired solution, in keeping with gold-standard practice among physicians. Any good doctor washes her hands between appointments to ensure that no infection is inadvertently passed from one patient to another or from any of the patients to the doctor. I asked if she would be willing to institute this as a standard operating procedure, a ritual of protection. She said she would. It then only made sense for her to also

* See Flemons & Gralnik, 2013, pp. 35–36.

wash her hands just before leaving the office for home, to ensure that any persistent patient symptoms with the potential to infect her would be safely washed down the drain before she headed out. So now instead of trying to resist the urge to wash in the manner of one of her patients, she was purposefully employing handwashing as a therapeutic ritual of empathic enclosure, marking the completion of each of her connections with her patients and then helping her to safely transition from work-mind to home-mind. It is now 15 years later, and she is still in practice.

Complementary Closeness

Empathy, and then the hypnosis that it makes possible, generates a kind of intimacy (from the Latin *intimus*, "innermost, deepest") with your clients. This only makes sense, given that you're sharing a mind. If you're going to work in this close manner, it is important for the well-being and safety of both you and your clients that you clearly distinguish therapeutic rapport from friendship or romantic intimacy.

With friends, and especially with lovers, closeness and trust are advanced via mutual sharing, opening up, and vulnerability. When one person offers a revealing story or emotion, the other responds in kind. However, in therapeutic relationships, intimacy is made possible not through mutuality but through a commitment to complementarity. When your clients reveal themselves in stories or disclose fears or yearnings, you don't reciprocate with personal stories or disclosures of your own; instead, you respond with empathic curiosity, maintaining the focus on their experience and their search for change.

Protecting the complementary shape of therapeutic interactions ensures that your shared-mind empathic (and, later, hypnotic) connections with clients stay ethical and safe. Your professional participation clearly demarcates and defines you as different from your clients. It is this contextual distinction that allows you the freedom and safety to connect so closely, so intimately, empathically dissolving boundaries of identity without breaching the boundaries of ethical practice.

Intraventive Empathy

Sometimes contributions to change are better characterized as *intra*ventions (from the Latin *intra-*, "on the inside, within" + *venire*, "to come": to come from within) than as *inter*ventions (from the Latin *inter-*, "between" + *venire*, "to come": to come between) (Flemons, 2002, p. 77). The distinction turns on your position and intent relative to your clients. If they experience you as an outside expert whose advice or input they are seeking, then you are well situated to *inter*vene, to introduce some difference into their lives. This could be an idea you'd like them to consider or take into account, an activity or approach you'd like them to try, or an interruption in some pattern they keep repeating.

However, if your clients are experiencing you as an inside consultant (from the Latin *com-*, "with, together" + *selere*, "take": to take together, to take counsel), as someone with whom they are sharing their mind, then you are in a position to *intra*vene, to float a possible change in how they are thinking, feeling, acting, interacting, or orienting—to themselves, to their problem, to their significant others. Intraventions tend not to be scrutinized so much as they are explored and/or enacted, as they emerge from within the fabric of your relationship, from within the developing sensibility that you share. This is, as I noted earlier, particularly the case with suggestions that follow an invitation into hypnosis. Avolitional responsiveness is facilitated by boundary indifferentiation in your clients' relationship to you and to their body/experience. Nevertheless, the development of therapeutic intraventions needn't wait till you've formally begun hypnosis. You can approach your empathic interlacing as an opportunity for introducing the sorts of shifts in orientation that make therapeutic change possible.

Empathy as a practice is often equated with active or reflective listening. Indeed, this is pretty much how I've characterized it up to this point—you reflect back what you glean from listening closely to the details and to the emotional tenor of your clients' stories, as well as from attending to their emotional engagement in the telling of the stories. But if you listen with a commitment not only to accuracy but also to establishing an orientation for change, then your participation will expand from offering sensitive reflections to include the offering of therapeutic possibilities. I think of this as *refractive* listening. You'll continue accurately noting the composing elements of their experience, but, in addition, you'll listen for and, when possible, implicitly or explicitly mark elements that could prove helpful in the development or therapeutic application of hypnosis.

For illustration, let's take a look at a conversation with Norma, who had been mandated to therapy after getting arrested for shoplifting.

> **NORMA:** {dejectedly, with both defiance and shame} When I went to the [clothing store where I was caught], I was in a state—I'd just had a horrible fight with my ex-husband. . . . I went to the store because I was worked up. . . . I had no plan to take anything, not even to buy anything. . . . I just like browsing through the racks, touching the clothes: It calms me down.

With Norma saying so much so quickly, I had many choices in what to focus on in an empathic response—the arrest, the ex, her upset, the lack of an intent to steal, the calming effect of browsing. I began by acknowledging the emotional state she was in following the fight.

> **DOUGLAS:** The argument left you upset, agitated.
> **N:** Very. And I didn't want my kids to see me that way.

I made a mental note of her having the strength and resolve to shield her kids. This could prove important later.

> **D:** You wanted to protect them, and you needed a way to settle your jangled nerves.
> **N:** Both. . . . I don't drink. If I did, I'd probably have just gone to a bar.
> **D:** A lot of people turn to alcohol at times like that. Your method of calming down is easier on your liver.
> **N:** {small laugh} Yeah.
> **D:** But when you head to the store at such difficult times, you don't necessarily have to buy something? So it isn't retail therapy.

N: {smiles} Right, no.

D: Somehow, it's the touching that makes a difference?

N: The feel of the different fabrics—it soothes me.

D: Your fingers do the browsing.

I was attributing agency to Norma's fingers.

N: {smiles} Exactly. Running different textures through my fingers. That has always been my way.

D: Your fingertips know something about how to use the sensation of touch to deliver relief.

This sensory-based, non-effortful way of relaxing could have an application at some point, perhaps as a means of inviting hypnosis or of altering an experience within hypnosis.

N: I don't know why.

D: Right, but even though *you* don't know *why*, your *fingers* know *how*.

In distinguishing body-based knowledge from conscious under-standing, my statement began to lay the foundation for trusting her body's know-how. But I was getting ahead of her—she didn't endorse the point I was making.

N: I guess.

Clearly her touch-based know-how was double-edged, because she ended up getting in trouble with the law.

D: At some point, then, touching turned into taking?

An empathic connection can allow you to explore painful or delicate details while helping clients save face. It was important, going forward, to help disentangle touching from taking. That way, Norma could hold on to a resource and let go of what got her into trouble.

N: I suppose. I was getting back into my car and reaching into my purse for my keys, and I found a couple of blouses and some underwear. I hadn't realized I was taking them. I'd been in such a fog.

D: You must have been shocked to discover them there.

N: I was . . .

There was a hesitancy in her voice.

D: But not entirely?

N: {deflated} This wasn't the first time it had happened.

D: Where you discovered that you'd shoplifted?

I continued to characterize what happened in keeping with how Norma described it: The act of stealing eluded her conscious awareness; it was only after the fact that she'd come to her senses, when she'd stumbled upon the distressing realization that she had once again stolen.

Some therapists might take it upon themselves to challenge such a claim, but I'm not interested in serving as a proxy for a prosecutor or judge. Rather, I commit to empathically developing framings that facilitate avolitional change. This version of what transpired lent itself well both to face-saving and a therapeutic shift in course.

N: Yes. . . .

Norma said that she'd been apprehended when she attempted to take the stolen goods back into the store to surreptitiously return them.

D: So you were both shocked *and* dismayed.

N: I was. I'm a Christian and a mother. Not a thief.

D: What you did doesn't reflect your beliefs and your devotion to your children.

N: Not at all.

D: Sounds like when you were fighting with your ex, you lost touch with yourself.

This empathic hunch once again refracted the sense of touch as an important element in her well-being.

N: I did.
D: And that browsing the racks of clothes with your fingers was an attempt to get that connection back.

Through our empathy-infused conversation, I developed an understanding of what, from Norma's perspective, had transpired the day she got arrested. However, this wasn't just a neutral depiction or a reiterated version of how she was thinking and feeling about it when she'd arrived for the appointment. Rather, it was a shared, therapeutically refracted sensibility—one that, by this point in the conversation, could transition easily into hypnosis.

This brings us to the other responsibilities involved in creating the conditions for hypnotherapeutic change. In the next chapter, I take a close look at what is involved in orienting clients to the experience of hypnosis. Then, in Chapter 5, we'll delve into the process of inviting it.

4

FORMULATING HYPNOTHERAPY

The very fact of diagnosing a person with some sort of medical condition is a form of medical treatment *which can be expected to have an effect.*

—Daniel Moerman (2002, p. 25)

All creative acts are forms of play. . . . Without play, learning . . . [is] impossible.

—Stephen Nachmanovitch (1990, p. 42)

In Chapter 1, I drew on Daniel Siegel and others to establish that "mind is [not] simply brain activity" (Siegel, 2012, p. xix). An accurate conception of hypnosis depends on the recognition that the body is mindful and the mind embodied. But then, Siegel, along with Bateson (2000) and Barrett (2020), helped me to trace the communication pathways of mind beyond this "skin-encapsulated" self (Watts, 1961, p. 11), pointing out that conversation between and among people can be usefully understood as a shared-mind phenomenon. And then, finally, I distinguished hypnosis as a distinct form of connected knowing, of shared-mind communication. The invitation of hypnosis facilitates an indifferentiation of the defining boundaries of the everyday circumscribed self and, in so doing, frees up the potential for avolitional responsiveness to proffered suggestions.

In this chapter, I'm once again reconfiguring boundaries, but this time in relation to the question, "When does hypno*therapy* begin?" Much of the heavy lifting (or, I guess, since this is hypnosis, the effortless floating up) of therapeutic change follows the invitation and evocation of hypnotic experience. This makes good sense. Once you're connected with your clients and once the boundary distinguishing awareness from the rest of the self has been at least somewhat indifferentiated, avolitional responsiveness is potentiated and can be usefully applied to the altering of problematic experience. A similar sensibility can be found in Zen.

In some forms of Zen practice, the intense contemplation of a koan (a conundrum that eludes conceptual or logical analysis, usually presented in the form of a phrase or story) is undertaken within zazen (sitting meditation), once the mindful awareness of the breath has established a mind-body bridge and a concomitant steadiness of attention:

> Here the technique is to come to [mindful] attention . . . and then to introduce the [koan] . . . to be meditated on, usually by reducing it to a word or phrase that you repeat with the breath. You concentrate on it, not ignoring but not grabbing onto all your various thoughts and speculations about it, until it is reduced to its nub. Staying with that, you break through finally to release and insight. (Fischer & Moon, 2016, p. 10)

Most clinicians don't look to hypnosis as a means of creating insight (save, perhaps, for psychoanalytic practitioners), but hypnotherapy, like Zen, uses the flow capabilities of a mind-body connection to facilitate a non-effortful, nonlogical—often an *analogical*—pathway for releasing clients from the bindings of their problem. In Chapter 6, I explore some of the ways this can be carried out. Here, though, I want to extend backward the temporal boundaries that etch the outlines of the hypnotherapeutic process. It's not wrong, just limiting, to view the beginning of hypnotherapy as the point at which you begin making use of clients' hypnotic responsiveness in altering their problem. A more accurate, more encompassing accounting would locate the actual beginning back when you and your clients first meet, at the point at which you start the formulation of problem dissolution and resolution and establish the parameters of and possibilities for your work together.

Hypnotherapy takes shape in the way you ask about and respond to your clients' reasons for contacting you; delve into their current and prior experience of their problem, tracking not only exacerbations, but also variations and exceptions; find experiential descriptions and definitions of categorical diagnoses; tease out skills and other resources; ask about any concerns they might have; and talk about their understanding of and expectations regarding hypnosis and the therapeutic process as a whole.

To illuminate how to begin formulating hypnotherapy from the outset, I'd like to walk you through some of the first session with a couple I saw intermittently for three years.* Along the way, I'll augment the discussion with some stories of my work with other clients, too.

Grace and Leo, white and middle-class, were recently married. Leo was an architect; Grace, a math instructor at a local community college. Having been together for two years before their marriage, they wanted to start a family. However, their aspirations were currently limited by what Grace described as "an intense fear of anything in the medical realm"—seeing blood and needles, undergoing a medical procedure, being in a doctor's office for a checkup, seeing a family member's scar, or visiting a hospital. She said she couldn't "be a part of, see, or hear of anything medically related" without becoming nauseated and, two thirds of the time, passing out. She also would sometimes faint when experiencing pain.

I saw them twice during that first trip, each time for three hours. Both Grace and Leo attended the first appointment; Grace came alone to the second. Seven months after that, they flew down to Florida again, and I saw Grace twice, for a total of three and a half hours. Eighteen months later, we again met for two sessions, the first lasting two hours, the second, one and a half. Finally, a year after that—three years from the first appointment—I saw Grace

---

* For his dissertation research, one of my former doctoral students, Carlos Ramos (2018), undertook a detailed conversation analysis of this session. Some of the following discussion benefits from his discerning eye and committed parsing.

twice, for two hours each time. Leo attended part of both of these final sessions, for a total of about an hour.

Over the three years, Grace had the occasional setback, which we would address at the next appointment, but during this time, she became increasingly comfortable with medical-related conversations, settings, and procedures. Soon after the first two appointments, she described herself as being "more welcoming to the discussion of hospital situations and the observance of needles (on television)." In addition, during a discussion with colleagues at work about surgery, she said, "everyone looked at me, aware of my phobia, to see a reaction." However, "they observed that my face turned red rather than the usual white," which she found to be "a neat experience." Grace "was able to laugh it off and feel fine." Five months later, at her annual physical, her doctor suggested she get a tetanus shot, as it was four years overdue. She had refused every year earlier, afraid of "passing out," but this time she felt an urge to do something different. Contrary to the nurse's suggestion that she lie down, Grace decided to sit up for it, and afterward she felt "fine and accomplished."

After the third set of appointments, Grace needed to get some lab work done. Feeling "eager" and "excited" to undertake the challenge, she did not pass out, and she described the experience as "so positive." When the results came back, the doctor expressed a concern about the possibility of diabetes, so more data were needed. Grace obtained a glucometer and gave herself needle sticks for two weeks. She "poked [herself] over 15 times," describing the procedure as being "so much fun" that she even "tested Leo as well."

Grace was five months pregnant when she and Leo came for their last two appointments, so we focused on preparations for the birth, which, because of medical complications, needed to be a C-section. Following these sessions, she "was able to freely converse with a doctor regarding the C-section, spinals, and IVs"; and the blood draw—five vials—for her pre-op labs was, she said, "perfect."

Grace initially thought she would want "to be 100 percent knocked out" during the C-section, but when the time came, she opted to stay awake so she could meet her baby immediately. She needed no antianxiety medication, and after the birth, her nurses said she was "a rock star," requiring far fewer pain medications than is usual. Her baby was healthy, and they went home two days later. Grace said the experience was "the best thing I ever did for myself."

Many of the 17 hours that we worked together were devoted to self-hypnosis training and to the hypnotherapeutic altering of Grace's experience, but the first one and a half hours were dedicated to formulating the framework for these shifts, to establishing a context for the changes to come. Let's take a look at how you can do this, starting with the nature and quality of your curiosity.

COMMITTING TO THERAPEUTIC HERESY

According to the *Oxford English Dictionary* (*OED*), the Greek origins of the word *heresy* have to do with the ability "to choose." Within certain religions and other cohesive groups and cultures throughout history—cults, political parties and movements, art and music traditions, academic and scientific disciplines—those choosing to question the received wisdom or orthodoxies of their community have been taken as a dire threat to truth and the cohesion of the social order. Heresy is the belief-system version of treason, so it's not surprising that heretics in religious traditions have been routinely punished, with the severity ranging from public disgrace, disqualification, or excommunication, to imprisonment, torture, and death. Even in the face of such risks, heretics have been willing to question authority, to call BS, creating the conditions for change or even revolution.

We therapists can be characterized as professional heretics, with particular skills and tools for carrying out our duties. We don't risk being excommunicated like Martin Luther, imprisoned for life like Galileo, or burned at the stake like Joan of Arc, so I want to be careful not to aggrandize what we do. Nevertheless, when we empathically enter the world of the client, our ability to effect change is grounded in our willingness and ability, as shared-mind insiders, to heretically question the authority of a problem that has been constraining choices, determining thoughts, hijacking emotions, shaping identity, and/or hardening beliefs. Such questioning is the first step in liberating those held in the problem's thrall. An excellent example can be found in Dr. Frieda Fromm-Reichmann's work with

a young woman who from the age of seven had built a highly complex religion of her own replete with powerful Gods. She was very schizophrenic and quite hesitant about entering into a therapeutic situation. At the beginning of the treatment she said, "God R says I shouldn't talk with you." Dr. Fromm-Reichmann replied, "Look, let's get something into the record. To me God R doesn't exist, and that whole world of yours doesn't exist. To you it does, and far be it from me to think that I can take that away from you, I have no idea what it means. So I'm willing to talk with you in terms of that world, if only you know I do it so that we have an understanding that it doesn't exist for me. Now go to God R and tell him that we have to talk and he should give you permission. Also you must tell him that I am a doctor and that you have lived with him in his kingdom now from seven to sixteen—that's nine years—and he hasn't helped you. So now he must permit me to try and see whether you and I can do that job. Tell him that I am a doctor and this is what I want to try." (Bateson, 2000, p. 226)

In this instance, Fromm-Reichmann gave voice to her heretical questioning, confronting the problem head-on from inside the logic of her patient's belief system: "Go to God R and tell him that we have to talk." Questioning clients' foundational assumptions and convictions about the problem is essential to the process of creatively formulating an effective therapeutic response; however, posing such questions directly to the clients is not. Indeed, this most often isn't warranted and could easily undermine your relationship with them.

The most important elements in adopting a commitment to therapeutic heresy is taking nothing for granted; staying open to discovering that the problem has different qualities, or perhaps a different scope or shape, than the clients are assuming; and looking for ways that the problem or an apparent limitation can be understood, repurposed, and implemented as a resource or strength for initiating and developing therapeutic change (see Chapter 6).

The first step is to take in and get a feel for how your clients are showing up for their first appointment. What is their take on you and hypnotherapy? Are they reluctant? Hopeful? Afraid? Impatient?

MANAGING CLIENTS' ORIENTATION

Early on, you'll want to get a sense of how your clients are orienting to their presenting problem, to their significant others, to you, and to the prospect of hypnotherapy. This information is easiest to acquire if you're able to meet, at least in the first session, not only with clients themselves but also with one or more of their significant others. Of course, though I was able to do this with Grace and Leo, this often isn't practical or possible, and there are circumstances where it wouldn't even be advisable. Such was the case with a woman who once reached out to me because she wanted to quit smoking. Her husband, who traveled without her for extended periods of time, had been complaining for years about her habit and had issued a standing threat to leave the marriage if she didn't take care of her addiction. For obvious reasons, my client wanted to keep our appointments a secret. She said she was quitting for herself, not him, and didn't "want him to be able to take the credit for her kicking the habit." She was also afraid of the derision she'd have to put up with if she tried and failed to leave cigarettes behind. I suggested in that first session that she do her best to keep to herself not only her sessions with me but also, for as long as possible, her nicotine-free success. She loved the idea of being able to say to him, "Cigarettes? What cigarettes? I haven't had one in months."

You can develop a first-session appreciation for your clients' initial orientation by weaving questions such as the following into the conversation:

- How did you find me? Do you have any questions about me or what I do?
- What inspired you to come at this point in time? Why now?

- How did you get the idea to pursue hypnotherapy?
- What do you know about it?
- What are you hoping might be possible?
- Who is most committed to your getting relief or discovering things can be different?
- In what ways is the current state of affairs intolerable?
- How have you been coping with it?
- Prior to coming here, what have you done to try to solve your problem?
- How have family or friends tried to help?
- What has worked? What has helped a little? What hasn't helped at all or has made things worse?
- What advice have you been given?
- Are there any other professionals involved, and if so, what do they think about your coming to see me?
- Once things are different, what do you anticipate missing about how things are now?

Answers to these sorts of questions will help you develop a clear conception of the context informing your clients' reaching out to you.

Commitment

People sometimes come to a first appointment at the urging of someone else or because they've decided they "should" make a change. You'll want to scope out and take into consideration what is prompting their presence in your office. If you fail to do so, you can end up three steps ahead of them, looking back with frustration at their seeming lack of motivation. As I discussed in the last chapter (and will delve into in more depth in Chapter 5), you do your best work when you get and stay in sync with clients.

I knew that Leo's brother, Jeremy, had suggested that Grace and Leo see me, so I commented on that as a way of initiating a conversation about their reasons for being in my office.

DOUGLAS: {to both of them} So this was Jeremy's idea, I guess, eh?

LEO: Well, he recommended it because Grace has needle and

doctor phobia and stuff like pain [phobia], you know? So
we're . . . so I definitely want to have a kid, so, we're trying to
find a way {short laugh} . . .

Answering first, Leo clarified that Grace was the one who needed
help and that her phobias were standing in the way of his being able
to have a child. This alerted me to the possibility that Grace had
accompanied her husband at his behest, or at her brother-in-law's
urging, rather than as a result of her own discomfort and desire for
change.

> D: {to Grace} And do you want one as well?
> GRACE: Ahohhh. {short laugh} Want one but I don't want to go
> through . . .
> D: Ah-ha. So if you found yourself more comfortable around
> doctors and hospitals and all that kind of stuff, then the
> prospect of having a child—it would feel different for you?
> G: Yeah.

Grace's desire to avoid fear-provoking situations had been
eclipsing her desire for a child. My empathic restatement of this
uncomfortable position helped me pose a question not in terms of
what she didn't want but, rather, in terms of what might be possible. Notice that I didn't describe her *powering through* or *overcoming*
her fears but, rather, *finding herself* more comfortable. This phrasing
suggests the possibility for avolitional change. I'll have more to say
about this in Chapters 5 and 6. I also inquired about the possibility
of her feeling *different* about having a child, not about feeling *committed* to having one. I was taking care not to impose Leo's desire
onto her.

I then asked Grace what she thought when Leo told her about
his brother's idea that they come and see me. She said that they had
seen a doctor back home, who had scared her by saying her condition could worsen as she got older. He had suggested medication or
cognitive-behavioral therapy (CBT), which, she was told, could take
a long time. She said she was thus "willing to try this [hypnother-
apy] first." Had she said she "*wanted* to try this first," it would have

indicated more of a commitment. I continued to sense that she was following Leo's lead, perhaps somewhat reluctantly.

You will retain your flexibility and better support your clients' taking the initiative for their own well-being if you eschew any urge to become a cheerleader or salesperson. Your role is not to impel, implore, entice, or convince but, rather, to be available for and committed to facilitating change, should clients request your services. At this early point in the interview, Grace had yet to make such a request. To help me get more in sync with her tentativeness, I started with the possibility that hypnosis might not help, and I endorsed regular therapy back home as a viable alternative.

> D: The way that CBT would work if you did that with a therapist up where you live is that they would probably look at your ideas and beliefs about medical people, people in authority, about medical situations, and they'd help you change your beliefs. . . . So if what we do isn't helpful, I definitely recommend that you pursue [psychotherapy] up there. Hypnosis is sort of a fast track to doing what they would do slowly.

Grace's interest in hypnosis was in part prompted by the idea that it could make a difference in her symptoms more quickly than regular therapy.[*] In case she or Leo harbored any concerns that the potential for expediency might come at the expense of sustainability, I went on. If she were to decide not to pursue hypnosis, I wanted to ensure that it was an informed choice.

> D: Some people who don't know very much about hypnosis, and that includes mental health professionals, have an idea that hypnosis, because it can work so quickly, is . . . just a surface change, it's not a significant change. But they've actually got it upside down. The reason hypnosis can work quickly is because it's operating at the level of your automatic reaction, which is where the problem [can be most expeditiously addressed].

---

[*] If Grace had known then that our work together would span three years, perhaps she would have made a different choice.

This brings us to the importance of ascertaining your clients' take on hypnosis and hypnotherapy.

Understandings and Expectations

Clients' apprehensions about trying hypnosis and misapprehensions about what it is can undermine your work together. As you provide clarifying explanations and descriptions, you are shaping their expectancy and developing their anticipation, preparing them for a meaningful experience. Kirsch (1990) outlined how to clear up problematic misconceptions:

> [Clients] can be told that there is nothing mysterious about hypnosis; that it is a normal state of focused attention rather than a profoundly altered state of consciousness; and that it will not feel much different from meditating or relaxing. Most importantly, they can be informed that they will remain in complete control of themselves; that they will only experience those things that they wish to experience; and that they will be able to remember everything that occurred within the hypnotic session. (p. 164)

I endorse Kirsch's first set of recommendations but would modify the ones he deems "most important." For reasons I discussed in Chapter 1, I avoid promoting or endorsing "control" as a viable strategy for managing mind-body complexities. Indeed, it is the effort to control symptoms that puts people at odds with their mind and body and often exacerbates their suffering. So instead of talking with clients about their ability to retain control during hypnosis, I reassure them that their mind and body will be collaborating fully with me in shaping and discovering what transpires. It is possible that they will experience something valuable but uncomfortable,* so I don't promise that their wishes will dictate the content of what happens. Instead, I tell them that they'll never be *stuck* experiencing something they'd rather not have to deal with. And every once in a

---

* You'll see an example of this in Chapter 6, in my work with a man named Azran.

while, I've had clients who can't remember everything, or even any-thing, that transpired,* so if the question comes up, I typically say that they'll *probably* remember most everything that occurs and that if for some reason they don't recall and want to know, I'll be happy to fill them in.

I asked Grace what she knew about hypnosis. She laughed and said "nothing" and asked if, during the process, she would know what was going on.

> D: Most people, most of the time, hear everything, are aware of what's happening. Sometimes, with some people, they lose track of elements. . . . For example, . . . there might be a point at which you just stop really hearing my voice, like it fades in and out. . . . The teenagers that I see, I tell them that, and I say, "So I'm one of the few adults in your life who says, 'It's okay for you to ignore me.'" Because there will be times when you don't listen to me. And it doesn't really matter.
>
> L: I'm pretty good with that with my mom. {laughter}
>
> D: Yeah, tune me out, right?

There's not much to be afraid of if you can just tune out what's happening, and Leo's funny comment about ignoring his mother further supported the idea that Grace was free to disengage if she chose to do so.

> D: It's all, however, cooperation. So I don't do anything *to* you. Every step of the way is something that we do together. And if there's anything that doesn't feel right, you just [reorient]. . . . And you don't have to do anything to [reorient]. You'll just come out.
>
> G: Is it scary?
>
> D: Is it scary? Most people find it the exact opposite. A lot of people, when I say, "Okay, so you can come back," they're slow in coming back, because they're having too good a time. It's like, "Why would I want to come back? This is too nice."

---

*This was the case with a man named Alastair, whom I talk about in Chapter 6.

You'll invite a broader range of possible responses if you characterize hypnosis as both unusual *and* normal. That way, clients can find
the experience remarkably odd without being disconcerted and find
it unremarkably ordinary without being disappointed.

You're best-off setting expectations so that clients won't shrink
from dramatic or intense responses but also won't ignore or discount subtle ones. I should have done more with Grace to protect
against the latter possibility. I could have clarified, for example, that
some clients find that hypnosis doesn't seem much different from
their regular awareness. That way, if she were to be underwhelmed
by what transpired, she'd be able to interpret what happened for her
to be within the normal range of hypnotic experience. As it happened, she *did* end up being impressed by what she experienced, so
this didn't become an issue; however, added insurance never hurts.

> D: Sometimes there's an element for some people . . . that
> [hypnosis] can feel delightfully weird. . . . [But] it's a natural way
> in which our minds work. So it's not . . . anything abnormal. It
> facilitates stuff happening that normally we can't *make* happen
> but [that becomes effortlessly possible]. . . . For some people,
> their body may feel very, very heavy.

It can help not only to speak in generalities (e.g., "some people
notice this or that; others experience something quite different")
but also to ground your explanations in actual examples.

> D: I was doing a demonstration with one of my students a couple
> of days ago, and she said she never felt her body feel so heavy
> in her whole life. For some people, their body feels so light, they
> feel like they're floating. And they're not even really aware of
> being in their body—they feel like they're floating above it.

In the formulation phase of your work together, you also have
the opportunity to begin orienting clients to the associative structuring of hypnotic communication and hypnotherapeutic suggestion. As I explain and elaborate in Chapter 5, the avolitional nature

of hypnotic change is easily introduced and developed through the offering of correspondences, whether in the form of analogies (similes or metaphors) or, less poetically, juxtaposed events or actions.

The logic of such correlations looks something like this:

If X can happen, then Y can happen.
or
As X happens, Y can happen.

For example, I said this to Grace as I was explaining how hypnosis works:

> D: So physiological sensations can change. . . . And this is why [hypnosis] is very helpful with pain. It's not uncommon to be able to, to have a part of your body get numb. And if one part of your body can get numb, then another part can get numb, and there's a way, then, to . . . diminish the pain significantly as a result of your body's natural ability to . . . move sensation.

Here is a streamlined, more generalized, version of the associative logic:

If one part of your body can experience a hypnotic response, then so can another part.
and
If a hypnotic response can be shared with or expanded to other parts of the body, then hypnotic responsiveness can be directed toward ameliorating a problem.

In other words, implicit in my description of the hypnotherapeutic ripple effect of developing numbness is the assumption that something analogous can be effective in response to fears:

If hypnosis can be used in this way to alter pain, then it can be used in analogous ways to alter fear and the tendency to faint.

A little later, I made the same point more explicitly:

> D: Hypnosis is a way of you and I together being able to access
> that part of you that works on automatic, the part of you that
> responds without you having to consciously think and without
> you being able to consciously stop whatever's going on. . . .
> [And] that automatic part of you . . . is able to learn a different
> way of responding.

To underscore the point, I told a story about a class demonstration
I once did with a woman who was afraid of geckos. By detailing
what transpired, I was further elaborating the correlative structure
of hypnotherapeutic suggestions:

> *If hypnosis can be used to alter a fear of lizards, then it can be used*
> *in analogous ways to alter a fear of blood, needles, and other doctor-*
> *related cues.*

> D: This woman worked in the same building as I did at my
> university, and she was very, very afraid of lizards. And we live
> in South Florida, so there are lots of lizards.

Fear-inducing cues were omnipresent.

> D: One day, a lizard went under the filing cabinet in her office,
> and she said there was no way that she could stay in her office,
> knowing that the lizard might come out at any time. This fear
> was getting in her way. At the condo where she lived, she had
> to pass under a trellis in order to get to her front door, and she
> worried about possible lizards in the trellis. It would sometimes
> take her several minutes to get up the nerve to go under it. And
> she noticed that her son was now doing the same thing, and she
> didn't want to pass this anxiety onto him.

Grace was considering becoming a mother, so I thought this might
have some resonance for her—resolving fear as a gift for a child.

D: And so she wondered if there was anything I could do to help her. I was teaching a class at the time on hypnosis, and I asked her if she would like to come in for an hour, and she could help me demonstrate for the class how to work hypnotically with problematic fears. So she agreed and came in the next time the class met.

This illustrated hypnosis as a collaboration—the woman agreed to come to class to help me help the students—and hypnotherapeutic change as something that could happen in a short amount of time in less-than-ideal conditions (in this case, in the course of an hour in front of a bunch of strangers).

D: I invited her into hypnosis, . . . and she was very good at visualization. She started to see a little lizard. She played the piano, [so I invited her to play some catchy tune in her imagination]. She started to see this little lizard with a top hat and a cane, and it stepped onto the top of the piano she was playing, which became a makeshift stage. And this was before the Geico commercials {Grace laughs}.

And, funny, the lizard started to dance while she was playing: [a little soft-shoe]. Well, she got to laughing at this absurd sight and continued to play and continued to laugh. When she came out of hypnosis, her way of relating to lizards was profoundly different—so different that a couple of days or maybe a week later, she called me and asked me to come down to her office. . . . I walk in, and she's standing in the middle of the room and she's saying, "Hey, Douglas, look at that," pointing to a lizard on the floor, a few feet from her. And I said, "Well, that's cool. How you feel?" She said, "I feel fine." I said, "Would you like to pick it up?" She said, "No, {Grace and Leo laugh} but I'm fine with it being there. It's cool."

The hypnotic change wasn't from abject fear to deep love but, rather, to comfortable tolerance. That's all Grace needed. After all, she wasn't wanting to pursue a career as a doctor or a nurse (although

I've resolved needle- and blood-related fears with other clients who were already in or about to enter health-care work settings). Milton Erickson (and, later, Steve de Shazer, 1985) advised psychotherapists to think small: What *incremental* shift can you initiate? If a change is seemingly inconsequential, it appears and can develop under the radar, without being subjected to judgmental scrutiny and/or unhelpful efforts to encourage it.

Fears of Hypnosis and Hypnotherapy

Sometimes clients are intrigued by the potential for hypnotherapy to help them, but they are afraid of your "messing with" their mind. I once worked with a novelist who was as grateful for our talk-therapy sessions as she was adamant about my not employing hypnosis. At one point when I floated the possibility of using hypnosis, she pointed to her head and said, "This is how I make my living. I can't risk anything gumming up the works."

If you empathically respect the sanctity and ecology of your clients' mind-body connection as you intraventively invite, rather than interventively implore, the development of avolitional shifts in their experience, then the possibility of iatrogenic effects is minuscule. But hypnotherapy is a collaboration, so if your clients are harboring problematic ideas or fearful expectations about hypnosis, then these will weave into what transpires, and you'll need to address them, the earlier the better. I didn't try to persuade the novelist that hypnotherapy would be safe. I know that I never attempt to exercise any undue influence over the delicate balance of anyone's mind; however, it would have been oxymoronic for me to attempt to convince her of that. We found ways of addressing her concerns without my inviting her to become of one mind with herself.

I asked Grace whether she had any other questions or concerns. She told me she was afraid that just talking about her problem could result in her fainting in my office.

> D: [pointing to the couch where she was sitting] Right. So the
> nice thing about this couch is, it's very comfortable. {Grace and
> Leo laugh} And if you were to, if you were to pass out, it would

actually be very helpful. Because if you end up . . . having a child, you will watch that baby learn to walk when he or she is somewhere in the neighborhood of 11 months to a year and a half. Okay? Do you want a boy or girl?

We detoured for a minute and determined that they both wanted a boy.

> D: So, at 11 months or so he starts to walk and what you're going to see happen again and again, is he's going to get up and he's going to fall down, and he's going to take a step, and he's going to fall down, and he's going to get up, and he's going to learn how to walk by falling. And so [it will help] if you can manage to faint a couple of times while we're doing this today {Grace laughs}, because you don't have to worry about getting hurt. And your [body] is really good at dropping your blood pressure.

A strategic therapist might have said something similar, believing that paradoxically "prescribing the symptom" would contribute to a resolution of the problem. However, I didn't prescribe fainting; I simply made it clear that she could pass out safely and comfortably on the couch and that doing so would create an opportunity for learning how to respond differently to needles, blood, doctors, and so on.

Grace suffered from two-tiered fear. Not only was she afraid of "medical stuff," she was also afraid of losing consciousness when she happened upon or needed to face it. I was making it possible for her to let go of the second tier of fear as a precursor to and context for changing the first.

Hypnotherapists establish the necessary safety for clients to turn toward and encounter dreaded objects, thoughts, feelings, impulses, or actions and to discover and learn new avolitional responses to them. Over the course of the first two hours, I used the word *comfort* or *comfortable* 33 times (Ramos, 2018, p. 119) and the word *blood* 50 times. I didn't just repeat them over and over; they found their way into anecdotes and stories about other clients, research studies, and hypnosis demonstrations.

For example, early on, I offered a graphic description of a hypnotic demonstration (involving a needle) that I hadn't been part of or even seen; I'd heard about it from one of my students. There was a certain amount of buffering, then, embedded in this three-steps-removed story. From the look on Grace's face and the sound of her voice when she vocalized a response, I could recognize that she still found it disturbing; however, despite the fact that she had fainted in response to friends or family talking about medical procedures, she didn't get light-headed.

> D: The other day, one of the students in my class [described] a demonstration of a guy doing hypnosis. The student said the hypnotist's assistant put a blood pressure cuff on [the subject's] arm, and it read normal. And then . . . the hypnotist . . . [had the subject] lose all the blood in his arm. [T]he subject did that. And they took his blood pressure again, and it was zero—there was no blood in his arm. So then they took the back of his hand and they put a needle through it,
> G: Ahghhh!
> D: and there was no blood.

In unhooking the usual pairing of needle and blood, this story contained within it a template for our hypnotherapeutic direction—a dissolution of Grace's experiential pairing of medical-related cues and fainting.

> L: How?
> D: Because there was no blood pressure in his arm. And then the hypnotist had the subject put the blood flow back in there, and the blood pressure again registered normal.

Hypnosis facilitates a more focused or intense version of avolitional mind-body changes that can happen in response to everyday circumstances. By normalizing hypnotic phenomena, you normalize hypnotic and post-hypnotic responsiveness.

> D: Now it seems weird, that that would be possible. But . . . we're all capable of [changing blood flow]. If you get very scared,

the blood drains from your face. You know that. . . . If you get shocked by something, if something really scares you, you'll go white. Why do you go white? Because blood drains from your face. . . .

I was reading an article recently about both men and women's response to seeing erotic stimuli. We, all humans, if you see a naked person, and they're a naked person of the gender that you find attractive, you get an automatic body response—blood [engorges your genitalia]. We're wired so that this image produces this effect. And it's an effect that's produced by a movement of blood in your body. . . .

I was laying the groundwork here for the possibility of hypnotically inviting blood to move into, rather than out of, an area of the body. Later in the session I built on this by telling a story about a client who sought help because of blushing, which, of course, is the opposite of what happens to Grace. And then I generalized the explanation:

D: Your mind-body connection works so that . . . thoughts and images can flow through your physiology. . . . If you have the ability to have a *drop* in blood pressure, then you also have the ability to have a *rise* in . . . blood pressure.

You may remember that at the beginning of my discussion of this case, I described one of the first changes Grace noticed after we started our work together. While listening to colleagues talk about medical procedures at work, she and they were surprised to discover that her face turned red, rather than white.

As I mentioned earlier, it helps to set a goal of minimal, effortless change:

D: So that kind of ability to move blood around is just a given. All we do with hypnosis is to give you access to the ability to adapt the flow, so that you stay safe. It doesn't mean that you have to end up *loving* needles or *loving* doctors or *loving* blood. But [you could] be like my colleague at work, where the lizard's just no

big deal. "Yeah, it's there." "Did you want to pick it up?" "Nah."
You might decide you don't want to become a phlebotomist.

G: I'm a teacher.

Grace could relax into knowing that she didn't need to move all
the way from feeling terrified by medical-related situations to loving them, to wanting a career in a medical field. All that was needed
was for fear-inducing cues to lose their potency or significance, or
for them to cue a different body response. No big deal.

This resonates with the general goal of hypnotherapy—to facilitate changes in the mind-body relationship. Through a close interpersonal connection with the therapist and a close intrapersonal
connection between mind and body, clients are afforded the opportunity to shift from fear to non-reactivity, from non-reactivity to
dispassionate interest, from dispassionate interest to curiosity.

FINDING AND DERIVING CLIENTS'
SKILLS AND RESOURCES

In Chapter 1, I introduced Milton Erickson's utilization approach to
hypnotic invitation and hypnotherapeutic change, and I will return
to it in more detail in Chapters 5 and 6. As a resource-focused
method for inviting hypnosis and hypnotherapeutic change, utilization orients you to consider and treat *all* client attributes, behaviors,
beliefs, and responses as potential contributors to the hypnotherapeutic process. Virtually anything the client is doing, thinking,
feeling, saying, or communicating can be brought into service to
enhance both your shared-mind connection with the client and the
client's mind-body connection with their own self.

Some skills and abilities are easy to recognize and employ—
a vivid imagination, an artistic sensibility, a practiced capacity to
deeply relax, a history of in-the-zone athletic prowess, or a skill in
other flow activities, such as meditating, playing chess, or practicing
a musical instrument. Other experiences may require some refine-
ment or tweaking before they can be applied resourcefully.

Part of the logic of utilization involves embracing as part of a solution (for going into hypnosis or for resolving the problem) what in the client's experience has been considered wholly problematic, such as one or more of the symptoms of the problem itself. Both Grace and Leo viewed her fainting as a troubling, potentially dangerous weakness. I mentioned in passing a quite different way of understanding it.

> D: There's an evolutionary reason, some people think, for the reaction that you have to blood. . . . If your blood pressure drops, you bleed less. And there's some thought that [people] . . . like you have evolved so that if you see blood and your blood pressure drops, it means that if it's *your* blood that you're seeing, you will bleed less, and you're less likely to bleed out if you . . . have some kind of injury.

This allowed us to laugh about Grace's problem having to do with her being more highly evolved than either Leo or me.

To locate and employ skills and resources, I invariably ask about and listen for how clients devote their time and attention to their work and play activities, how they relate to others, and how they relate to themselves, both when they're relaxed and when they're struggling. Grace, for example, was a swimmer who, when she got in the zone, would sometimes lose track, mid-swim, of the number of laps she'd logged. She was also a college instructor. In her first two years on the job, she'd had to contend with disrespectful students, particularly one male student who considered females inferior and another who sexually harassed her. Initially, her department head was not supportive. Her challenges as an instructor could have been chalked up to her anxiety; however, I was interested in learning about the character trait(s) it took to persevere.

> D: Boy, that took a lot of courage to be going to class every day to deal with that kind of thing.
> L: Especially by herself.
> D: How did you muster the courage to go back every day?
> G: It was tough.

Eventually, she learned how to nip potential problems in the bud.

> G: I think it was that summer, I was teaching one of those
> summer-session courses, and some guy made a joke or
> whatever. I just clearly said, you know . . . "It's not okay."
> D: Uh huh.
> G: And that was that. But I knew I had to [address it] at the first
> experience of it.

When listening for strengths and resources, I don't want to simply catalog a list; I want to flesh out the client's descriptions of the inner workings, as often it is these that can be transported into new circumstances.

> D: Okay, so how did you find the idea of what to say and how to
> say it, and to be able to do it in the moment? How did you do
> that?
> G: Just learning from that last one, and not letting it go there . . .
> D: And it worked, right?
> G: Yeah. . . . You know, small things that you let go just get bigger
> and bigger . . .
> D: Small things that you didn't address at the time.
> G: Yeah.
> D: Right. So if you take care of them when they're small, they don't
> get big.
> G: Right.
> D: And you learned that.
> G: Yes.
> D: That's a source of confidence, to be able to take care of
> something when it's small.
> G: Uh huh.
> D: And in a way, that's going to be what happens with any change
> in your blood pressure.

I was interested not only in Grace's courage and her ability to proactively address problems, but also in her problem-solving approach when learning and teaching math. She said she wasn't good at quick computation, which I characterized as a preference for methodically working out solutions:

D: You like figuring it out.

G: Yeah.

D: So how do you do it when you're figuring out,

G: A computation or a proof?

D: Either. What's your process?

G: With a lot of it, it's just out of a book and it spells it out for you, so I'll just go through it quick once and then I just try to do it on my own.

D: So you learn the logic of it over *here*, and then you can take that and apply it [elsewhere].

G: Yeah, to other ones.

D: To whatever problem.

My empathic statement both specifically captured the nature of Grace's math problem-solving process and, more generally and implicitly, set the stage for the application of the hypnotic changes to come: I was suggesting that upon learning how to solve a problem *here* with me, she would be able to apply that ability "to whatever problem."

In identifying and refining the characterization of clients' skills and resources, I am looking for ways that the heart of localized mastery in one area can be abductively carried to and implemented with other, analogous, areas of challenging experience. In this case, I was interested in how the essence of Grace's approach to working out math problems could be drawn on when solving the problem of her fears.

D: When you're working through a problem, do you see the next step? Do you just have a feel for what the next step would be? Do you work it out step-by-step? . . . How do you go into problem-solving mode?

G: It kind of flows, I think.

D: You have a sense of how it flows? . . .

G: I just do it. I don't know. I haven't thought about that. . . . It's just innate, I guess. . . . It just comes to me.

D: It just comes to you, okay.

Grace's description is an excellent example of the way many people experience flow-state epiphanies or discoveries—they just come to them.

By this point in our conversation, we had arrived at a recognition of Grace as a courageous, determined, highly evolved woman who had the ability to apply a laser focus to prepare for challenging situations that, when she was in the middle of figuring them out, created the conditions for a solution to just come to her. These were resourceful qualities to bring with us into our forthcoming hypnotic explorations.

ADAPTING THE PROBLEM DEFINITION

Embracing therapeutic heresy invites questioning the very definition of the problem. When Michael Yapko (2014) was a young psychologist, he approached Jay Haley, the founder of the strategic approach to therapy, for supervision on a tough case.

> So I came to him and said, "Jay, what would you do with a woman who is dysthymic, who has borderline personality disorder, who has PTSD and unresolved attachment issues?" There was this long pause before Jay finally said, "I wouldn't let her have those problems." (p. 246)

During the early months of the COVID-19 pandemic, I met with a woman struggling to cope with her fear of the virus and the demands it had placed on her time. In addition to washing, rebagging, and/or wiping down all of her groceries, she was cleaning the surfaces in her home for hours a day. She would order staples and other items online, but then, when the packages were delivered, she couldn't bring herself to touch them, so she left them on the front porch.

Boxes were stacking up outside, and stress was ramping up inside. Family members all thought she was over the top with her COVID precautions. They made a point of not taking seriously the government-issued guidelines and restrictions that she had taken to heart. Standing up to their dismissal of her as OCD crazy, she doubled down on her efforts to keep everyone safe. But the more seriously she took the pandemic, the less they needed or wanted to, as they were put off by her unsolicited advice on what they should and shouldn't be doing. The entrenched divergences between them widened.

Continually nauseated and tightly wound, my client was hoping that hypnosis could dispel her anxiety. At first blush, the request sounds reasonable, but it seemed to me that however painful she found the physical and psychological manifestations of her no-doubt-elevated levels of cortisol and adrenaline, her stress hormones were helping her to stay alert and informed, both of which were contributing to her making safer choices than the rest of her family. So rather than agreeing to mount a campaign against anxiety, I proposed, instead, that we look to augment her alertness by pairing it with an ability to relax.

Through interspersed meditation training and hypnotherapy, my client learned how to maintain her acute attention to potential risk while getting in sync with herself and developing calm awareness. She was also able to bring this balance into her conversations with loved ones, which shifted their interactions significantly. She let go of trying to keep them safe, of insisting on what they *must* do.

An essential precursor to bringing meditation and hypnosis into the mix was the heretical formulation of the goal: Rather than focusing on the eradication of something construed as a problem (anxiety), we would collaborate on adding skills (getting in sync with herself, releasing thoughts and tension, developing calm awareness) to a resourceful quality she already possessed (alertness).

Something similar transpired in my first session with Grace and Leo. Grace said that she suffered from syncope, the medical term for fainting, which was related to her needle, blood, and pain phobias. She also had been diagnosed with social anxiety disorder, as well as, they said, "some kind of mood disorder." All such diagnoses are categories that coalesce an array of symptoms and/or a series of disconcerting incidents into an abstract entity, a label, which becomes self-referentially confirming. Grace, Leo, their families, and the involved medical professionals all deemed that she was afraid of needles *because* of her needle phobia; that she would faint when anticipating or experiencing pain *because* of her pain phobia; that she was afraid to answer the phone *because* of her social anxiety disorder. Her diagnosed mental health disorders designated conditions that she *had*, and, in so doing, they also defined who she *was*—they characterized her identity.

Like any belief system, your identity, your sense of who and what you are, frames and thus shapes how you orient and respond to challenges and opportunities, and it determines the choices you consider and enact. Vigorous identities (e.g., athlete, parent, artist, inventor, explorer, teacher, etc.) invite galvanized, inspired, focused responses, while enervated identities (a patient or victim who is mentally ill, traumatized, depressed, high-strung, etc.) trigger halfhearted, helpless, disarrayed responses.

Changing an enervated identity directly can be a daunting undertaking, so, like Jay Haley, I sidestep the necessity of doing so by arriving at a changeable problem definition. Sensitive to the way negation works (see Chapters 1 and 2), I don't generally dispute diagnoses and other identity-defining labels head-on. If I were to do that, my clients would be caught between competing expert opinions: "I know your psychiatrist has diagnosed you with a mood disorder, but I believe she's mistaken." Instead, I shift the conversation from the abstract, categorical level of the diagnosis or "condition" to experiential descriptions of the symptoms that compose it, and we then explore how these component strands can be altered. By sidestepping the label, I can help make a difference to the symptoms that define it, thus altering the problem from the inside, which can then inductively contribute to the development of a more enlivened sense of identity.

PREPARING TO TREAT SYMPTOMS
RATHER THAN DIAGNOSES

A client diagnosed with an anxiety disorder asked me why she had been having panic attacks. In addition to dealing with anxiety, Meika was also sensitive to antihistamines, alcohol, and caffeine. If she took in just a little of any of these substances, she would experience an outsize effect—feeling "agitated" or "weird"—which sometimes would give rise to one of her "full-blown" panic attacks. Self-conscious about her sensitivity, anxiety, and proneness to panic, she construed them as stemming from or evidence of a characterological weakness. This enervated identity stood in contrast to that of her grandmother, who had been a robust, courageous woman. Friends and acquaintances viewed Meika as a strong, capable person, but she worried that they didn't see the "real" her.

An identity-level—categorical—answer to Meika's question would have been circuitously succinct: "You have panic attacks because you have an anxiety disorder." And then any hypnosis we did with this as a point of departure would have been organized by this confirmation of the diagnosis. We'd be looking at ways to help her cope with anxiety or overcome anxiety or counteract panic. Instead, I offered an extended answer to her panic-attack question, one that took into account her family history and the mind-body self-referentiality of her unfolding experience. I wanted to formulate an understanding of what had been happening to her that rendered it hypnotically treatable:

DOUGLAS: Sounds like you're very sensitive to antihistamines and caffeine.

MEIKA: Way too sensitive.

D: A little goes a long way.

M: I basically can't tolerate them. . . .

D: You sip a little coffee and your heart registers the caffeine.

M: Immediately.

D: And then you immediately notice that it speeds up. . . . You're, like, the opposite of oblivious.

M: {laughs} No one would accuse me of that, no.

D: Your body is a live wire, attuned to what you take in, and then your [awareness] is tuned in to your body. Like someone with perfect pitch who suffers when a singer doesn't quite hit her notes. . . . You can tell when something is off, and it pains you.

I was describing the *process* of what happens—the details of experience rather than the criteria of a diagnosis.

M: Yeah.
D: You suffer from a precision . . . of discernment.

If you value strength and you view sensitivity as a weakness, then you will exert yourself in trying to overcome it. If, however, you recognize your sensitivity as a gift of refined perception and attunement—like someone with perfect pitch—then you can be annoyed by it, but it is a valued quality rather than a source of shame, and it is an ability that can be developed.

D: When you recognize a quickening of your heart or a tightness in your chest or something, it unnerves you.
M: I worry that something's wrong.
D: Something feels off-kilter.
M: Exactly.
D: Which immediately triggers the release of stress hormones. . . .
M: I definitely feel stressed.
D: Yeah, but actually the word *stress hormone* is a misnomer. Adrenaline, cortisol, norepinephrine: They should be called *rise-to-the-occasion hormones.*[*] They're released when you're face-to-face with a threat or a challenge. They speed up your heart and increase your blood pressure, they improve your oxygen intake, they [energize your muscles] and get more glucose to your brain. . . . You know when you get butterflies? Your digestive system gets suppressed so you won't waste

---

* I borrowed this relabeling of the term *stress hormone* from my colleague and friend Dr. Jim Hibel, who in turn got it from his daughter-in-law, the developmental neuroscientist Dr. Leah Hibel.

energy digesting your last meal when you've got something
critical to take care of. The whole cascade of body reactions
[happens] so you can show up for something that's a big deal.
The hormones show up so you can show up.

M: But they make me feel horrible. I hate the feeling. . . .

D: Yeah, if you were oblivious, . . . you'd probably barely register
them. But you've got this high-fidelity connection between your
mind and body—you're tuned in to what's up.

M: I want them to stop.

D: Of course you do.

Meika's *reaction* to the effects of the hormone release would set off
an escalating feedback loop.

D: It's like, you notice a problem and you call 911. The operator
dispatches some first responders—those rise-to-the-occasion
hormones—who rush to the scene to help. But what's been
happening, you start to feel the effects of the hormones doing
what they're supposed to, . . . like you're hearing the sirens of
the first responders arriving, and you [think,] "Oh my God,
sirens! There must be something wrong. I better call 911!"
So you call 911 again, upset by the sirens, and the operator
says, "Oh, no! You sound distraught. You must need more
first responders." Soon the sirens of the second wave of first
responders start screaming, . . . so you call 911 again to report
a still bigger emergency. The operator sends a third wave. . . .
Doctors call this a panic attack.

This description defined panic not as a concrete entity but, rather,
as a reflexive communication spiral between Meika's finely focused
awareness and finely tuned body.

D: Your thought in coming here was, "How do I get rid of my
anxiety?" But your discernment and your body's response are
finely adjusted to keep you safe. The problem isn't that first
wave of first responders. The problem is the second and third

wave. . . . Unless you're facing a true emergency, you only need
the first wave. More than that is just redundancy.

M: So then where does hypnosis come in?

D: Well, maybe the sirens don't need to be so damn loud. Or
when you hear the sirens, when that adrenaline is first
kicking in, you find yourself thinking, "Oh, whew, you've
arrived! Just in time! What a relief! Thanks for coming," and
you don't find it necessary to call 911 a second or third time.
Or you call [the first time] and the operator isn't so quick to
dispatch. . . . Or maybe you discover that even that [initial
call] isn't necessary.

These proposed changes, metaphorically described, all offered
some slight alteration in the sequenced pattern of escalating interaction among awareness, thoughts, and body response. Offering them
helped prepare the ground for modest, achievable hypnotic shifts in
experience that could—and actually did—have far-reaching conse-
quences: Following the ensuing hypnotherapy, Meika reported no
further panic attacks.

This is one of the reasons why I don't talk about or even personally conceptualize hypnotherapy as capable of *curing* ailments,
as this characterization only concretizes the problems clients initially present, and it would set up the clients and me as the problem's adversaries. Instead, as you've seen throughout this chapter, I
develop the understanding that clients can adapt and apply abilities
and skills they already possess, as well as those they can learn in
the course of our hypnosis sessions, to the process of altering the
composing threads of their suffering.

FACILITATING LEARNING

Pain, anxiety, depression, addictions, compulsions, nightmares:
They often seem to have a mind of their own. Upending plans,
eluding efforts to contain or control them, somehow managing to
often be both omnipresent and unpredictable, they leave those suffering from them feeling edgy and helpless—victimized.

According to the *OED*, the word *victim* derives from the Latin word *victima*, which refers to "a living creature killed and offered as a sacrifice to some deity or supernatural power." A victim is someone who is out of options, depleted and vulnerable, whose fate lies in the hands of someone or something else. Given your clients' inability to dispel or dispatch their problem on their own, it can be alluring for both you and them to consider your hypnotherapy as the launching of a single-handed rescue mission. One way this is commonly undertaken is via the metaphor "mind as computer."

I've heard clients and therapists alike conceptualize hypnotherapeutic intervention as a task of "reprogramming the subconscious." The induction is thought of as a means of taking the conscious mind off-line so that the therapist can then go into the subconscious or unconscious and hypnotically overwrite the "faulty code" causing the problem. This orientation to hypnosis reinforces the clients' understanding of themselves as being without agency, positioned to receive, submit to, and enact, but not contribute to, the therapist's injunctions.

Of course, the presuppositions implicit in this programming metaphor aren't actually true. Regardless of what the therapist and clients assume, hypnosis is still a shared-mind phenomenon, with clients actively participating in what unfolds. Nevertheless, because expectancy plays such an important role in what happens in a hypnotic encounter, the effects of a misleading metaphor can be both insidious and extensive. A man once contacted me, asking if I would be willing to hypnotically correct the damage he believed had been caused by a previous, incompetent albeit well-meaning, hypnotherapist who, he said, had devoted several sessions to "reprogramming my unconscious mind." The man did not think of his description as metaphoric. He believed that the therapist had inadvertently introduced several literal coding errors that were now wreaking havoc with his well-being, and he wanted me to hypnotically reprogram the reprogramming. I considered accepting and utilizing his precise and rock-solid convictions about what he needed from me, but I was concerned that the implicit assumptions embedded in his metaphoric understanding posed too great a risk. I didn't want to iatrogenically create further entangled difficulties, so, much to the man's dismay and disgruntlement, I declined to work with him.

An alternative formulation of hypnotherapy, one that pays heed to its relational realities, treats it as a therapeutic jam session. Your induction—or *invitation*, as I prefer to call it (as I discuss in the next chapter)—engages your clients' ability to relate to themselves and to you in a way that alters or redefines the usual cloistering boundaries of the circumscribed self. This shift makes possible the effortless, flow-state freedom of collaborative, imaginative transformations. Clients aren't kicking back while you kick in; they are full participants in what plays out, with their agency stitched into their embodied engagement. However, because this engagement is flow based, the agency isn't undertaken and can't be recognized in terms of effort or trying. It is in evidence, instead, in their willingness and ability to curiously engage in the play of their imagination, to dissolve the everyday boundaries imposed by fear-based recoiling and/or prosaic reckoning. I'll say more about this in Chapter 6, but I should clarify here that play doesn't imply frivolity; it can be deadly serious and deeply meaningful. As Gregory Bateson noted, "*Play* . . . is a word for a context of learning" (Bateson & Rogers, 1975, p. 6).

The therapist's role in this learning context is not to indoctrinate, not to "plant" suggestions, not to "reprogram" unconscious mentation. Rather, it is to establish trust and safety in the hypnotic relationship and to facilitate a range of possibilities for relevant trial-and-error discoveries, for reorienting to challenges, and for learning and adopting new connections and patterns of response. Holding this as a guiding commitment, you can communicate something of its essence to your clients. This is how I described it to Grace and Leo:

> D: Hypnosis gives us a way for you to unconsciously learn something new, easily and comfortably. And then, with that new learning [established], to be able to then automatically respond differently to whatever it is that you're [dealing with]. Now, there's nothing really mysterious about that, because we all have an ability to unconsciously respond to something automatically. You drive?
>
> G: Yeah.

D: So when you drive, if you suddenly see red lights flash from the car in front of you, some guy stopping too quickly, you see the red and your right foot automatically goes from the gas to stomp on the brake, without you having to think, "Hmm, I wonder if there's something I should do?" So you automatically respond before you ever think about it consciously. You unconsciously learn stuff like this all the time. And that learning, the establishment of that habit, makes it possible for you to be safe. Hypnosis is just really a way to be able to automatically learn a different way of responding automatically to stuff that in the past would send you in one direction but now sends you in a different direction.

Near the end of the appointment, I circled back to address how learning to learn math could be applied to learning to learn a response other than fainting:

D: Your skill in algebra probably contributed to your skill in geometry. Some people are only good in one or the other, . . . but some are able to take a learned skill in one area and apply it to another: geometry becomes easier because of your grasp of algebra, or vice versa. And the movement from algebra to geometry, or from geometry to algebra, isn't all that different from applying [a learned skill in] math to [learning a new skill] in social situations.

In both cases, a steep learning curve depends on a comfort with trial-and-error discovery:

D: And I think college kids and we ourselves somehow got the mistaken idea that to make a mistake is bad or wrong, instead of it being the central brilliance of learning—an absolutely essential step to learning. Which is why if you could manage to faint a couple of times while you're here it would be very helpful. Because if you can learn the mechanism by which something happens—"How did I do that, that which I don't want to have happen?"—then you can learn how to do something else instead.

If you formulate hypnotherapy in the sorts of ways I've been suggesting in this chapter, then by the time your clients are ready for
you to invite them into hypnosis, you, with your heretical sensibility
providing guidance, will have shifted the conversation from intrac-
table diagnoses to changeable symptoms. And you'll be working
with resourceful, informed collaborators, curious to discover how
they, with effortless agency, can avolitionally respond to opportunities for embodied learning.

INVITING HYPNOSIS

The greatest killer of creativity is interruption.
—John Cleese (2020, p. 46)

*There is a phenomenon called entrainment, which is the
synchronization of two or more rhythmic systems into a single
pulse. . . . It is entrainment that provokes the trance states in the
samä dances of the Sufis. When improvisers play together, they
can rely on this natural phenomenon to mesh the music so that
they breathe together, pulse together, think together. . . . In
entrainment, the voices are not locked in exactly; they are always
slightly off from each other, finding each other again and again in
micromoments in time, weaving in and out of each other's rhythms.*
—Stephen Nachmanovitch (1990, pp. 99–100)

*The most basic devices of poetic speech are themselves, looked at
closely, secret compartments, unnoticed places in which paradoxical
expansion is stored. Image, metaphor, simile, allusion . . . —each in
some way slips past the narrow blunting of a relationship to the
world that is overly literal. These seemingly various Houdini
freedoms share one quality in general: each creates and requires a
mind doubled, able to take up two thoughts at once. The capacity
comes so naturally we mostly don't see it. Yet it is impossible: How
can a thing say, and mean, both itself and something else?*
—Jane Hirshfield (2015, pp. 277–278)

Hypnosis inductions create a liminal space, a context for clients to
transition from the distractibility and judgment-laden intentionality

of everyday conscious awareness to the absorbed, open-minded effortlessness of flow-state engagement. Some transitions are protracted, resembling the way some people wade gradually from beach to ocean, perhaps pausing or even retreating a few times before their body adjusts to the temperature difference of the water and they commit to floating or even submerging. Other transitions are more contracted, not unlike how some people, without a moment's hesitation, dash from the beach and dive headlong into the first approaching wave.

Regardless of length and trajectory, I prefer to characterize the facilitation of the transition into hypnosis as an *invitation* (from the Latin *invitare*, "to invite"), rather than an induction (from the Latin *in-*, "into" + *ducere*, "to lead": to lead into), as this underscores the cooperative nature of what happens. You can't—and thus shouldn't bother trying to—"hypnotize" your clients, any more than it is possible or advisable to try to "therapize" them. Neither you nor they can unilaterally invoke or command mind-body connectivity or avolitional responsiveness. As Jeff Zeig (2014) put it, "Hypnosis is elicited, not induced" (p. 25).

Usually by the time you and your clients are prepared for you to begin your invitation, you've helped to orient their expectations about hypnosis and hypnotherapy, responding to their questions and concerns, making note of their resources, and defining resolvable therapeutic goals (see Chapter 4). And, from the outset, you've been empathically connecting with them. If they've been agreeing with your articulations of their experience, then, on issues relevant to your work together, the self-defining boundary that distinguishes them as separate (and you as other) has become less distinct. You and they have become more of one mind (see Chapter 3). These developments all serve as stepping-stones for the elicitation of hypnosis.

One way to set the process in motion is to ask a question about getting underway: "Are you ready to start?" or "Would you like to do an experiment?" or "Shall we begin?" Such queries make clear your commitment to consensual engagement—you're providing reassurance that you'll wait to proceed until you get a thumbs-up—

but they also heighten anticipation: Something different is about to occur. This brings us to the invitation itself.

Regardless of length and style, most hypnotic invitations accomplish three interrelated tasks. First, they absorb clients in such a way that the boundaries of everyday conscious awareness—and the circumscribed self it reflexively defines—are relaxed. As you engage clients in the process, you indifferentiate the boundary-defining differences between you and them, as well as those that isolate their circumscribed self from their body and unpremeditated experiences (urges, emotions, sensations, perceptions, imaginings, fleeting thoughts, etc.). As the invitation proceeds, clients get more in sync with you and with themselves, allowing for a sense of flow (Csikszentmihalyi, 1990). Such shifts in relationship enable effortless responsiveness to suggestions.

This brings us to the second task. At some point, you will implicitly and/or explicitly suggest that clients can discover the possible or inevitable development of one or more avolitional actions or experiences—an expanding and intensifying feeling of relaxation; eyelids that find themselves unable to open or to close; a hand that feels so light that it floats up on its own or so heavy that it can't budge; a numbness in a hand or some other part of the body; one finger that can lift spontaneously when the client thinks *no,* and another, when they think *yes*; perceiving something not physically present or not perceiving something that is; a hypnotic dream or a distorted sense of time; and so on. These sorts of suggested changes often serve as the foundation for, or an experiential opening to, subsequent hypnotherapeutic shifts in clients' problems (see the illustration at the end of this chapter and all of Chapter 6).

More immediately, clients' recognition of their nonpurposeful responsiveness to your suggestions aids in the first task of your invitation—altering the defining boundaries of conscious and self-conscious awareness. Usually, the circumscribed self not only tracks what "its" body is doing but also considers itself the instigator of whatever action is performed. This everyday sense of identity is upended by what you and your clients are accomplishing together. Your clients are presented with experiential indicators of a decentralized, distributed self—an engaged, responsive mentality with communication capabilities that extend throughout the body, encompassing processes of mind that aren't always or can't be consciously apprehended or directed.

The third task of your invitation is to implicitly frame and/or explicitly name your and your clients' interactional engagement *as* hypnosis or some other form of flow absorption distinguishable from everyday awareness. There's nothing special about the word *hypnosis* per se. Indeed, because of widespread misconceptions about what hypnosis is and how it works, the use of the term can complicate and even undermine avolitional experience.

> A key problem is the word hypnosis itself. You might say to your client, "Let's do hypnosis" and they promptly . . . run screaming from your office. You say, "Let's do some focusing and relaxation" and they say, "Fine." They don't have any difficulty with the *experience*. They only have difficulty with the *label*. I think that the label baggage in and of itself should give us pause to think about how we want to frame what we do. (Yapko, 2014, p. 240)

Unless your clients are committed to a particular framing (e.g., if they've come to you *because* you practice hypnotherapy), it doesn't matter whether you identify what happens with them as *hypnosis, focused relaxation, brain-body training, mind-body coordination, guided meditation, applied flow,* or some other analogous term. What *does* matter is that you define it in *some* way. By categorizing it, you demarcate a border, setting off the experience as a distinct and special form of connected knowing. Outside of it—in the time preceding and following it—everyday conscious awareness rules the day. Inside of it, out-of-the-ordinary changes in mind-body communication and relationship become anticipated and recognized, observable as avolitional shifts in action, emotion, cognition, perception, and imagination. The framing of the experience reflexively contributes to and potentiates the extent of the changes themselves. For convenience and clarity, I will continue using *hypnosis* to name this context of connected knowing and avolitional change, but when I'm working with clients, I adapt to whatever they're comfortable with.

Below, I'm going to articulate some of the guiding principles and practices of the second task of hypnosis invitations—the offering of suggestions—before moving on to the third, the verbal and nonverbal cueing of hypnotic communication and experience *as* hypnosis. I'll then illustrate both by taking a close look at a demonstration I conducted on Zoom for a doctoral family-therapy class during the COVID-19 pandemic. But first, I'm going to delve into the challenges of the first task: getting in sync with clients and facilitating their getting in sync with themselves.

You may want to augment and contrast what I have to say with approaches to inductions offered by other authors (e.g., Gafner, 2006; Gafner & Benson, 2000; Gibbons & Lynn, 2010; Jensen, 2017; Rosen, 1994; Short, 2017; Zeig, 2014). You'll find broad agreement among them that both what you say and how you say it make a difference when you're inviting and developing clients' hypnotic experiences. Some clinicians, such as Gafner (2006), concern themselves so much with the precise wording of inductions, they support, even advocate, coming into your sessions with a prepared script and reading it aloud:

> If therapists need, for example, a confusional induction, or an induction for children, they can just pick up [my] book and read . . . it. . . . In the case of a complicated, precisely worded induction, I choose to read it because I simply can't remember the whole thing. (p. x)

The responsibility of helping clients transition into hypnosis can feel overwhelming at first, so there's something both alluring and reassuring about the idea that you can undertake the process by just reading aloud what you or someone else has written down. Such a pre-prepared approach is in keeping with what happens in research studies, where the same induction is read or a recording of it is played to all subjects as a means of ensuring standardized conditions or treatments. However, given that the heart of hypnosis and hypnotherapy has to do with the shared mind of coordinated communication, I privilege close attention to the evolving connection with, and experiences of, my clients. This would be difficult, if not impossible, to pull off if I were reading from a page, rather than attending to how my clients are responding, moment to moment, to what I'm offering. Yapko (2014) put it this way:

> [Some clinicians] deceive themselves into thinking that hypnosis is somehow to be found in the script they read to the client. Some apparently believe that unless you say this magical incantation, these words in this scripted sequence, you are not really doing hypnosis. (p. 237)

Your language choices *do* matter. But your job is not to carefully recite pre-prepared text—it is to extemporaneously evoke hypnotic possibilities. You are an agent évocateur. Hypnosis is facilitated and enlivened in the warmth, hope, and potential realized in the constantly evolving relationship with your clients. So in this chapter, rather than presenting induction scripts for you to reproduce verbatim, I'll be offering a set of orienting ideas and illustrated guidelines. Once you get the gist of them, I encourage you to try putting them into practice. Words will come to you when you're clear about what you're undertaking, and, attuned to your clients' in-the-moment and after-the-fact feedback, you'll learn how to adapt and refine what you say and how you say it. Each invitation you offer may be drawn out or compact, elaborated or minimalist, as you make adjustments to accommodate the clients' level of trust, comfort, developing absorption, and unfolding shifts in experience.

GETTING IN SYNC

I was born and grew up in Calgary, Alberta, in Canada; when I was 30, I moved permanently to the United States. I eventually became an American citizen, but I retained my Canadian citizenship. A few years ago, pre-COVID, I flew back to Calgary for a family visit. When I landed at the airport, I presented my American passport to the Canadian customs official. Scrutinizing it, he saw where I'd been born, and he asked, with a critical tone, "Where's your *Canadian* passport?"

I told him I hadn't brought it with me. He looked disappointed.

"See, if you show me a foreign passport like this one, I could always say to you, 'No, sorry, I'm afraid you can't come into my country today.' But if you show me your Canadian passport, I'm gonna say, 'Welcome home, brother.'"

Clients can be as circumspect as that customs official, reluctant to let you cross the border into the domain of their (imagi-)nation. But if your empathic offerings are attuned and accurate, you'll earn a kind of home-country passport. Feeling understood and safe, your clients will find it easier to relax into trusting and connecting with you. And as you initiate your invitation into hypnosis, there are several ways you can consolidate and extend that connection so that it encompasses the relationship not only between you and your clients but also between their awareness and their bodily experience.

Using Permissive Language

Stage hypnotists can be a bossy, transgressive bunch. An illustrative example can be found in a brief television demonstration by Richard Barker, a well-known, skilled practitioner who bills himself as "The Incredible Hypnotist." Throughout the demonstration, Barker speaks quickly and authoritatively, holding and restricting his male volunteer's attention. Barker also physically intrudes on him many times, snapping his fingers next to the man's face; jerking each of the man's arms forward to throw him off balance; touching the man's head and face; prodding and pressing his shoulder, arm, and leg; and lifting up and then releasing the man's wrists so his hands plop onto his legs.

Barker starts by telling the volunteer what he wants him to do and how he wants him to think:

> **B:** I just want you to stare straight ahead and I want you to find a light to stare at. . . . And I want you to understand something: That the more you stare, the more tired you become, the more tired you become, the more you'll stare. That's very important.

Soon the volunteer is being told what he *will* do and is *able* to do:

H: You listen to the sound of my voice at all times, but you're able to focus, relax, and concentrate.

Barker prepares the volunteer to anticipate a signal for initiating a specific action: coordinating his breath with the hypnotist's:

B: I'm going to count to three but not before. When I do count to three, just take a deep breath in and out with me together.

Barker then tells the volunteer what to understand and what to do, tying the physical act of breathing to an assigned act of imagination:

B: Understand that every time you breathe in and out, you'll push all the aches and pains, worries and troubles away from you.

Continuing to direct the volunteer's attention, Barker builds anticipation for the arrival of the signal:

B: Get ready now. Keep staring at the light, 1, 2, 3, breathe in, that's it, and breathe out. Keep staring at the light. . . .

In the midst of detailing what the man will do next, he discreetly inserts a description of an anticipated change in his perception—on the next exhale, the man's head will be heavy:

B: Now the next time I ask you to take a deep breath in, you'll simply breathe in, you'll close your eyes. When you exhale, allow your heavy head to rest forward on your chest. . . .

And Barker ties the development of positive feelings to the predicted development of hypnosis:

B: The deeper you go, the better you feel, and the better you feel, the deeper you go. . . .

The transition into hypnosis depends on clients' (or, in this case, a volunteer's) accepting what the hypnotist presents. A dominating approach like Barker's, in which the subject is given no choice but to accept the hypnotist's directions and predictions, can be very effective with some people, as, apparently, it has been with the hundreds or thousands of volunteers on whom Barker has demonstrated his skills. In the video described above, the man went along with Barker's directives, and their pas de deux produced what appears to have been a hypnotic experience. However, had the man been at all reluctant to participate or less willing to give Barker the benefit of the doubt, the boundaries of his circumscribed self would have been fortified, rather than compromised, by the process, and a hypnotic relationship would not have developed.

Tell clients what they *will* do, what *will* happen, what they will experience, and you create a high-stakes scenario. If your predictions are borne out, as Barker's predictions were in this demonstration, then your words and the clients' experience will match, thereby facilitating the indifferentiation of the boundary of their circumscribed self. However, if your approach is off-putting and/or your assertions are doubted or inaccurate, then your clients' confidence in you, as well as in their ability to experience hypnosis, will be undermined, and the boundaries of their circumscribed self will be more definitively etched.

If you're committed to working collaboratively, rather than transgressively, your participation, and the process as a whole, will unfold much differently, beginning with how you construe and construct your invitation. Treat clients with the deep respect they deserve, and you significantly reduce the risk that they will recoil from you and from the hypnotic process. Such an orientation takes you and your clients into a world of floated possibilities, rather than imposed certainties, where you provide defining parameters within which clients can discover their creative responses to your invited syncing up. Your challenge is to facilitate your clients' easing into a flow-state relationship with you and themselves without inadvertently erecting barriers to the process. The best way to do so is to preclude the need for your clients to guard themselves against you or what you're offering, to question your credibility, or

to wonder whether they are or will be able—or, indeed, are willing—to experience the shifts you're describing. All such concerns
can result in clients erecting boundaries of self-protection and/or
self-definition, via the exercise or insertion of some form of negation: "I'm not comfortable with what you're doing"; "No, you're
wrong"; "Nope, that isn't happening"; "Nah, I don't feel that"; "No,
I can't; "No, I don't want to."

You can avoid such boundary marking by employing Milton
Erickson's permissive language practices (e.g., O'Hanlon & Martin, 1992; see also Chapter 1). It isn't a problem for you to be defini-
tive when you're describing a given or verifiable state of affairs (e.g.,
the presence of ambient sounds or an observable behavior), but you
can alienate your clients and undermine the hypnotic process if you
predict to your clients what *will* happen ("When I get to the number 3, you will drop even further into hypnosis") or claim what you
presume is currently happening ("You are becoming more and more
relaxed"). The alternative is to provide options and possibilities,
offering what *could* or *might* occur.

To illustrate how a permissive approach differs from the dominating style of stage hypnotists, I'm going to rework the example I quoted
above in a way that invites the volunteer into a connection with the
hypnotist and into avolitional experiencing. I'll keep my "cover" rendition as close to the original as possible so as to facilitate clear com-
parisons. In my version, the hypnotist starts by asking the volunteer
to look at a regular light with an attitude of absorbed expectancy:

> H: You know how, when you see something remarkable occurring,
> like say a sunset, it draws your attention so thoroughly?
> How, not wanting to miss what's going to happen next, you
> can't bring yourself to look away? I wonder if you could bring
> something of that quality of fascinated attention to one of those
> lights over there? Finding one that draws your attention and just
> keeping your focus there, even as your eyes begin to tire. In fact,
> the tiring of your eyes can be an inspiration to keep looking.

Soon the volunteer is given a heads-up regarding what he may
notice and what he can find himself able to do. Barker fended off

possible distractions by talking quickly and intensely, and by telling the volunteer to "listen to the sound of my voice at all times." An alternative approach is to take it easy, anticipating and accommodating possible distractions or hypnosis-related changes in perception:

> H: As we proceed, the sound of my voice might fade out from time to time. That's okay. No need to try to keep track of my words. You can always come back to them, like picking up a trail after not being sure if you've wandered off it. You can just relax into this special focus you're exploring, and you can stay in touch with my voice even if you're not consciously following it.

Rather than assigning the volunteer the task of obeying a signal for coordinated breathing ("When I do count to three, just take a deep breath in and out with me together"), the hypnotist can take on the responsibility of coordinating his breath with the volunteer's, naming the inhales and exhales as they occur (I'll explore this in more detail, below):

> H: As you breathe [waits for the volunteer's next inhale] in and [waits for the exhale] out, . . . in . . . and . . . out, you may come to recognize something intriguing.

The hypnotist then invites the volunteer to discover how his breathing can help coordinate an invited act of imagination:

> H: Every breath in is an in-spiration, a preparation, and every breath out is a release. As you breathe . . . in, you can prepare, and then as you breathe . . . out, you can, along with your breath, release any unnecessary tension, . . . release any aches or pains, release any unnecessary thoughts.

The hypnotist continues to encourage a connection between physical and imagined release, extending it now to the eyelids:

> H: Continuing to bring your close attention to the light, I wonder, on the next exhale, or perhaps the one after that, or maybe the

one after the one after that, whether your eyelids might just release their tension, too, just becoming comfortably heavy, relaxing all the way down.

If eyelids can become relaxed and heavy, why not the rest of the body? But out of a concern for the wellbeing of people's necks and spines, I don't encourage heavy heads to fall forward.

> H: That comfortable heaviness that allowed your eyelids to so comfortably close—I wonder how that feeling might radiate to or inspire other muscles throughout your body? Perhaps those closest at hand can be the first to catch hold of that ability to just let go—the muscles in and around your eyes, perhaps, or maybe your jaw. . . . On the other hand, what about distance learning? News travels fast. Will your feet be the first to take a nice slow step in that direction, into an inviting warm pool of relaxed heaviness?

By mentioning various options and posing questions of possibility, the hypnotist invites the volunteer to turn expectantly toward his body, not to the hypnotist, to discover what will avolitionally develop next. This reflects the hypnotist's commitment to embodied collaboration, not mindless obedience. And nothing is being demanded—even if news travels fast, the next step can be nice and slow. Some body parts were named directly (muscles around the eyes, the jaw, the feet); however, indirect mention was also made of the hands,* by way of common expressions ("those closest at hand," "to catch hold," "on the other hand"). Which will be the first to respond? It doesn't matter.

A permissive approach ensures that regardless of what happens, neither you nor your clients are wrong. You avoid being wrong by not making predictions that could end up not happening, and you ensure that your clients aren't wrong by not restricting them to a scripted, predetermined pathway into hypnosis. If you're not wrong,

---

* Erickson developed the technique of, and provided a rationale for, offering indirect suggestions (e.g., Erickson & Rossi, 2008b); however, he also would make direct suggestions.

your clients will be less inclined to harbor doubts about you and your abilities, and thus they won't find it necessary to distinguish you as an outsider. And if they're not wrong, they won't find themselves divided against themselves. Flow develops in environments of acceptance, where suggestions are just that—suggestions—and where barriers to hypnosis can be retrofitted as entrances. This brings us to utilization.

Utilizing

I mentioned in Chapter 1 that Milton Erickson reversed the conventional method of establishing hypnotic relationships. Instead of expecting his patients to fall in step with his presentation of some standardized induction procedure or script, he adapted his approach to the unique qualities of each person, offering inductions that accounted for and incorporated what his patients were thinking, feeling, doing, saying, believing, and/or noticing. McNeilly (2013) discussed the implications of adopting such a method:

> If we take note of words that a client uses, phrases that they repeat, [and] stories that they tell, [along with] their values, their concerns, [and] their doubts, [then] we can speak these back to the client. . . . We are literally speaking their language, and this allows for an easy translation of the session into each client's unique experience. . . . They can more directly, more easily, more transparently embody the experience as their own. (p. 25)

Developing a common language helps to establish the conditions for indifferentiating differences, for blurring the boundaries of the client's circumscribed self.

To support this blurring, to protect the conditions necessary for flow experience and hypnotic responsiveness, you must also have a strategy for keeping distractions or interruptions from undermining your clients' absorption in the hypnosis invitation. Stage hypnotists, and kindred spirits in the clinical-hypnosis community, tend to adopt attention-grabbing speech patterns, a commanding tone, and an authoritative—even authoritarian—presence to block or override—

to exclude—any threat to their subjects' narrow focus on them and what they are imposing. Erickson, in contrast, advocated a strategy of *inclusion*, rather than *exclusion*. When a threat to his patients' absorption would present itself, he would accept and embrace it, weaving it into the very fabric of what he was doing and saying. Erickson termed this orientation to practice a *utilization* approach and applied it not only to the development of hypnotic experience but also to hypnotherapeutic change. I'll talk about the latter in Chapter 6; here I want to focus on utilization in hypnosis invitations.

To get a feel for what's involved in a utilization mindset, it can help to recognize analogous flow-protection approaches outside the field of hypnotherapy. For example, mindfulness meditation practitioners also adopt an inclusion strategy for handling anything that could interfere with their absorbed, present-moment, sensory awareness, making a "soft mental note" (Goldstein, 2020) of whatever is disrupting their focus on the body. Whether the interruption is from outside sounds or an internal sensation such as hunger, "it all just gets included. . . . There's nothing outside of the practice. Whatever arises can be included. And that's the beauty of mindfulness meditation. In essence, nothing is a distraction, because everything can be included" (Goldstein, 2020).

The meditation teacher Jeff Warren brings this same attitude of inclusion (with a side of friendly good humor) to a guided meditation he offers on the Ten Percent Happier app called "Welcome to the Party":

> The whole principle of this "Welcome to the party" meditation is that everything and everyone is welcome. . . . You are an affable host. "So happy to see you," you might say, "Welcome to the party of my direct experience." . . . Make this your mantra: Welcome the insistent thought, welcome the annoying sensation, welcome the distracting sound. There are no enemies in this meditation, no problems—only new things to notice and to welcome. (Warren, n.d.)

Billy Collins (2019a) similarly embraces inclusion in his approach to writing poetry:

When you're writing poems, . . . there's no such thing as a distraction. If you hear something that's distracting you, put it into your poem. Maybe it belongs there. I was writing a poem once and we had a kitten in the house and the kitten kept jumping up on my lap and scratching me, and I kept picking it up and putting it down. Finally, I just started writing about the kitten. And the kitten found its way into the poem. Now it's . . . an immortalized kitten.

Of course, both meditation and the writing of poetry are solitary activities. Something of the interpersonal complexities of a hypnosis context can be found in improv theater, where two performers, provided with identities and some kind of setup, are invited to spontaneously compose a scene through close listening and open, in-the-moment responsiveness to what each offers the other. The comedian and actor Tina Fey (2011) outlined four rules for such improvisation, the first two of which are most relevant here:

The first rule of improvisation is AGREE. Always agree and SAY YES. When you're improvising, this means you are required to agree with whatever your partner has created. So if we're improvising and I say, "Freeze, I have a gun," and you say, "That's not a gun. It's your finger. You're pointing your finger at me," our improvised scene has ground to a halt. But if I say, "Freeze, I have a gun!" and you say, "The gun I gave you for Christmas! You bastard!" then we have started a scene because we have AGREED that my finger is in fact a Christmas gun. . . . Start with a YES and see where that takes you. . . .

The second rule of improvisation is not only to say yes, but YES, AND. You are supposed to agree and then add something of your own. If I start a scene with "I can't believe it's so hot in here," and you just say, "Yeah . . ." we're kind of at a standstill. But if I say, "I can't believe it's so hot in here," and you say, "What did you expect? We're in hell." Or if I say, "I can't believe it's so hot in here," and you say, "Yes, this can't be good for the wax figures." Or if I say, "I can't believe it's so hot in here," and you say, "I told you we shouldn't have crawled into this dog's mouth," now we're getting somewhere. To me YES, AND means don't be afraid to contribute. It's your responsibility to contribute. (pp. 83–84)

Saying NO to a distraction, disruption, or challenge—whether a sensation, sound, or thought; a persistent kitten; or an off-the-wall utterance from a fellow performer on a stage—is an exclusion strategy for protecting safety and comfort. It may work for a time to treat intrusions as annoyances to be shunned or shut down, but the boundaries erected by such efforts will tend to fortify the obdurate insularity of the circumscribed self. Saying YES, or better, YES, AND is a commitment to utilization—an inclusion strategy that indifferentiates unnecessary or problematic NO-imposed boundaries within and between people.

```
NO NO        NO NO   NO NO NO NO NO NO      NO NO NO         OR OR      OR OR      OR OR   OROROROROR
  NO NO        NO NO   NO NO NO NO NO NO     NO NO NO NO NO      OROROR     OROROR     OR OR   OR OR OROROROR
  NO NO        NO NO   NO NO              NO NO            NO      OR OR OR    OROROR     OR OR   OR OR     OROROR
  NO NO   NO NO   NO NO              NO NO                   OROROROR    OR OR OR   OR OR   OR OR       OROROR
NO NO NO NO   NO NO              NO NO NO                 OR OR  OR OR  OR OROROR   OR OR   OR OR        OR OR
  NO NO NO NO   NO NO NO NO NO NO      NO NO NO            OR OR   OR OR   OR OR OR OR OR OR   OR OR        OR OR
  NO NO        NO NO NO NO NO NO     NO NO NO           OR OR   OR OR   OR OR  OROR OR OR   OR OR        OR OR
  NO NO        NO NO              NO NO               OR OR OR OR OR OR OR   OR OR   OROROR OR OR   OR OR        OR OR
  NO NO        NO NO              NO NO            OR OR OROROROR OR OR   OR OR   OR OR OR   OR OR        OROROR
  NO NO        NO NO        NO          NO NO        OR OR        OR OR   OR OR   OROR OR   OR OR        OR OR
  NO NO        NO NO NO NO NO NO   NO NO NO NO NO NO    OR OR        OR OR   OR OR       OROROR   OR OR OROROROR
  NO NO        NO NO NO NO NO NO      NO NO NO NO       OR OR        OR OR   OR OR       OR OR    OROROROROR
```
,

For Erickson, "utilization was a central facet of all of [his] interventions [and] an integral part of his persona. [It] was a *life-style*, not merely a technique" (J. Zeig, personal communication, December 13, 2015). Indeed, utilization offers a YES, AND *orientation* to meeting challenges, one that invites and encourages flow, flexibility, and extemporaneous discovery.

Hypnotherapists recognize that for clients, distractions in the environment—intruding sounds, ambient temperature, kittens—can undermine focus and connection, and thus preclude flow, particularly before the clients have become internally absorbed enough for the disturbances not to be noticed. If the distractions are negligible or short-lived, you can probably get by with letting them dissipate on their own. But if they are prominent or persistent enough to draw your attention, then they could also be undermining your clients' connection with you and their absorption in the process, so they warrant a resourceful response, if only to render them inconsequential.

A simple, straightforward way to do this with a current or pre-dicted distraction is to just acknowledge its presence or possibility. In making a passing note of it, you help clients accept it as a given and thus disregard it as unimportant:

H: For the next little while, you may hear the traffic from time to time, . . . or some part of you may track the air conditioning as it cycles on and off. As background sounds come and go, your foreground awareness can become more and more focused.

You could also, à la Joseph Goldstein (2020), reference only "the bare experience of the sound [rather than] . . . naming it," intro-ducing the possibility that such sounds needn't be relegated to the background; indeed, they may assist in foregrounding an enhanced hypnotic experience:

H: For the next little while, you may hear sounds of movement . . . or sounds that mark a change in temperature. You might find yourself moving along with them, heading someplace important, . . . or you may discover how a shift in what you hear can cue a shift in how you feel.

A more Billy Collins or Tina Fey approach would involve transmuting such distractions into YES-AND *contributions* to the hypnotic process:

H: Horns blaring, engines racing: The cacophony of impatience and hurry *out there* puts into clear relief the breath-by-breath tranquility that can develop *in here*. And what a relief *that* can be. The cars can do all the fussing and rushing *out there* so that *in here* you're freed up to quietly settle in and slow down. And just as the air conditioner cycles on and off now and again, keeping the temperature comfortably constant, your breathing is also cycling—now in, now out, again in, again out—allowing your experience to begin comfortably changing.

I mentioned earlier that I would be taking a close look at a hypno-sis demonstration I conducted on Zoom for a class of family-therapy doctoral students. I'll get to that soon. But I actually did two demos that day, the second of which offered a rich opportunity for utilization. The woman who volunteered for it was interested in getting back into what she described as an intuitive relationship with her body, involving eating well and running more often. A few minutes into a hypnosis invitation with her, an interruption occurred, not feline, but canine, in nature. The student had her dog in the same room with her, and, for a period of time, it barked intermittently. My dogs heard hers and barked back, so some short call-and-response interactions ensued. Here's how I utilized one such interchange:

> D: {bark} When dogs communicate a desire, they {bark} have just a few ways of doing that, {bark} expressing excitement or displeasure with an anticipation of response. Bodies are not dissimilar. We have ways, often just a few ways, of communicating {bark} a need, a necessity, a desire, {back-and-forth barking} issuing a warning, {back-and-forth barking} . . . calling [out], . . . to alert, and then can settle down. And as you settle {bark} down beneath any need for alert attention, {two barks} go ahead and relax into your intuitive sensibility.

After the demonstration, one of the students asked the volunteer what it had been like for her when her dog was barking. She replied, "I did notice, . . . [but] after a while, I just started to . . . tune her out. So I could hear her barking but . . . it just seemed like she was in the background." By transmuting interruptions into contributions, you save yourself and your clients the trouble of having to guard against or unleash a campaign against them.

Sometimes the source of distraction is more inside than outside, or a combination of both. Erickson (2008a) once saw a woman who "had been defeated in her efforts to secure therapy by a compulsive attentiveness to the minutiae of the immediate environment," coupled with an "overpowering . . . need to . . . comment upon what she saw about her" (p. 274). She provided a running commentary of the objects in his office, "rapid[ly] shifting from one object or subject to another" (p. 274). Erickson inserted himself into her "verbal flow" by making a series of deliberate movements—extending a letter opener, polishing and then placing his glasses in their case, glancing over at his bookcase, and so on. Each time he gestured or motioned, his patient felt compelled to mention it in her running commentary. Gradually, Erickson "deliberately slowed" and inserted "slight, hesitant pauses" into his actions, and then he added "to his silent indication of objects an identifying word or phrase or comment" (p. 275). This served to calm his patient's pace, inviting her to become interactively engaged. Her frenetic soliloquy became part of a cadenced duet, which then made possible the development of hypnosis. But how?

By occasioning the pairing of his patient's descriptions with his deliberate movements, Erickson facilitated the gradual transformation of her autonomous, runaway listing into a coordinated, measured noticing. Her impulsive words and his deliberate actions synced up, which made possible the subsequent linking of his deliberate words and her avolitional responses. Such *interpersonal* mind-body entrainment lies at the heart of hypnotic and hypnotherapeutic influence (from the Latin *in-*, "in" + *fluere*, "to flow": to flow into). Language never merely describes; it is also always orienting and pointing—setting a tone, indicating a direction, prescribing a response, evoking a possibility. Interstitially insinuated as it is in the mind-body connection, language is able to invite and draw forth sensory, perceptual, cognitive, emotional, behavioral, and physiological change.

Another Erickson (2008a) case example illustrates the degree to which utilization involves the interpersonal—and thus shared-mind—entrainment of language and action, though in this case, the initial coupling was established between Erickson's words and his patient's compulsive behavior.

> A male patient in his early thirties . . . entered the office and began pacing the floor. He explained repetitiously that he could not endure sitting quietly or lying on a couch and relating his problems and that he had repeatedly been discharged by various psychiatrists because they "accused" him of lack of cooperation. (p. 275)

Erickson immediately took care of this problematic accusation by defining as cooperation a readiness on the part of his patient to undertake what he already felt compelled to do: " 'Are you willing to cooperate with me *by continuing to pace the floor even as you are doing now?'* His reply was a startled, 'Willing? Good God, man! I've got to do it if I stay in the office' " (p. 275).

Next, Erickson (2008a) secured permission to conjoin his verbal directions with the man's actions: "He was asked to permit the writer [Erickson] to participate in his pacing by the measure of directing it in part. To this he agreed rather bewilderingly" (p. 275). By asking the man to do what he was already doing—pacing this way and that, turning this way and that, walking away from the chair, walking toward the chair, and so on—Erickson synced his descriptions and directions with the man's behavior, indifferentiating the differences between them. Once this entrainment was established,

> the tempo of the instructions was [gradually] slowed and the wording changed to, "Now turn to the right away from the chair in which you can sit; turn left toward the chair in which you can sit; walk away from the chair in which you can sit; walk toward the chair in which you can sit," etc. (p. 276)

You can recognize in Erickson's description not only the utilization of the man's pacing but also an ever-so-slow introduction of expectancy—the anticipation of avolitional change: The chair is no longer just an object in the room being used to orient the directions; it has become "the chair *in which you can sit.*" I'll address this shift soon, but first I want to further explore the process of entraining the hypnotist's words with clients' actions.

Entraining

Watch two people agreeing with each other in an intimate conversation, and chances are you'll see them assuming the same posture or, if they're walking, adopting the same gait. The respective volumes of their voices and rates of speech will also likely be closely aligned. Such matching tends to happen unconsciously when people feel in accord: Their idea sharing and emotional rapport are reflected in the minimization of physical and vocal differences between them.

But the mirror inversion of this is also true. Reciprocated gestures, facial expressions, qualities of voice, body posture, and movement: These are not just demonstrations or reflections of a common mood, idea, or emotion; they are also *cues for* and *contributions to* shared thoughts and feelings. You may find that you can enhance your empathic grasp of your clients' experience if you match some of the physical and acoustic qualities of their presence, adjusting your pace, volume, posture, and countenance in ways that help you *embody* their sensibility as they relay their stories. Diminishing the visual and auditory differences between you and your clients further indifferentiates, for both of you, the boundaries that demarcate the clients' circumscribed self and that distinguish you as an outsider.

As you begin your invitation, you can go beyond an empathic mirroring of the physicality of your clients' communication; you can also couple what *you say* (and when and how you say it) with what *your clients are doing*. Here are some examples:

TABLE 5.1: Linking Words and Actions

CLIENT'S BEHAVIORS	YOUR WORDS
Shifts in seat	Feel free to adjust your position so you can get comfortable.
Shifts again	Making any necessary adjustments to settle in.
	Isn't it interesting how certain behaviors, such as
Blinks	blinking,
	happen automatically all the time without our consciously noticing it? If you add up all your {pause}
Blinks	blinks,
	they total something like 20 minutes of eye closure per day. That's a lot of not seeing that you're not seeing what's right in front of you, {pause}
Blinks	blink

	by {pause}
Blinks	blink.
	And they happen so effortlessly, so automatically.
Scratches face	It's like when you get an itch somewhere
	and you scratch it. You don't even have to think about it. Your hand, in the
Blinks	blink of an eye,
	lifts up and
Scratches nose	relieves the itch
	with a quick, light touch, without you having to plan or direct it. Your hand just handles it.

By folding in mention of or reference to avolitional or reflex actions in time with their occurrence, you initiate an interpersonal language-body connection between your words and your clients' avolitional experience that has later application in inviting hypnotic responses.

This coupling takes on a rhythmic quality when you entrain your speaking with your clients' breathing. To manage it, you of course first need to be able to *find* their breath, which isn't always easy. Some people breathe so shallowly or so deeply and slowly that it is hard to pick up visual cues of what their breath is doing or which direction it is headed. The easiest way to catch a glimpse is to look for movement along some edge—the top of the shoulder in contrast to the chair or wall behind it, the line of an open collar against the neck or collarbone, a bunched part of a shirt or blouse, standing out against the fabric next to it. All such places will tend to display—definitively, if only slightly—the movement of the chest or diaphragm. This monitoring is best done with the most motion-sensitive part of your visual field, your peripheral vision. And while it is tracking discreet movements in your clients' torso, the central part of your vision can continue to maintain socially appropriate eye contact.

Once you locate your clients' breath, you can time your words so that they synchronize with it. There are several ways to do this, the most direct of which is to name or allude to, as it's happening, the breath they're taking in or letting out.

TABLE 5.2: Synchronizing Words and Breath

CLIENT'S BREATHING	YOUR WORDS
Inhales	One way to get started
Pauses	is to
Exhales	just notice as you're
Pauses	breathing
Inhales	*in*
Pauses	and then
Exhales	*out*
Pauses	how your body
Inhales	*in*itiates the next breath,
Pauses	how it figures
Exhales	*out* {pause} the time for the
Pauses	next
Inhales	breath *in*, the
Pauses	next
Exhales	breath *out*

As you continue with your invitation, you may find it helpful further along to ease into talking a little quicker on your clients' inhales, pausing or talking at a regular rate during the pause between inhales and exhales, and then s l o w i n g   d o w n   y o u r   e n u n c i a - t i o n a little during exhales:

TABLE 5.3: Altering Tempo

CLIENT'S BREATHING	YOUR WORDS
Inhales	You can just find
Pauses	a
Exhales	c o m f o r t a b l e s p o t
Pauses	

Inhales	on the wall there
Pauses	or
Exhales	o v e r t h e r e
Pauses	
Inhales	Anywhere you like
Pauses	to just
Exhales	r e s t y o u r g a z e.
Pauses	

You may have noticed that I timed things so that I said the words *comfortable* and *rest* on the exhales. When we breathe out, we are, through the stimulation of the vagus nerve, cueing the parasympathetic nervous system to physiologically trigger a relaxation response. So another way of encouraging entrainment is to anticipate what you're going to say next and time your words so that anything having to do with *letting go, relaxing, slowing down,* and so on coincides with the exhale.

TABLE 5.4: Pairing "Relaxation" Words With Exhales

Inhales	You may find that
Pauses	as you
Exhales	r e l a x d o w n
Pauses	into your
Inhales	chair, it becomes possible
Pauses	to
Exhales	r e l e a s e a n y
Pauses	remaining
Inhales	tension in your
Pauses	body, to just
Exhales	l e t i t f l o w d o w n
Pauses	or maybe
Inhales	just evaporate.

You can further enhance the syncing up of your words and your clients' breathing by **emphasizing** the words you say on their exhales, perhaps through a slight increase or decrease in volume and/or by saying words such as *relax* with a more **relaxed** tone.

TABLE 5.5: Marking Exhales

Inhales	If it feels
Pauses	
Exhales	**c o m f o r t a b l e**
Pauses	to do
Inhales	so, you can
Pauses	just
Exhales	**a l l o w**
Pauses	
Inhales	your eyelids
Pauses	to
Exhales	**d r i f t d o w n .**

Concomitantly, you'll want to time your use of words having to do with upward motion or buoyancy so that they align with clients' inhales. You might experiment with intoning these words with a quality of lightness.

TABLE 5.6: Marking Inhales

Pauses	Isn't it
Exhales	i n t e r e s t i n g
Pauses	how
Inhales	uplifting it
Pauses	can
Exhales	f e e l t o d i s c o v e r
Pauses	that
Inhales	when one of your
Pauses	h a n d s
Exhales	**f e e l s h e a v i e r**
Pauses	than the other,
Inhales	it may be only a matter

Pauses	of
Exhales	**time** till the
Pauses	other
Inhales	hand discovers
Pauses	
Exhales	that it, in turn, is
Pauses	feeling
Inhales	lighter.

Although you can start getting in sync with your clients regardless of the current rate of their breathing, it is generally helpful once you've established some degree of coordination to invite a gradual slowing down. A more leisurely pace facilitates the relaxing of muscles and experiential boundaries, gives you time to formulate what you're going to say next, and gives your clients time to comfortably explore what's unfolding.

Sometimes your clients, perhaps nervous and self-conscious, will be breathing quite quickly as you begin your invitation. In such circumstances, it may be best not to bring attention to their breath, as this could actually increase their discomfort. And you wouldn't want to encourage them to try to slow their breath down, as this will put them at odds with their body, thus precluding the blurring of mind-body boundaries characteristic of flow states. You can still match the rhythm of their breathing, but you'll probably be best-off just marking this or that exhale or inhale every once in a while.

TABLE 5.7: Intermittent Marking

CLIENT'S BREATHING	YOUR WORDS
Exhales	You mentioned that
Inhales	you're not sure
Exhales	whether
Inhales	you'll be able to

Exhales	fully experience
Inhales	hypnosis, whether you'll
Exhales	be able, despite
Inhales	your best efforts, to
Exhales	**r e l a x**
Inhales	into the process.
Exhales	So I should
Inhales	clarify that
Exhales	there's no need
Inhales	for you to try to
Exhales	**l e t g o**
Inhales	of any concerns,
Exhales	no need
Inhales	to try to
Exhales	make anything
Inhales	happen or to
Exhales	**s l o w d o w n**
Inhales	your thoughts. You can
Exhales	just allow
Inhales	yourself to
Exhales	curiously explore
Inhales	whatever
Exhales	small shifts
Inhales	you may notice
Exhales	**e f f o r t l e s s l y**
Inhales	arising.
Pauses	
Exhales	**N o h u r r y .**
Pauses	
Inhales	Indeed,
Pauses	
Exhales	**t a k e a l l t h e t i m e**
Pauses	you need to
Inhales	investigate
Pauses	
Exhales	**l e t t i n g g o .**

Entrainment helps to establish a correspondence (from the Latin *com-*, "together" + *respondere*, "to answer") between your words and your clients' involuntary mind-body processes. To help your clients relax into the hypnotic experience, it will help for you to stay relaxed about the entrainment itself. You needn't account for and connect with every breath, every movement. You can treat entrainment as an attitude or an orientation to adopt and explore, rather than a requirement to fulfill.

As you and your clients get in sync, it becomes easier for you to invite avolitional responses to your hypnotic suggestions. Let's take a look at how to do this.

MAKING HYPNOTIC SUGGESTIONS

Hypnotic suggestions are floated possibilities that bring clients into a liminal space, a context for transitioning from the dissociative perspective-taking and willful action of the circumscribed self to the associative awareness and effortless action of flow-based experience. Whereas some clinicians, as I mentioned earlier, manage the challenges of this transition by outsourcing the process to a scripted induction, I prefer to be guided by orienting ideas and methods that allow and encourage me to extemporaneously adapt what I say in accord with my clients' unfolding experience and my commitment to staying in sync with them.

When you offer an ordinary, non-hypnotic suggestion to your clients that they accept—where they might want to park, say, when they come for their first appointment—then their acceptance of it is consciously decided, and the resulting change in their subsequent behavior is purposefully implemented (e.g., choosing to steer into the lot you recommended rather than the one they'd intended to use). In putting your suggestion into action, they exercise volitional agency.

Now, when you offer a *hypnotic* suggestion to your clients that is accepted—say, that a hand can become so light and airy that it begins to float up—then their response will be realized without the exercise of conscious choice and intentional effort. For example, a finger on one hand—who could have guessed which one it would be?—jerkily begins to lift up, followed by a second, and then a third finger, until soon the whole hand is haltingly but steadily achieving liftoff. There's still agency involved, but it is *a*volitional.

Our regular discourse is riddled with the common assumption that the thoughts we have and the actions we take are marinated in conscious choice and intent. This is evident in the following explanation offered by a client during a first appointment: "I called you because, after weighing my options, I've decided I'd like to give hypnosis a try." The circumscribed self is implicated every step of the way.

An exception to this implication occurs when we describe the making of a choice or the taking of an action for which we'd rather avoid responsibility: "It's been decided," said the father to his son, "that you're grounded for a week," or "Your favorite vase," said the son to his mother, "got broken." Passive-voice and vague constructions (e.g., "It's obvious," said the man to his partner, "that we need to break up") manage to leave the subject—the protagonist—of the sentence out of the picture. But, in general, despite brain-based evidence to the contrary (see Chapter 1), our language constructions—in both thought and conversation—broadly reflect the widely and deeply held presupposition that our circumscribed self is definitely in the picture and, in fact, is in charge of the show.

Hypnotic suggestions are a necessary exception to this tendency. Indeed, your challenge is to invite avolitional action without inadvertently invoking the machinations of the circumscribed self; otherwise, you'll be sending mixed messages that may complicate your clients' ability to respond without intention and effort. For example, you obviously wouldn't want to say to a client, "Decide which hand you want to lift and then watch as you yourself raise it." A suggestion worded this way would confusingly call the client's circumscribed self into service.

One way to suggest avolitional agency is simply to attribute volition to the unconscious: "Your conscious mind can watch while your unconscious mind begins to lift one of your hands off your lap." By definition, if the unconscious is responsible for making something happen, clients won't be consciously aware of it, and so the suggested behavior, if it occurs, will feel avolitional.

Another way to help ensure that your language choices align with the idea of avolitional agency is to trade in the conscious assumption of *volitional causation* (e.g., "Because you decided to lift it, you can raise your hand") for what we might call the hypnotic assumption of *avolitional emulation*:

> H: *Just as* a helium balloon, lighter than air, tugs to go upward,
>   and
> *just as* an elementary-school girl, knowing the answer to the teacher's question, can't keep her hand down,
>   and
> *just as* the minute hand of the clock on her classroom wall, as it slowly, confidently, makes its way from the bottom to the top of the hour,
>   and
> *just as* a seabird catches an updraft off the ocean and takes a free ride into the sky,
>   *so too* your hand can find its own unique, uplifting way of defying gravity.

The expression of avolitional emulation can take many different forms, but all are grounded in the idea that

> *if **that** can happen **there**, then **this** can happen **here***
> or
> *as **that** happens **there**, **this** can happen **here**.*

In the logic of hypnosis, change isn't singularly motivated and consciously instigated by a circumscribed self. Rather, it is associatively inspired and supported within a distributed self, within a shared interpersonal mind and an inclusive body-mind. To transport this orientation to change into the formulation of our suggestions, it can help to turn to the language of the poets, as they, too, in their

connected knowing, embrace an associational sensibility, an attention to *correspondences.*

The Nobel poet Octavio Paz (1974) said that the medium for
communicating correspondences is *analogy,* a term he used to refer
to both simile and metaphor. "Analogy," he said, "conceives of the
world as rhythm: everything corresponds because everything fits
together and rhymes" (p. 63). He went on:

> Analogy exists only by virtue of differences. Precisely because
> this is *not* that, it is possible to extend a bridge between this
> and that. The bridge is the word *like* or the word *is*: this is like
> that, this is that. The bridge . . . establishes a relation between
> different terms. . . . Analogy does not eliminate differences: it
> redeems them. (pp. 72–73)

Metaphor "asserts an identity between two different things. And
it is wrongest when it is most beautiful" (Percy, 1975, p. 66). Envi-
sioning one thing as another (X *is* Y), metaphor "systematically
disorganizes the common sense of things—jumbling together the
abstract with the concrete, the physical with the psychological, the
like with the unlike—and reorganizes it into uncommon combina-
tions" (Geary, 2011, p. 2). For instance, if you were Emily Dickinson
(2019), you might say that " 'Hope' is the thing with feathers" (p. 94).

Simile, like metaphor, links disparate things, but it inserts the
word *like* or *as* into the equation, so the metaphoric assertion of
identity (X = Y) becomes an assertion of similarity (X ~ Y): Either
X is *like* Y—

> I ask them to take a poem
> and hold it up to the light
> *like* a color slide
> (my italics; Collins, 1988, p. 58)

—or some quality of X is *shared by* Y: We say someone is as strong *as*
an ox, nutty *as* a fruitcake, or blind *as* a bat.

Geary (2011) characterizes simile as "just a metaphor with the

scaffolding still up" (p. 8). The inclusion of *like* or *as* in their articulation renders similes a little more rational, a little less dreamlike,
than metaphors; however, such scaffolding is incredibly useful in
guiding your clients' attention and imagination to the avolitional
change you have in mind:

> H: And just as that minute hand on that elementary-school
> clock ever so gradually, ever so effortlessly, hesitates its way
> upward, higher and higher, one of your hands can explore that
> inexorable feeling of being uplifted, like clockwork, in small,
> minute steps.

Let's play this out a bit more. Let's say that you have a client who
describes a gnawing, burning pain in her stomach, a pain that her
doctors have concluded, after thorough investigation, has no discernible physical cause. You and she agree that she would feel much
less distressed if her stomach pain were to diminish, perhaps by
her stomach developing a feeling of numbness, or maybe by some
other means. You would invoke the willful intent of her circumscribed self if you were to say, "I want you to control that gnawing
pain, that burning in your stomach, by deliberately making it numb.
Come on! Try harder! Choose comfort, not pain! Just do it!" Instead,
you might offer something like this:

> H: I don't know when you'll first notice the quality or the location
> of that gnawing, that burning in your stomach starting to
> change in some way. I've noticed with campfires that after a
> while, if you don't put another log on, the heat concentrates
> in the embers. It's not dancing all over the place; it becomes
> collected, contained. It settles in, settles down, like a dog that
> ages out of that puppy stage of grabbing onto your hand with its
> teeth and just gnawing away. Gradually, one by one, the puppy
> loses its puppy teeth and, week by week, loses its need to gnaw.
> But such changes can be difficult to detect midstream. As your
> body a little bit ago started easing into hypnosis, you recognized
> at some point that your hands felt numb. You were able to
> notice the result of a process of change without having to track,

perhaps without even being able to track, its development.
Starting in one particular place in one particular hand and then
the idea of that—the *feeling* of that, the possibility of that—can
grab hold, catching on, and spreading like wildfire throughout
your hands.

This extended suggestion is organized in terms of several analogies, several correspondences between

- the burning in the stomach and the burning of a campfire;
- the gnawing in the stomach and the gnawing of a puppy on a
  hand;
- the settling down of a campfire when it is no longer being
  stoked and the settling down of a puppy as it gets older;
- the difficulty of noticing the process of a puppy growing up
  and the difficulty noticing the development of numbness in the
  hands;
- the grabbing hold of a puppy and the grabbing hold of a feeling
  of numbness;
- the spreading of an idea, feeling, or possibility and the
  spreading of a wildfire.

By virtue of these analogies, the hypnotic suggestion implies several possibilities for how *emulation*, rather than intentional effort,
can inspire avolitional change:

- Just as the heat in a campfire becomes concentrated in
  the embers, so too the burning in a stomach can become
  concentrated, collected.
- Just as campfires and puppies settle down, so too the burning
  and the gnawing in a stomach can settle down.
- Just as a puppy loses its teeth, so too the pain in a stomach can
  lose its teeth.
- Just as a puppy lets go of gnawing, so too the pain in a stomach
  can let go of its gnawing.
- Just as a puppy can grab hold of a hand, so too can numbness
  grab hold of a hand.

- Just as a wildfire can spread quickly, so too can numbness spread quickly (note that numbness is now associated with fire, creating the intriguing ironic possibility that the fire in the stomach can be an expedient delivery system for numbness).

In Paz's connected world of poetry, correspondences can be found anywhere, so anything and everything can be meaningfully—analogically—juxtaposed. Transported into the mind of hypnosis, this sensibility gives rise to the recognition that something happening or changing *there* can be emulated by, or perhaps complemented by, something happening or changing *here*. Analogies convey this orientation toward possibility, but so can, albeit less poetically, bare-bones correlations. You can create change-oriented correspondences simply by juxtaposing any two

- **coincident actions:**
  As X happens, Y can happen.

    H: As you listen to the sound of my voice, you can find yourself relaxing.

    H: As the cars outside rush to wherever, you can settle in and drift to nowhere in particular.

  While X happens, Y may happen.

    H: While you explore the comfortable movement of that sensation in your legs, you may find that it can develop other pleasant qualities.

- **developmental actions:**
  Before X happens, Y can happen.

    H: Before you reorient to your regular awareness, you can take a moment to consolidate your learning in a place you can easily access later.

Now that X has happened, Y is able to happen.

> H: Now that your breathing and your pulse have slowed down, your movement into hypnosis can pick up momentum.

> H: Now that your eyes have closed, the doorway into your imagination can open even wider.

After X happens, Y may happen.

> H: After you satisfy the next itch on your face with that nice, easy, automatic movement of your hand, you may notice just how lasting that relief can become.

> H: After your eyes close, you can go anywhere at all.

- **interdependent actions:**
  Because X is happening, Y can happen.

> H: The spinning of the room can help you locate the still point around which it is rotating.

> H: Your open eyes allow you to take in the details in your surroundings, ensuring the necessary safety for you to turn your gaze inward, noticing colors or shapes, perhaps even images.

If X can happen, then Y can happen.

> H: If, when you exhale, you effortlessly release carbon dioxide you don't need, then you can also effortlessly let go of any thoughts and sensations you don't need.

> H: When you touch-type, your fingers convey an idea in your mind up onto a computer screen, and they do that without your having to hunt-and-peck the letters on your keyboard. Go ahead and allow your fingers to convey the feeling of

numbness they've developed up into the incision from the surgery, and you know they know how to do that without your having to get involved in the nitty-gritty details.

The analogies and juxtapositions you invoke in service of inviting avolitional change will benefit from the responsive timing, pacing, and expressive voicing of your words. It will also help when describing movement or change if you choose adverbs and verbs that in and of themselves evoke a quality of effortlessness. Thus, you might suggest that a thought, image, perception, sensation, or body process can *casually, comfortably, dreamily, easily, effortlessly, gradually, incrementally, languidly, slowly,* and/or *smoothly* find itself *absorbing, ambling, blending, bubbling up, condensing, cooling down, dissolving, draining, drifting, dripping, dwindling, easing up, emerging, enveloping, evaporating, evolving, fading, feathering, flickering, floating, flowing, fluttering, gliding, hovering, immersing, letting go, loosening, marinating, meandering, melting, percolating, relaxing, releasing, resonating, rippling, saturating, sauntering, scattering, settling down, shifting, sinking, skimming, sliding, slowing down, softening, swaying, tacking, trickling, unfurling, unraveling, wandering, warming up,* or *weaving.* All such descriptors invite and evoke relaxed, seemingly negligible, and therefore easily accepted, shifts in experience that, because they are modest, can discreetly continue developing without getting squelched along the way by judgment, critical scrutiny, or a concerted effort to help.

FRAMING HYPNOSIS

In the practice of mindfulness meditation, and mindfulness in general, practitioners are committed to maintaining sensory-based awareness. As you breathe in, you know you're breathing in, and as you breathe out, you know you're breathing out (Goldstein, 2016, p. 50). You "sit and know you're sitting; walk and know you're walking; stand and know you're standing" (p. 56). The resonance between doing and awareness-of-doing maintains a mind-body connection, concomitantly helping to dissolve the boundaries of the circumscribed self.

But something else is going on as well. In their mindful practice of reflective, sensory-grounded awareness, meditators are explicitly, but also implicitly, framing—contextualizing—their undertaking as mindful. Such framing places them within the tradition of mindfulness—and, for some, more generally, Buddhism—and this creates an interesting paradox. The commitment to unalloyed, non-labeling attention unavoidably imbues the practice with labeled meaning. Just as you can't not communicate (Watzlawick et al., 1967), you can't not contextualize. Hypnotherapists embrace this truth and make it a defining feature of their practice.

In hypnosis, clients, like meditators, experience something of a boundary-dissolving, flow-creating resonance between awareness and experience. However, the hypnotherapist's response to this is, in many respects, the opposite of the meditator's. Meditation students are advised to "just practice . . . in a certain posture. Do not think about anything. Just remain on your cushion without expecting anything" (Suzuki, 2006, p. 46). The hypnotherapist, recognizing that expectancy is central to clients' ability to respond to hypnotic suggestions (Kirsch, 1990), is continually, both explicitly and implicitly, defining clients' experience as unique and special.

For example, as he offered a hypnotic induction, Milton Erickson, at some point along the way, might make observations such as these: "As I've been talking to you, your blink reflex has changed. Your pulse rate has changed. Your swallowing reflex has altered. Your muscle tone and motor tone have changed" (Zeig, 2014, p. 127).[*] Such noting implicitly frames and validates for clients that out-of-awareness shifts in body functioning, along with unwilled shifts in experience, are signifiers of the nature and range of hypnotic responsiveness. Their avolitional experiences are reiterated and further realized when they can recognize and verify what's

---

[*] Zeig characterizes such descriptions as the equivalent of the lights and sounds provided by biofeedback machines, which give people privileged access to brain and body operations that otherwise would escape their notice.

happening. Hypnosis develops as a flow-based context in which clients come to expect and acknowledge these changes and abilities.

Moerman (2002) highlighted that the meaning or sense a person makes of their experience self-referentially influences—contextualizing, intensifying, enhancing—the experience itself. Kirsch (2011) made a similar point regarding the reflexive effects of clients' construing that they are in an altered state: "This perception can heighten [their] expectancies for responding to suggestion and can lead them to focus more on the task at hand, rather than just letting go and passively allowing their minds to wander" (p. 359).

As I discussed in Chapter 3, implicit and explicit context setting begins right at the outset of your contact with your clients. The way you formulate hypnotherapy for them—answering their questions, explaining what hypnosis is and isn't, indicating the sorts of experiences they may have—does much to orient their curiosity and anticipation. But there are a number of other ways that you can offer context cues or markers that define what's transpiring as a definable context, a ritual space, for problem resolution.

Vance (2016) described the way the "theater of medicine" puts "us in the frame of mind that we are receiving treatment and build[s] our confidence in it" (p. 38). The doctor's manner ("a kindly hand on your shoulder, eye contact, a sense of confidence and authority") is a context marker for this theater, as are "all the accoutrements, such as the white coat, the fancy tools, the jars of Q-tips and gauze." Theater-of-medicine context markers can unconsciously trigger a patient's placebo response, "communicat[ing] to our subconscious that it's time to feel better" (p. 38).

My first exposure to what Vance might call the "theater of hypnotherapy" was in 1985, during a 10-hour hypnosis workshop offered to students in the clinical master's program in which I was enrolled. After providing a rudimentary explanation of inductions and therapeutic applications of hypnosis, the instructor put us to work, half of us talking, the other half listening. He brought out thick, soft mats so the induction recipients could comfortably recline, and then he dimmed the lights and put on some ethereal music. I appreciated the vibe he created, but I didn't recognize it as theater. I mistook the context markers he supplied as essential ingredients for successful hypnosis.

I suspect I attributed so much importance to the ambient cues because I couldn't quite believe that I, alone, could facilitate hypnotic changes in clients' experience. The very first workshop participant with whom I practiced promptly fell asleep as I talked. Although that wasn't quite the effect I was aiming for, I was shocked that it could happen. I left the workshop stoked, but with a serious dependency on softness: soft lighting, soft music, soft furniture.

Luckily, my supervisor was supportive of my introducing hypnotherapy into my sessions at my practicum placement. Trouble was, I saw clients in a windowless therapy office, harshly lit with undimmable florescent bulbs, so for mood lighting my choices were harsh bright or pitch black. Did I lobby for the institutional purchase of a nice floor lamp? Yes. Was I successful? Nope.

And then there were the hassles with the cassette tape of New Age music I played on the boombox I lugged in every week from home. I knew nothing about utilization at the time, so I had no idea what to do on those occasions when the tape ended, abruptly and loudly clicking off, while the hypnosis was still underway. So I purchased a longer cassette—an hour of music on each side. But either the tape was too thin or my boombox was too old, for it didn't take long for the tape to get mangled in the machine, right in the middle of a hypnosis session:

> D: As the music garbles into strangled silence, its expiration can serve as inspiration for the choking off of your problem's oxygen supply.

Nah, I didn't say that. I don't actually recall what I did to try to salvage the situation, but I do remember that it prompted me to start reading. Before long, I came across a comment of Milton Erickson's, I don't know where, that cured me of my dependency on these particular context markers. He said that if a therapist were to consider music important for conducting a hypnosis session, it would be more effective for the patient to *imagine* it than for the therapist to supply it. And then at some point in my reading, I saw a picture of Erickson's office, with nary a comfortable recliner or boombox in sight. So much for the necessity of ambient softness.

There are many other ways of using context cues to explicitly and implicitly define the hypnotic process as distinct from regular awareness, to set off its physical, temporal, metaphoric, and experiential borders. None is essential but all can helpfully contribute to the moment-to-moment construction of a meaningful liminal space for hypnotherapeutic change. I'll offer a few examples.

Physical Context Marking

If your office is big enough to have a couple of different seating choices, you might experiment with designating one of them the "hypnosis chair." When you and your clients are ready for you to begin your invitation, suggest that they first move to this seat. If you do this consistently, both you and your clients will come to associate their entering into hypnosis with the process of their physically relocating to, and orienting in, the new chair. This can contribute to the expectancy and subsequent experience that something uniquely different and special happens there. Which chair you reserve for this purpose doesn't matter.

Temporal Context Marking

You create temporal context cues anytime you verbally distinguish hypnotic from non-hypnotic awareness, relative to whichever one your clients are currently experiencing:

H: Before you begin moving into hypnosis, I have one more question.

H: Ready to embark?

H: Before you start reorienting to regular awareness, take a moment to get your bearings so you can easily return here the next time.

H: Before you return to the new normal of your everyday awareness, devote a minute to consolidating the significant learning you've been immersed in.

H: Welcome back!

H: Anything you can describe, now that you're back, that you couldn't bring into words when you were in the midst of it?

Metaphoric Context Marking

It is pretty common to ascribe metaphoric dimensionality to hypnotic experience. There is of course no actual physical "depth" to hypnosis, but familiar spatial cues provide useful three-dimensional GPS coordinates for distinguishing inside from outside and for graphically capturing the clients' degree of absorption and imaginative engagement.

H: As I count backward from 10 to 1, you can, each step of the way, find yourself going deeper and deeper down into hypnosis.

H: When you're ready to go still deeper, you can let me know with a signal from your *yes* finger.

But just as it doesn't matter *which* chair in your office you identify as the "hypnosis chair" (if you decide to do that), there is no universal or necessary directionality ascribed to flow experience. My wife, Shelley, for example, floats *up* into hypnosis, and my mother used to get pulled *headlong* into the novels she devoured.

H: As I count up from 1 to 10, you can, each step of the way, find yourself, as the song goes, defying gravity, picking up speed for liftoff, effortlessly floating up higher and higher into hypnosis.

H: When you're lucky enough to pick up a really captivating novel, one you just can't put down, it doesn't take long to get drawn into it, forging ahead, page after page, to find out what happens next. I wonder what you'll notice happening next as you make your way into this hypnotic experience, your curiosity and sense of possibility lighting the way. Not long till you're at page 17, {pause} then 23, {pause} 31 {pause}. Soon, I'm going to ask you to bookmark where you are so I can check in with you. Then, once you've filled me in on the developments, you can easily return to just that spot.

Experiential Context Marking

The experiential framing of hypnosis is accomplished through both entrainment and endorsement. Entrainment, you'll recall, involves matching what you say and how you say it with your clients' automatic behaviors—their breath, gestures, and physiological changes (such as physical relaxation). This necessarily creates odd, noticeable pauses, as well as recognizable shifts in pace, pitch, and tone. Such an altered communication style indirectly marks the context (i.e., the nature of your interaction and the meaning attributed to it) as different from what was happening only a few minutes earlier.

Endorsement, or what in the hypnosis literature is called *ratification*, involves mentioning or acknowledging avolitional changes you and/or your clients are noticing:

H: In the last few minutes, your facial muscles have relaxed and your breathing has slowed and deepened.

Such comments make explicit hypnosis-defining indicators that avolitional change is underway. Something analogous occurs when you warmly confirm, mid-hypnosis, the experiences your clients report to you:

H: And what's happening now?
CL: I can't feel my hands.
H: No you can't, can you?

or

H: What are you noticing now?

CL: Colors!

H: Yeah. Aren't they so beautiful?

CL: So vibrant!

H: Such rich intensity!

By endorsing what clients report, you provide insider witness confirmation of the details and significance of their experience. In the process, you highlight and contextually mark the uniqueness of what's transpiring, which enhances your clients' expectancy and allows you to bring forth and utilize its hypnotherapeutic potential. You'll see a few examples of this in the following "case" illustration.

"CASE" ILLUSTRATION

To illustrate the process of context marking and of offering and developing suggestions, I'm going to walk you through relevant portions of the Zoom hypnosis demonstration I mentioned earlier. I was working with a student in the class, Taylor, who was interested in discovering whether hypnosis could make a difference with the stress-related pain in her neck and upper back. She said her neck often "hurt like hell," at times becoming so stiff that she wouldn't be able to turn her head. Her doctor had run a bunch of tests and concluded that other than inflammation, nothing was wrong. She'd been pursuing "a whole slew of treatments"—including a heating pad, an ice pack, daily prophylactic ibuprofen/NSAIDs, and sometimes CBD—for two years, but nothing had helped. She was having to just "suffer through."

One of the semester-long assignments for the class she was taking (and I was visiting) involved establishing a daily meditation practice. After a stress-filled first week of school, Taylor had started meditating for five minutes every day, and this seemed to be making a difference. At the time we worked together (the third week of the semester), she hadn't taken the medication for a few days, as she hadn't felt like it was necessary.

My hypnotic invitation with Taylor segued quite soon into

experiments devoted to altering her tension and pain. Such utilization of hypnotic experience to effect therapeutic change is the primary focus of the next chapter; however, we'll get an early start on
it here. Just as the experiential border between regular and hypnotic
experience is often not crisply delineated—clients can find themselves straddling the border for a while before drifting or meandering into hypnosis—so too the boundary between hypnosis
and hypnotherapy can become experientially indistinct. In liminal
spaces, borders invite border crossings—transitions (from the Latin
transire, "to go or cross over").

There are countless ways to invite a person into hypnosis. Rather
than attempting an encyclopedic accounting, I'd like to use the par-
ticularities of this invitation with Taylor to highlight some of the
guiding principles and practices I've been talking about. I began by
asking Taylor about her understanding of hypnosis, clarifying that
it involves collaboration, not imposition, and that it has something
to do with getting into a flow state. I was interested in finding out
about activities, in addition to meditation, where she lost track of
time or would get so absorbed that she lost track of herself. She
said she liked to paint using watercolors or mixed media. She would
"just pick colors and . . . just go with whatever" she was feeling at
the time, and there was "no rhyme or reason" to the abstract paint-
ings she created. I offered an empathic clarification that underscored the extemporaneous-discovery quality of her art, a quality
shared with hypnosis.

> DOUGLAS: Okay, so you have some medium—[mixed-media
> paper, canvas, watercolor paper]—and you put some color on
> it through, through a brush or something. Based on where that
> [brushstroke is made], you then make a choice for the next, the
> next shape, the next color?
> TAYLOR: Yeah.
> D: So you're discovering it on a moment-to-moment basis, I guess,
> are you?
> T: Yeah, yeah. . . .
> D: Picasso said that the mark of an artist is knowing when to stop.
> How do you know when you're done?

My question defined the moment of bringing a flow-state experience to an end as itself an aesthetic choice. It also established the fact of Taylor's artistic identity.

> D: And when you're . . . engaged in that process of creation, you lose track of time. Do you lose track of the pain as well when you're doing that?
> T: Yeah, I would say so.

One way to alter pain is to forget about it. Her experience in flow-state absorption offered a good foundation for hypnotherapeutic possibilities.

I further oriented Taylor's understanding of (and thus also her expectations about) hypnosis by reassuring her that she could easily stop the process anytime she chose to do so. The use of a painting metaphor to make this point served to further associate the two contexts.

> D: And anytime, like Picasso, . . . you know that you're ready to stop, . . . you can . . . put . . . your paintbrush down and . . . engage at that point in . . . regular awareness.

I delineated in Chapter 2 some of the similarities between meditation and hypnosis, and I demonstrated there how to use a modified meditation approach as a means of initiating the mind-body connection characteristic of hypnotic experience. I offered something similar here, utilizing Taylor's familiarity with meditation to begin the transition into hypnosis.

> D: There're so many different ways of making the transition from regular awareness into hypnotic awareness. One way is to do it via what you have already been learning with meditation. So why don't we do that?
> T: {nods}
> D: Because I'm also interested in you being able to augment your meditation with what we're going to do right now, so that it's oriented toward relief and adjustment.

Clients who have a meditation practice already in place are well positioned to infuse it with hypnotherapeutic possibilities, such as activating hypnotic relief of pain.

> D: So, you could just find your breath and . . . in doing so, there's this simple process of following alongside or through it. So that as you're breathing out, your awareness is breathing out. As you're breathing in, your awareness is on the breathing in, so that [your awareness and your breath] are synced up.

Both meditation and hypnosis begin by concentrating the attention. Bringing focus to the breath or an internal sensation prompts a mind-body connection and initiates entrainment.

Anytime a commitment to absorbed connection is made, the potential for distraction comes into play. To take care of this eventuality, I offered the most basic of utilizations—acknowledging the likelihood of possible sources of interruption as a way of preemptively rendering them unremarkable and thus non-distractible.

> D: Of course, there's so much else going on besides just the breath that other things will occur to you. Thoughts will occur. Given you're an artist, images, no doubt, will occur—colors, whatever. And the fact that you have your colleagues on the Zoom call may occur to you from time to time.

In addition, I floated the potential for avolitional emulation:

> D: But just as you get absorbed in the concrete creation of an abstract painting, you can get absorbed in the concrete discovery of your internal experience in a way that leaves behind whatever isn't relevant.

For the next few minutes, I guided Taylor in syncing up with her breath and taking care of distractions. I then made the first of several intermittent requests for details about her internal experience. Such information always provides rich opportunities for utilization. However, before asking for an update, I explained that while providing it she could (note the permissive wording—I didn't say she *would*) maintain her present "level of engaged flow." This implicitly framed—context-cued—her current mind-body experiencing as different from her usual mode of awareness.

Getting verbal feedback from clients during hypnosis is invaluable for helping to guide the process, as you'll see below. But sometimes clients find that reporting on what's going on for them is just too disruptive or irritating, or they can't, even with repeated encouragement, bring it into words. At such times, you might choose instead to ask clients to find a finger on one of their hands to effortlessly lift as a way of signaling "yes" in response to questions you'll be posing from time to time. Once they can move one of their fingers to where you can see it (sometimes the movement is slight, despite their proprioceptive sense that it was demonstrable), you can then request that they find and show a *no* and an *I don't know* finger. These ideomotor finger signals (Erickson & Rossi, 2014b) can then provide simple answers to questions designed to keep you apprised of relevant developments in their experience. This method of communication was not necessary with Taylor. I began with a temporal context marker.

> D: We're gonna do some experimenting, [but] before we embark on that, I want to check in with you. So you can keep your eyes closed and you can stay at whatever level of engaged flow that you're at right now. But then free up your voice box to talk with me a bit. {pause} As you're sitting there, what is it that you're noticing?

My question was poorly posed. Rather than remarking on Taylor's physical location ("As you're sitting there"), which reoriented her to surroundings, I should have preserved the distinctiveness of her hypnotic experience, saying something like this, instead: "I'm sure a lot's been going on inside; what is it that you're noticing?"

> T: My eyes squeeze a little bit
> D: Uh huh.
> T: around the outsides.

D: You can feel them squeezing on the outside.

T: Yeah.

My simple empathic comment served as an experiential context marker, confirming the sensory reality of an involuntary sensation. Taylor's agreeing with it furthered our attunement, making it more likely that she would entertain my next, tentatively proffered, statement about the mindfulness of the body:

D: Yeah. As if they kind of have a mind of their own.

T: {nods} Yeah.

D: So let's, let's start . . . the first experiment with that.

Scientific experiments allow for the making of discoveries and the forming of experientially grounded understandings. In hypnosis experiments, these discoveries and understandings are *embodied*— clients arrive at a felt sense, a felt sensibility that emerges from avolitional changes in their experience. In hypno*therapy* experiments, clients experience avolitional shifts in their experience of their *problem*, making possible a reconfigured relationship to it. I'll elaborate on this idea in Chapter 6.

D: Your eyelids *always* have a mind of their own. When you're not engaged in hypnosis, as you are at the moment, they're making decisions several times a minute to close on their own. So they're exercising a lot of decision making on their own. And sometimes they're making decisions that you disagree with, for example, I would imagine you've had some late nights where you're trying to get some reading done and your eyelids are pretty determined to close and you're determined for them to stay open,

T: {nods}

D: and they at some point, they win. So . . . let's just reverse that and go ahead and allow yourself to consciously *try* to open your eyes and allow your eyelids to exercise their own sensibility, their own independence.

T: {struggles but succeeds in opening them}

D: Great, you can overcome it. Great. And now notice how the eyelids are feeling. That's right.

T: {eyelids flutter and blinking slows}

Taylor later told me that she felt she couldn't keep her eyelids open, no matter how hard she tried. She was surprised by how heavy they felt.

D: So you can keep trying to keep them open and discover that with each {Taylor blinks} blink {pause} that's right, your eyelids exercise *their* ability to make choices, to experiment with how *they* feel.

T: {continued, slowed-down blinking}

D: Right. You can keep that conversation going between trying to open and letting close.

I was promoting a conversation, a meeting of minds, across the experiential division between intentional effort and nonintentional effortlessness. This division is often crossed in the day-to-day functioning of a few of our body processes.

You can't directly decide to slow down or speed up your digestion or heart rate, or to increase or decrease your blood pressure or immune system's T-cells. You can, however, purposefully swallow, blink, or take a breath. Of course, when you're not actively engaged in making any of those actions happen, your body kicks in, monitoring the need and activating the reflex. This dual-realm characteristic of blinking and breathing, particularly, establishes them as easily accessed bridges across the mind-body gap. You can utilize either or both to invite clients to transition from volitional to avolitional responsiveness.

D: And what are you noticing now?

T: They feel, they feel heavy.

D: They *do* feel heavy, yeah. *So* **heavy**.

With both word and tone, I empathically endorsed the visceral quality of Taylor's experience. Such context-cueing endorsements further attune therapist and client, but they also inductively frame the client's experience as indicative of hypnosis.

> D: So you can invite, with every {Taylor exhales} exhale, you can invite that heaviness to {Taylor exhales} express itself.

Once an avolitional shift in experience occurs, you can then invite an avolitional change to this change—some kind of meta-avolitional development that nuances, concentrates, moves, modulates, extends, or otherwise transforms it.

> D: To even expand, intensify. To move from your eyelids outward, upward, downward, inward.

I was concerned about the well-being of Taylor's neck, so I wanted to ensure that as the heaviness made its way into the rest of her body, her head could continue to comfortably support itself. I offered an anecdote that illustrated a compatibility between two seeming opposites—something can be both heavy *and* buoyant, analogically conveying a suggestion for avolitional emulation:

> D: It's important for your head to be able to remain afloat as it explores the expansion and intensification of heaviness. So allow it to explore, take on the characteristics of a ship's hull. Shipbuilders figured out a long time ago that ships don't float because they're light. They can be incredibly heavy. All that's necessary is for the shape of the hull to be constructed in such a way that the water that's displaced is heavier than the shape that's displacing it. So your head can be wonderfully heavy and still float. . . . It's an odd irony, an ironic sensibility, that it can feel heavier and heavier but be easier and easier to float.

Metaphors that exemplify and convey ironic or paradoxical truths succinctly and graphically communicate the both-and sensibility that X needn't be stopped or eliminated for Y to be possible or realized. Something heavy can float; a person can get so hot that they feel cold; liquid nitrogen is so cold that when touched it feels like a burn; and so on. I'll have more to say about this in the next chapter.

Having introduced the image of a ship floating on the water, I shifted to another water-based metaphor to further encourage absorption in the hypnotic process.

> D: One of the meditation teachers you may come across in your readings has a lovely metaphor that busyness of the mind is like the surface of the ocean and once you get below the surface everything is still. So as you submerge into . . . {Taylor exhales} **stillness**, let's do another check-in. Tell me what it is that you're noticing now.

This was much better phrased than my first checking-in. Here I emphasized the continued development of her hypnotic experience ("As you submerge into stillness").

> T: {long pause} My fingers feel, like, tingly.
> D: Mm-hmm
> T: Almost like I can't tell where they are.
> D: Yes. Tingly, and their location—"to be determined." {laughs}

Hypnotic changes can feel weird, so bringing a sense of humor into your voice when endorsing what clients tell you is a way of indirectly communicating that everything is safe.

> T: Mm-hmm
> D: Yeah. And how's your head feel?
> T: {pause} Stuck.
> D: Mm-hmm. Stuck in what way?
> T: I feel like I can't turn it.
> D: Is it okay for it to keep still for the time being?
> T: Mm-hmm
> D: Okay.

Stuck implies a problem in need of intervention; *still* is descriptive of the same lack of movement but implies tranquility—a condition that doesn't need to be solved. I'd just introduced this sense of stillness when referring to the ability to submerge beneath the busyness of the mind, so I simply repurposed it here. By asking whether it was okay for the experience to continue "for the time being," I was clarifying that Taylor had full collaborative input into what was transpiring, and I was implying that the experience would soon change. Nevertheless, given that she had told me before we started that her neck, when stiff, would "hurt like hell," it would have been wise to slow down and gather some more information about the stuckness. It's never a good idea to try to discount or pay insufficient attention to a client's experience. In my rush to make the feeling "okay," I missed an opportunity to obtain and work with a more granular appreciation of what was going on with her neck. Instead, I went back to the tingling sensation in her fingers.

> D: Would it be okay if the tingling that you noticed in your fingers, if that were to {Taylor exhales} develop in some interesting way?
> T: Mm-hmm
> D: Okay. So the indeterminacy of location and the tingling expression frees up that sensation to travel.

Associational logic occasions and facilitates hypnotic change, identifying the relationships or conditions that render it possible and marking the pathways along which it can develop. I proposed a change through an intercontingent correspondence: *"Because* the tingling began in your fingers and you're not sure where your fingers are at the moment, *therefore* the sensation can move."

I often make mention to clients of easily recognized or commonly understood processes that illustrate, indicate, or metaphorically imply the sorts of changes that could now or soon develop. I spoke about communication channels throughout Taylor's body that make possible the coordination of seemingly disparate parts or processes, such as the syncing up of hands and feet when walking or dancing. This allowed me to juxtapose two coincident actions to suggest a coordination between the heaviness and the tingling.

> D: As the heaviness from your eyelids expresses and explores, in some interesting ways, that tingling can find its own communication channels to develop, not unlike the way a painting develops, stroke by stroke, each one engaging you in the creative discovery of what the next color, the next shape, can be, will be, should be, is.

After giving some time for this utilization of her painting skill to develop, I checked back in.

> D: What are you noticing now?
> T: {pause} I think my right side had more tingling.
> D: Uh huh. The right side *had* more tingling. And now, what's the case?
> T: {quietly} I feel it everywhere.
> D: You do, don't you?

More insider, context-marking endorsement: I was confirming her experience in a way that implied that we were meeting in our mutual knowledge.

> D: Tingling can travel everywhere. And what about the heaviness?
> T: Still here. Doesn't hurt.
> D: And does the everywhere-tingling extend into your neck, yet?

Taylor's neck was the most important place for the tingling to end up, so even though she said the sensation was everywhere, I didn't want to take for granted that she could feel it there, too. In asking about it, I used perhaps the most important insurance word in English: *yet.* "Has it arrived in your neck, yet?" If she were to answer *no* (which indeed she did), then this denial has baked into it the reassurance that it will just be a matter of time until it does.

T: Nn-nnh

D: Not yet?

T: No.

D: Okay. But throughout your body you notice it?

T: Mm-hmm

D: Okay. If you were to paint a sensation of comfort extending from the top of your head all the way down to the bottom of your back, if you were to express that in color and shape in whatever medium, what would be the first stroke of that?

Here I again utilized Taylor's identity and knowledge as an artist to more explicitly introduce the potential for an avolitional development of comfort. I employed the subjunctive mood (what *would be* the first stroke?) to ease her into this shift in experience, and I inquired about tangible qualities—medium, color, and shape—to encourage a movement from idea into a visualized, hallucinated reality.

T: I think it would be blue.

In keeping with the tentative way I posed my question, her initial response was more hypothetical idea than sensory realization, so I increased the resolution of my inquiry. Her response suggested further immersion in what she was inventing.

D: Uh huh. Blue. And what quality of blue?

T: Deep.

D: Deep blue. Go ahead, and if it's okay, allow that to be placed in some medium in a way that feels right.

The passive-voice construction of the suggestion (she could allow the color *to be placed*) heightened the avolitional quality of the proposed application of the pigment. As I moved on to invite her to alert me when she discovered what occurred to her, someone's cell phone started ringing. I utilized the sound and then utilized it stopping, but I did so without directly naming it, instead incorporating it as a contributing sound effect:

D: And when it's made itself known, [when] it's apparent, let
    me know, {cell phone starts ringing} as if it's calling to you
    {ringing stops}— a call that can be answered just through its
    application.
T: Deep blue.
D: Using what size of brush?
T: {long pause}

I could have continued to wait for Taylor to respond, but I guessed
that I was asking too much of her, moving too fast. Three weeks
after the demonstration, she told me that, at the time of working
together, she was finding it "difficult to form words/sounds," as if
her "throat and vocal cords were also stuck, or maybe recognizing
stillness/rest for the first time." She'd noticed that since the demonstration, she'd been feeling less "pressure to respond to others so
quickly." She was now, in general, responding "to others, including
clients, slower and more thoughtfully."

Because of the way the perception of time distorts during flow
experience, I could have encouraged her to "take **all** the time
you need in the next 10 or 15 seconds to find the words needed
to describe what you're recognizing." Inside of this seeming paradox would have been the permission to comfortably bring her
awareness into language within the outside time constraints of the
demonstration.

Alternatively, I could have elaborated on descriptive details
related to the act of painting. This also would have ensured that
she didn't feel put on the spot, allowing her to continue exploring
the emerging hallucinated reality of painting the sensation of comfort as I talked, perhaps, about the balance and slight weight of the
brush held lightly but securely in her fingers; the precise yet relaxed
movement of her hand, knowing just where and how to move; the
fine bristles of the brush, able to hold, transport, and then smoothly
release the blue pigment; and so on. Instead, I relayed a brief (and
true) anecdote about a conversation I'd just had with another artist
client. The story provided a vehicle for encouraging further sensory
embodiment in the process of painting.

D: I was talking to an artist today. He was telling me that every aesthetic choice he makes feels *emotional*. And that made so much sense to me—that he would get the **feel** of it, that it would be profoundly sensory based. There's a synesthesia kind of quality to aesthetic choices, where you can almost *taste* the quality of it, the *feel* of it—a knowing that extends down through the felt sense of it, the felt sensibility of it. {pause} And what are you noticing, Taylor?

This wasn't the first time I had asked Taylor this particular question. By checking in, in this or in similarly neutral ways (e.g., "What's happening?" or "What are you experiencing?"), you are able to gauge how, and to what extent, your clients are responding to your various suggestions. The feedback you garner provides in-the-moment guidance for how and where to proceed.

T: My neck feels tingly, too.
D: It *does*, doesn't it?

The tone of my voice as I offered this context-marking endorsement implied that I was empathically alongside her, inside the feeling.

Because the tingling had now permeated her neck, too, and it had done so while I'd been riffing on art and synesthesia, I decided to continue developing the metaphoric linking between the application of pigment and the development of comfort. Only this time I stirred healing into the mix.

D: And allow those tingles to allow the muscles and other supporting fibers of the medium to make some necessary adjustments. You know how with watercolor you sometimes will wet the paper before you apply the color in order to produce a certain effect. Allow the tingles to prepare the medium for an aesthetic application of healing. {pause}
T: {head lifts}

Taylor later said that the tingling was everywhere in her body and that it helped her straighten up, perhaps even overcorrecting a little.

I was thinking at the time about an electrical-stimulation machine that my physical therapist had once used on my sprained ankle. I circled back to the complementarity of movement and stillness that I'd introduced earlier, bringing in the image of the ocean and connecting it to the color of the pigment.

> D: And in the stillness of that process to discover the movement underneath the surface. . . . {pause} Under the waves at the surface of the ocean is stillness. But that stillness is composed of movement—movement of water molecules, movement of current. Deep blue that can free up the ability to **drift down**. And what's happening now?
> T: I feel like there's a tightness in my shoulder.

When hypnotic and hypnotherapeutic shifts have begun to free up and take hold, it is helpful to treat *any* reported or evident avolitional development as constructive, even if initially it seems problematic. You can potentiate your capacity to respond resourcefully by asking yourself correspondence-inspired and utilization-inspired questions about what you're seeing and/or hearing:

- If *this* could develop, what *else* could develop?
- How might this development be encouraged to continue evolving in helpful ways?
- How might this development *here* reflect or facilitate the arising of a complementary development *elsewhere*?

With such an orientation in place, you can, with full-tilt, confident curiosity, inquire about specifics.

> D: A tightness in your shoulder, and in which one or both?
> T: The left.
> D: The left. Okay. Tightness in your shoulder and what else are you noticing?

You never know when your curiosity will make it possible to roust a detail that can be warmly endorsed and cultivated:

T: The tightness isn't in my neck.

D: It isn't, is it?

T: Nn-nnh

I figured that with such changes underway, it was safe to return to Taylor's visual imagination and see if any therapeutic changes could be further developed through the metaphor of painting. I kept the pressure off by employing the words *yet* and *would be* to ease her into any discovery:

D: And have you found yet a color to complement that deep blue?

T: For my shoulder?

D: Or anywhere. Just keep playing with that painting. Keep it as a project. The second step after the first deep blue would be **what**?

T: Green.

D: Green. Yeah. So discover what shade and what placement of green as you tune in to the sensation there in your left shoulder.

Having initiated a movement in that direction, I left it to develop on its own as I shifted over to telling a story about another client.

The associational logic of hypnosis and the relational nature of information and mind together inspire this hypnotic practice of introducing possibilities through correspondences. When two or more items of interest are juxtaposed in close spatial, temporal, and/or ideational proximity, the perceiver derives meaning from the inevitable, automatic interweaving of comparison and contrast. Think of the way voices interweave in Bach's two-part and three-part inventions; the way stand-up comedians deliver a punch line that crashes into and topples the audience expectations that they've just set up; or the way images collide in an Imagist poem:

The apparition of these faces in the crowd;
Petals on a wet, black bough.
(Pound, 1957, p. 35)

The action happens—the music, the laughter, the luminous recognition—in *the relation between* the juxtaposed elements.

With this idea in mind, I shifted from Taylor's visualizing of brushstrokes to telling a story of a client I'd once seen who sometimes in stressful social situations (and once when she was driving) would have to fight against her eyelids inexorably clamping shut. During hypnosis with that client, I told Taylor, I arranged a conversation with her eyelids and introduced the possibility of their not having to be the singular point of contact for meeting all the demands she was facing. I invited them to distribute this burden fairly and equitably among other muscles in her face and throughout her body.

> D: When other muscle groups in her body participated in sharing
> the responsibility for responding to her situation, her eyelids
> no longer felt the full weight on their shoulders. She was freed
> up to be able to have her eyes open to what was occurring,
> regardless of where she was or what she was facing.

I then directly juxtaposed the composition of Taylor's painting with a suggestion informed by the story I'd relayed:

> D: Just as green complements blue, you might allow other muscle
> groups elsewhere in your body to feel the tingle of possibility,
> to share, to distribute, the focused digesting of your stress
> outward so it's not borne just in one localized place but can
> be distributed through your body. If you were to try to . . .
> do a push-up with just your fingertips, it would be so much
> pressure . . . in [a] concentrated area. It would be so difficult.
> Share that around and it becomes almost effortless. Hardly
> even noticing. Go ahead and allow some other particular
> muscle group or some distributed area to volunteer to
> participate in upholding your ability to face all that you face,
> to help to shoulder the responsibility of that. And notice what
> happens as you do that. {pause} And what's happening, now?
> T: Other parts of my body are helping.
> D: Yes.

T: My arms.

D: Your arms, right. Excellent. Anywhere else?

T: Mm-hmm. My legs, too.

D: Oh, wonderful!

T: My shins.

D: Your shins, yeah. So strong.

We have many expressions in English that reference the body when metaphorically describing actions. I just made mention of "shouldering responsibility," and I went on to use a few others. They proved helpful in promoting a mind-body connection.

D: Your arms helping you to embrace that responsibility, giving you a leg up and allowing you to move forward. And as they do that, what do you notice now? In your shoulder.

T: It doesn't hurt.

D: It doesn't, does it?

T: Nn-nnh

So much of facilitating hypnotic change involves introducing a possibility, giving it time to develop in the background, and then checking back in. Now that her neck and shoulder were no longer hurting, I wanted to go back and keep developing the potential for her artistic imagination to contribute to a sustained change.

D: No. Deep blue then green then what's next?

T: Yellow.

D: Yes, yellow. Something so light and warming about yellow. So as the yellow takes shape alongside or integrating with green and deep blue, bring your aesthetic eye to your neck and your shoulders, your arms, your legs, your shins, and discover if there's anything else to introduce to further the development of this learning.

I approach all therapeutic change as a process of learning. More on that in Chapter 6.

D: Bring your aesthetic sensibility into play. And what comes to you?

T: I'm at a riverbank.

Taylor's response took us into new metaphoric territory. Notice that she didn't say she was *thinking* of a riverbank or even *seeing* it—she was *there*. The hallucinatory quality of her avolitional experience was denser than it had been earlier. She later told me that, at the time, she was standing at a brook deep in the woods behind the house where she'd lived when a little girl. It had been a happy place, one she had shared with her sisters and father. Now, in the hypnosis, she was there by herself as an adult, among bright green trees.

D: You're at a riverbank, uh huh. And is it a slow-moving or fast-moving river?

T: Just a trickle.

One of the most delightful things about working extemporaneously is the improv thrill of utilizing whatever arrives. Nevertheless, we were near the end of our allotted time, so I didn't have the luxury of exploring at length with Taylor where the river could take us. Indeed, I gave it rather short shrift, extracting and weaving into what we'd been doing only this quality of "trickling." I found it metaphorically resourceful for freeing up a stuck, "frozen" neck.

D: Just a trickle. Where I am up here in North Carolina, if you leave just a trickle going in your hose then it won't freeze at night. It's nice—just a little movement keeps things from freezing up. All it takes is a trickle to distribute, to keep things moving inside of the stillness. And to keep the learning going. No rush. But the learning that you've undertaken here and the learning that will take you forward as you find your way into flow can allow a tingle of discovery in a trickle of flow, distributing, sharing, relieving. Nothing needs to move quickly, can develop trickle by trickle, tingle by tingle, deep blue, green, yellow, and then, it can always be on the tip of your tongue: "What's next?" . . . And what are you noticing now?

T: I can feel my heartbeat.

Our limited remaining time once again constrained my choices for how to respond to this visceral awareness.

> D: Yeah, the source of the rhythm of the flow. {pause}

Her ability to feel her heart inspired a descriptive phrase I used a minute or so later, when, as you'll see below, I made reference to her being able to make a "heartfelt discovery."

> D: Anything else?
> T: Just peace.
> D: Yeah. So you can continue this learning every time you meditate, without making any effort.

This is a permissively worded post-hypnotic suggestion. Such suggestions highlight a significant learning from the hypnotherapeutic context and associate it with some future context—in this case, the practicing of meditation—where its avolitional realization will be a welcome and reliable resource. I elaborated a little more on how this learning could show up during future meditations before I invited Taylor to reorient to her regular awareness.

> D: You don't have to try, just the same way you open up to discovering what next color to place, where you can bring the tingle of that into your meditation practice, inviting the rest of your body to help your shoulder with whatever it is that you're facing. And what a heartfelt discovery *that* can be. When you're ready, you can begin reorienting to your surroundings, to the room you're in, to the headphones that you're wearing, to your feeling your fingers, you can, there they are! {laughs}

It is a good idea to protect some time at the end of your sessions—after you've brought the shared-mind experience of hypnosis to a close by inviting a reorientation to regular awareness—to check in and get some retrospective feedback from your clients on what they found significant. What you learn can be invaluable, helping you to correct any misconceptions or misunderstandings you might be harboring and helping you to prepare for a possible next session. In this particular circumstance with Taylor, where I was doing a demonstration, I left it to the course instructor to follow up the next week. I then followed up myself a few weeks after that. Taylor reported that since our session, she hadn't taken any anti-inflammatories. She was continuing to notice a "tingle" and "trickle" when her neck would start to get tense, with other areas of her body lending a hand to keep her neck from freezing. She felt that she was handling her stressors better and had been thinking about "stillness" rather than "stuckness."

As you've seen, the liminal space of hypnosis facilitates transitions across borders, indifferentiating differences between self and other, between the circumscribed self and the rest of the self, between awareness and experience. This establishes a resourceful context for facilitating the dissolution of the borders defining and entrenching our clients' problems. This brings us to the last chapter, which concerns itself with inviting therapeutic change. But because my demonstration with Taylor has already eased us into this realm, you'll find it so easy, so natural, to just turn the page and discover that you already know so much about how to transmute, to dissolve, to indifferentiate problems.

6

INVENTING CHANGE

I believe that to solve any problem that has never been solved before, you have to leave the door to the unknown ajar.
— Richard Feynman (1998, p. 27)

Jede Krankheit ist ein musikalisches Problem, die Heilung eine musikalische Auflösung.
Every disease is a musical problem; every cure, a musical solution.
— Novalis

Your task is that of altering, not abolishing.
— Milton Erickson (2015, p. 92)

I finally discovered the only reliable liberation from suffering: not trying to get rid of the problem.
— Yongey Mingyur Rinpoche (2019, p. 94)

You invite hypnosis, but you *invent* hypnotherapeutic change. According to the *OED*, the word *invent* derives from the Latin *invenire*, which means "to come upon, discover, find out, devise, contrive." At its etymological core, invention entails both searching *and* tinkering, both detection *and* construction. Your work with clients requires this double focus: a commitment to finding *and* repurposing or retrofitting clients' resources in service of hypnotherapeutically resolving—often *dissolving*—their problem.

As I detailed in Chapter 4, a resource-infused approach to hypnotherapy begins with how you construe and orient to the problems from which clients seek relief, whether from grief, anger, panic, addiction, phobias, depression, PTSD, anxiety, dishonesty, insomnia, physical pain, compulsions to act, perseverating thoughts, or distorted realities. Most people, clinicians included, conceive of these and other problems as reified, isolable afflictions that are best defeated and ousted, or at least restrained and contained. Such attitudes, and their concomitant efforts, establish and entrench *opposition*—negation—as the primary strategy for handling problems. When people battle against something afflicting them, marshaling resistance to it, their countering efforts inevitably heighten its profile, further entrenching its status as an adversary, as *other.* This creates another level of distress, given that the problem is actually a *part of* them—a part of their inclusive mind-body self. Their efforts to heal, to make whole, ironically and painfully serve, instead, to further divide them from themselves.

Novelist, essayist, and migraine sufferer Siri Hustvedt (2008) captures how ingrained this strategy of opposition is:

> Our culture does not encourage anyone to accept adversity. On the contrary, we habitually declare war on the things that afflict us, whether it's drugs, terrorism, or cancer. Our media fetishizes the heart-warming stories of those who, against all odds, never lose hope and fight their way to triumph over poverty, addiction, disease. The person who lies back and says, "This is my lot. So be it," is a quitter, a passive, pessimistic, spineless loser who deserves only our contempt.

The hypnotherapeutic alternative to battling *against* afflictions is not *giving up* or *giving in*; rather, it involves nonconfrontationally *engaging with* them. The associative foundation for this approach can be seen in meditation, where practitioners avoid going into battle against problems not by lying back in resignation but by sitting up with an attitude of clear-eyed, radical acceptance:

> We bring alive the spirit of Radical Acceptance when, instead of resisting emotional pain, we are able to say yes to our experience. . . .
>
> Saying yes does not mean approving of angry thoughts or

sinking into any of our feelings. We are not saying yes to acting on our harmful impulses. Nor are we saying yes to external circumstances that can hurt us. . . . [Saying] yes is an inner practice of acceptance in which we willingly allow our thoughts and feelings to naturally arise and pass away. (Brach, 2003, pp. 82–83)

In meditation, accepting whatever comes into your awareness allows you to

move closer, observing it with an unbiased interest. . . . When we're neither pushing away from a negative situation nor wallowing in it, we can respond with a new form of intelligence rather than with the same old knee-jerk reaction. Often it's not a matter of solving problems; sometimes a problem dissolves when you shift your relationship to it in a particular way. (Salzberg, 2011, p. 109)

When you aren't mounting a campaign against a problem, when, instead, you're approaching it with curiosity, your shift in orientation facilitates the softening of the sharp-edged borders that have been defining both the affliction and your circumscribed self in contradistinction to each other. The dissolution of boundaries opens new ways of relating, of being, of becoming.

I once worked with a cancer survivor who had been enduring excruciating pain following several surgeries. When I followed up with her three months after she stopped seeing me, she attributed the significant diminishment of her pain to acceptance. She said that when she first came to see me, she was wound tight with anger and resentment at the cancer and at the brutalizing treatment regimens she'd been through. Uncoiling from her indignation and prevailing sense of injustice had proved profoundly beneficial, she said, not only psychologically but also physically.

In a similar way, Hustvedt (2008), after a lifetime of battling headaches, reconceived and reembodied her relationship to them:

I am a migraineur. I use the noun with care, because . . . I have come to think of migraines as a part of me, not as some force or plague that infects my body. . . . The very moment I stopped thinking of my condition as "the enemy," I made a turn and began to get better. I wasn't cured, wasn't forever well, but I was better. Metaphors matter.

Metaphors matter, as do labels, because they determine your orientation—and thus the options and degree of agency available for responding—to whatever is challenging or vexing you. Defining herself as a migraineur helped Hustvedt not fight back against the pain of her current headache or against the seeming inevitability of the forthcoming ones, and this helped a settling down of both mind and body: "Acceptance, even physiologically, has a calming effect on the body. In other words, if you are in a state of resignation or acceptance, you're less tense than if you're going to war. And I think with a number of illnesses, this is probably a somewhat healing factor" (Gross, 2010).

Something similar operates in 12-step programs. Participants who embrace the resignation inherent in the identity-defining designation of *alcoholic* or *addict* are relieved of their doomed hope that they might eventually prevail in their battle against their compulsion to drink or use. The label (along with the rituals of proclaiming and witnessing designed to reiterate and reinforce its contextualizing protection) delivers the acceptance and surrender necessary for participants to no longer be at odds with themselves. It takes the autoimmune-like fight out of them.

As with Alcoholics Anonymous and Narcotics Anonymous, hypnotherapy facilitates changes by relieving clients of their hopeless, countering efforts to dominate and/or shield themselves from their problem, and by liberating them from the helplessness of feeling trapped and victimized by it. However, it doesn't accomplish this shift through the congealing of a resigned certainty (e.g., "Hi, my name is Jack, and I'm an alcoholic"; "Hi, Jack"). Indeed, it heads in the opposite direction, into an unveiling of creative *un*certainty, of unscripted discovery. Therapeutic change unfolds in a shared-mind environment of avolitional exploration, an exploration grounded in trust.

In this chapter, I'll offer some illustrative examples of some of my and my clients' shared hypnotherapeutic explorations, mindful of Billy Collins's (2012) sage counsel to people aspiring to become poets: "Those who want to write good poems should be reading good poetry, not how-to books. Indeed, every fine poem *is* a how-to manual." The same could be said for those intent on learning the art of hypnotherapy. Early on, I probably benefited most from watching demonstrations and reading case transcripts of skilled clinicians partnering and co-inventing with resourceful patients and clients. However, before you can appreciate and learn from reading or hearing a well-composed poem, you need an attuned eye and ear so you can recognize the craft stitched into the lines. And to derive useful—applicable—technique and inspiration from hypnotherapy case stories and transcripts, you need a way of grasping the associative logic informing both the clinician's words and the clients' shifts in experience. So, as I have done in previous chapters, I'm going to augment the describing and showing of hypnosis-facilitated therapeutic changes with some orienting ideas and principles, some up front and others along the way. Let me start by talking about the nature of problems.

THE NATURE OF PROBLEMS

Hypnosis involves avolitional responsiveness to suggestions for experiential change in action, sensation, perception, conception, and/or imagination. Hypno*therapy* involves avolitional responsiveness to suggestions for experiential change in some kind of avolitional affliction. Zeig (2014) points out the import of this rhyming between the nature of problems and a hypnotic method for resolving them:

> The avolitional quality of . . . hypnosis parallels the avolitional quality of the symptom, which can add to the therapeutic effect. . . . By definition, both hypnosis and symptoms occur, to some extent, "out of conscious control." Some of the effec-

tiveness of hypnosis perhaps stems from the possibility that the problem is addressed at the level of experience from which it is generated. Because the problem is experienced outside of conscious control, it can be addressed through hypnosis at an "unconscious" level. (p. 77)

This chapter is devoted to exploring ways of addressing avolitional problems through hypnosis, but the logic of how to hypnotically address problems won't make much sense until you have a clear understanding of what it is that you're addressing. A few pages back, as well as earlier in the book, I made the point that although we all experience problems as isolable, othered entities, they are actually part of the weave of our inclusive self—they are a part of us, not apart from us. This is why our efforts to control, constrain, or eradicate them almost always end up reinforcing or even intensifying them. How this comes to be can be more easily appreciated if problems are treated not as things but as *patterns*—as knotted complexities, knotted relationships of interaction and reflexive intra-action.*

I've spoken throughout the book about the degree to which reflexivity is a defining feature of so much of our experience, including the self-referential awareness involved in the distinguishing of a circumscribed self. It is also certainly integral in the reflexive definition and perception of problems. We all experience perception as a process of passively receiving information that comes to us, which we then react to, contemplate, organize, and perhaps communicate. However, perception is, as I talked about in Chapter 1, a *proactive* process. We don't simply take in neutral sensory details; rather, our perceptions are in part constituted by our previous experience, expectations, and pattern recognition. We certainly make sense of what we sense, but we also, in part, make—construct, contribute to—the sensing itself, both external and internal. Let me give you an example.

---

* Karen Barad separately developed the notion of intra-action as part of her investigations at the intersections of ethics, ontology, and epistemology (see Barad, 2012).

A dermatologist was set to begin cutting out a basal cell carcinoma on the left side of my friend Kathee's nose. The process—called the Mohs procedure—involves removing an area of tissue and examining it under the microscope to see if there are clear margins all the way around. If there aren't, the doctor cuts a larger swath and takes a look at the new specimen under the microscope. This cutting-and-checking process continues until no evidence of cancer remains. Each successive tissue removal requires the initial administration of a local anesthetic.

Knowing that getting a needle stick in the end of her nose would be incredibly painful—perhaps as bad, she speculated, as a man getting one in the tip of his penis—Kathee told the doctor she would be okay going through the elaborate step-by-step procedure as long as he didn't try to keep her from saying Oww!! when it hurt. She knows that it helps her to give voice to her pain. He told her it wouldn't be a problem. They started in.

The needle did hurt, and Kathee did say Oww!! more than a few times. At some point the doctor said, "I want you to do something for me. Next time you are going to say Oww!! I want you to say Yay!! instead." She thought it was a frivolous request, but she agreed. And so the next time she needed to vocalize her pain, she said Yay!! To her surprise, she noticed that it made a remarkable difference in the nature of the sensation: It was much less painful. The doctor continued the slice-by-slice removal procedure, and when he was done cutting, he said, "Now I have to stitch you up, which is going to feel even more intense than what we've already done. So instead of Yay!! I want you to yell Hurray!!" Kathee took his suggestion, and when she yelled Hurray!! the diminishment of her pain level was even more pronounced.

Calling out and thus hearing sounds of celebration (Yay!!) and completion (Hurray!!), rather than pain (Oww!!), qualified and modified Kathee's perception of the very sensation that was giving rise to the exclamation. Sensation and vocal expression were inextricably, reflexively linked.

Such Ouroboros-like circuits pervade our lives.* All problems have something of this fold-back quality, a self-referential looping that contributes to the pain we experience in response to them. You were introduced to this notion in Chapter 4, in my characterization for Meika of how panic attacks spiral into existence. Something sparks a concern, which occasions the release of rise-to-the-occasion hormones to help in the preparation for taking care of the concern. But the perception of the sensory effects of the hormones being released (dry mouth, nausea, agitation in the limbs, tightness in the chest, etc.) triggers more concerns, thereby signaling the need for more hormones to meet the perceived growing crisis. More hormones produce more effects, which produce more concerns, which produce more effects. In short, panic entails freaking out about freaking out. The release of hormones spirals from incremental to exponential.

The reflexive looping of other problems can be similarly traced. All display a Gordian-knot quality. People are pained by their pain, get depressed about feeling depressed, feel hopeless about their hopelessness. One of the most complex knots that binds clients is addiction.† Talk to adherents of AA, and they will tell you that alcoholism is a disease for which there is no cure. This conceptualization is an essential component of their framing sobriety as necessitating the resigned acceptance I mentioned earlier. A different understanding emerges if you instead view addiction in terms of the various relational and reflexively layered entanglements composing it. I'll sketch out a few of them. It isn't the whole story, but such an intra-active and interactive mapping offers up a different orientation for inventing therapeutic responses to any kind of problem.

At its simplest level, an addiction involves a person with some form of chronic suffering, who makes use of a quick-acting source of pleasure—alcohol, say; or food or sex; or a narcotic, a stimulant, or gambling; or whatever else—to provide relief, if only through distraction, from the pain or problem. Like all sources of pleasure, it is effective as a quick-hit, but time-limited, solution: The benefits

---

* The Ouroboros is an ancient symbol of a snake eating its own tail.
† I first outlined this patterned view of addiction in Flemons and Green (2018), pp. 30–35.

of the dosage don't sustain without its being continually readministered. When a ready supply becomes unavailable for whatever reason, the person faces a second source of suffering—not just the reasserted in-your-face presence of the original problem but also, now, the added screaming absence of the relief: a double whammy. Craving ensues.

The knot of self-referential coiling is tightened still further when the commitment to securing and indulging in the pleasure-source eclipses consideration of other relationships. Perhaps the person goes into debt, or steals, lies, or cheats to obtain the source. Or perhaps while experiencing the pleasure, the person becomes dangerous, unpredictable, or unreliable. All such actions skew and strain relationships with significant others and within the self, giving rise to still more suffering. Once this happens, the addictive cycling becomes fully recursive, the loop fully closed: The need for fast-acting relief is intensified by its attainment—the source of pleasure stokes the suffering for which it enticingly offers a solution.

The final Gordian cinching of all confounding problems is secured by negation-fueled and purpose-driven efforts to solve them. People anxiously try to stop feeling anxious, hopelessly try to stop feeling hopeless, get angry at themselves for feeling angry, or addictively fight against their addictive looping. At the core of all such countering gambits is the dream of dispatching the problem, or of smiting it.

This is how Alexander the Great famously solved the puzzle of the original Gordian knot. Back in 333 BCE, he was marching his army, in conquest mode, through what is now Turkey. Entering the city of Gordium, he came upon an ancient chariot with its yoke secured by a confounding tangle of cornel-bark rope. Other men had tried to loosen the mysterious knot, but all had failed. Tightly bound with no ends exposed, it concealed the secret to its unraveling.

According to local legend, the wagon originally belonged to the father of King Midas, a man named Gordius. An oracle had predicted that the person who freed the chariot from the clustered tangle would go on to rule the known world. Alexander tried prying the knot apart for a while, but he soon grew impatient.

Deciding that it made no difference *how* it was loosened, he brought his sword up and, in a single stroke, sliced it in half.* True to the oracle's prediction, he then went on to conquer much of Asia.

I wonder if the allure of quick fixes would be so embedded in the Western imagination had Alexander's method of sword-slicing problem-solving not been so revered for the past two and some millennia. What if, stumped and humiliated, Alexander had gone back to his tent, raging to his wife—let's call her Alexandra the Wise—that the damn knot presented an incomprehensible jumble of impossibility? In my retelling, Alexander drinks himself into a stupor and drops into a sloppy sleep. Alexandra tucks him in and then steals away to the chariot.

As an experienced carpet weaver, Alexandra knows her knots. By the light of the moon, she brings her practiced eye to the twistings and tanglings of the rope, and she discovers not a chaotic snarl but an intricate motif. Given the subtle patterning on the surface, she is able to intuit how the complex knot must likely be braided inside, beyond where her eyes can see. She calls to the cooks already manning the breakfast fire to bring her a cauldron of steaming water and a jug of olive oil. Soaking the desiccated cornel-bark thonging until it is pliable, she then douses it with the oil.

With deft hands small and strong enough to now find tight but lubricated spaces between the strands, she's able to slip her fingers far enough inside the knot to locate both ends of the rope, tucked in close to where she thought they might be. Instead of pulling on one or the other, she alternately pushes each end deeper and deeper into the center of the cluster, carefully watching what happens on the surface. A strand over to the side quivers. To make room for it to move more freely, she gently rotates it laterally along its length, rolling it back and forth, back and forth. She finds its diametric twin

---

* In Plutarch's biography (1919) of Alexander (written about 100 CE), he makes passing mention of another version of the story told by his—Plutarch's—father, Aristobulus (section 18). In this rendition, Alexander easily undid the Gordian knot, simply by removing the wagon's linchpin to expose the ends of the rope. But other details of Alexander's life are more consistent with the impetuous sword-slicing scenario. For example, Plutarch describes how, in a fit of pique-stoked rage, Alexander ran a spear through his best friend, Cleitus, only to instantaneously regret his action (sections 50–51).

over on the other side of the knot and does the same with it. When both have some play in them, she firmly pushes on each at precisely the same time, and one of the buried ends releases. The reverse engineering of the puzzle has begun.

By the time Alexander staggers out of his tent the next morning, hungover and groggy, the chariot has been unleashed. The oracle's prediction turns out to be mostly, though not completely, accurate. Alexandra the Wise goes on not to conquer the known world but to weave it into a confederation of diverse, mutually respected cultures.

If only. We can't rewrite the history of bloody conquests, but we *can* adopt an Alexandra- rather than Alexander-inspired sensibility when encountering the elaborate twisted skeins of our clients' Gordian knots. Rather than striving to smite—cure, choke, banish—them, we can hypnotherapeutically invent ways to collaboratively unravel the strands that constitute them and bind them in place. Below, I'll illustrate hypnotherapeutic responses to knots of addiction (specifically, to porn) and also to knots involving pain, panic, urges, habit, trauma, compulsion, insomnia, embarrassment, and body reactions. Along the way, I'll interlace principles and practices related to pattern unfurling and re-forming, encouraging you to trade in your sword for some warm water and olive oil.

The hypnotherapeutic resolution of afflictions is best realized within safe contexts for creative exploration. Such contexts make it possible for you and your clients to playfully engage with what has to date been othered and shunned—to collaboratively and meaningfully invent avolitional shifts in the strands of problematic experience. There are several ways to do this. If a symptom is already in evidence in your session, or if it is able to show up if you invite it to attend, then you can work with it extemporaneously in real time, improvising therapeutic responses to ongoing developments and shifts in its expression. If the symptom is a threatening or anticipated presence in the client's life but is not currently being experienced, then you can invoke it in the imagination or allude to it metaphorically, inventing avolitional alterations in the present that can be manifested or realized at a later time.

CREATING A SAFE, PLAYFUL CONTEXT
FOR DISCOVERY AND LEARNING

> *In play we manifest fresh interactive ways of relating. . . . We toss together elements that were formerly separate. Our actions take on novel sequences. To play is to free ourselves from arbitrary restrictions and expand our field of action. Our play fosters richness of response and adaptive flexibility. . . . Play enables us to rearrange our capacities and our very identity so that they can be used in unforeseen ways.*
> —Stephen Nachmanovitch (1990, p. 43)

People often expect—and some fear—that doing something significant about their problem will be arduous and painful, requiring a serious attitude and unshakable resolve. As Waldman (2021) notes, the need for therapy is pervasively promoted in our culture, along with the idea that it involves commitment and effort: "We're doing the work. We need to do the *work.*"

It helps if clients don't give up too soon, so some degree of perseverance is probably necessary, and it takes courage and a degree of trust to try something different. But particularly with hypnotherapy, which is such a decidedly uncontentious approach to change, the play of the imagination, and the learning that this affords, dances circles around a furrowed brow and steely determination any day.

The invitation of hypnotic experience facilitates the altering of the boundaries of the circumscribed self, creating a context where established beliefs, constrained options, and well-worn habits can give way to fresh discoveries, unfettered possibilities, and new-learning experiments. Hypnotherapy is a playground where the rules of engagement, the patterns of intra- and interaction (with the body and the problem; with others; with present circumstances and unfolding experience; with expectations for the future), can be altered and thus transformed. Playfulness and learning were clearly in evidence in my hypnotic work with a bright-eyed, 10-year-old vegetarian named Katherine.

Two months before we first met, Katherine was a Rollerblading, kayaking, gymnastics enthusiast. Then, not long into summer, she broke her foot, and all action-oriented activities screeched to a halt. Boredom set in. Netflix set in. With busy hands having not much to do, hair-pulling set in. Eyelashes were the first to go, then eyebrows. Katherine's mother, Liz, bought her a pair of cool, no-prescription glasses, which supplied excellent prophylactic protection, but Katherine's hands then headed further north, pulling extensively along her hairline, which, of course, kept receding.

Funny, artistic, and curious, Katherine was a precocious autodidact. She had learned to ride a bicycle pretty much on her own at four, when she convinced Liz to take off her training wheels and allow her to fall over a bunch of times in pursuit of balance. Currently, with no formal ballet training, she was teaching herself how to dance en pointe. And she loved drawing. She'd get a complete picture in her mind's eye of, say, a family member or a horse, and then, pencil in hand, she'd sketch the image onto the paper in front of her.

Commenting on Katherine's natural inclination for trial-and-error learning in her pursuit of bicycle and en pointe balance, I suggested we approach hypnosis in a similar way—as a series of trial-and-error experiments. She agreed. She'd actually had, she said, some previous experience with hypnosis, so we wouldn't be starting from scratch. She'd discovered that if she imagined one hand holding a stack of books and the other a helium balloon, they each became respectively heavy and light and moved in opposite directions.

Katherine was excited, she said, about my hypnotizing her. Respectful of her independent spirit and commitment to self-directed learning, I told her that, actually, her hands were already a step ahead of me. Not only did they have experience with imaginary books and balloons, they also knew how to become hypnotized anytime they acted with a mind of their own, such as when they were drawing. Our experiments would simply be providing opportunities for them to further develop their abilities. We would have time for the first experiment before the end of the appointment.

Reasoning that the trajectory of her pulling had been northward, moving from lashes to brows to head, I wondered aloud what would happen if her hands simply continued in the direction of their trekking. I invited Katherine to imagine both hands becoming lighter and lighter, lifting up and, on their way, lightly touching down to brush first her eyelashes, then her eyebrows, and then her hairline, before continuing further north, to where they could float lightly above her head, like a conductor's hands leading an orchestra. Which hand felt lighter? She said the right one. I asked it to share with the left the special knowledge of how to lighten up and to explore the good feelings that could develop in both hands.

At the next appointment, Katherine reported a change, but she attributed it to her playing video games while watching Netflix. She'd found a way to keep her hands busy doing other things. This meant that the pulling had now been mostly relegated to the 15 minutes in bed before she fell asleep and first thing in the morning before she got up and started reading. We did some more hypnosis-infused experimenting. She discovered her hands could feel too heavy to budge even though she was trying her best to move them. When I suggested that she share some of that learning with her eyelids, with one holding a little stack of books, and the other, a tiny balloon, her head immediately tilted to the side. With her hands too heavy to move, she imagined pulling a hair out and feeling the satisfaction of that. Then, at my suggestion, she did the same thing in slow motion. And then even more slowly. And slower still. Each time, the feeling of satisfaction was able to extend longer and longer. What she couldn't do was feel the sensation of the hair follicle growing back, like a seed sprouting and heading up into the sunlight. The growing back, she said, didn't feel like anything at all.

As you can see, Katherine wasn't the only one in experimental mode. I, too, was trying this or that possibility and, based on how she responded, either pursuing it further or abandoning it for some other option. As when you're learning to ride a bicycle, the mess-ups and no-goes are essential components in the developing acquisition of new knowledge and new habits of action. Katherine was learning how to lose the habit of pulling; I was learning how best to facilitate that learning.

When she returned the following week, Katherine said she'd gone a few days with quite diminished pulling, but then she'd started up again on a day when she was particularly bored. We talked more about how, six years earlier, she'd fallen off her bicycle, again and again, as she'd gradually found her balance, taking the learning from each spill back onto the bike and into her subsequent steering and pedaling. During the week, she'd practiced pulling in her mind's eye while her hands stayed in her lap, unable to move, but she'd found that it wasn't all that satisfying.

As I've been emphasizing throughout the book, hypnosis and hypnotherapy are fundamentally collaborative ventures. Your job isn't to conjure up and unilaterally implement some dynamite intervention; rather, it's to feel your way forward in sync with your clients, seeking feedback—some verbal, some nonverbal—and utilizing whatever they have to offer. So I asked Katherine what she thought the next step should be for heading in the right direction. She immediately responded, "A whole day without pulling." I said I thought that this was too much change, too fast. She disagreed; I allowed her to convince me. Together we decided that the forthcoming Sunday would be a good day to conduct the experiment. She wouldn't have any competing activities, and she'd have several days ahead of time to train with her hypnotic experiments, which, she said, she was getting good at.

Katherine told me at our appointment the following week that on Sunday she'd managed to go the whole day without pulling, but it had been exhausting, largely the result of her having to exercise sheer unrelenting determination. Inspired by a fun mud-run 5K she'd participated in several months earlier, she'd set herself several challenges throughout the day, including a stint at watching Netflix while literally sitting on her hands. At other times she'd used her hypnosis training to invite her hands to become too heavy to move and, at other times, to lift up in her imagination higher than the top of her head. The next day, she'd pulled a lot. We met on Wednesday morning. She'd anticipated Tuesday night that she wouldn't pull prior to our appointment, but she was wrong.

We tried some further hypnosis experiments, most of which she didn't like. Katherine then mentioned that she and her mother had been talking about how and when they would celebrate her letting go of pulling. They'd decided that once Katherine had gone a whole week pull-free, Liz would allow her to ride her bicycle alone to an ice cream store on the edge of their neighborhood, something Katherine had never been allowed to do before. Once there, Katherine would order and enjoy a cone of her favorite flavor—"Honeycomb." I abandoned the direction I'd been pursuing and hopped onto Katherine and Liz's inspired transportation device.

Katherine's bicycle was white, a color that, I mentioned, was unique, in that it contains all the other colors. She could, I said, right now during hypnosis, start off on that ride to the ice cream shop, and her bicycle could easily become whatever color best suited the occasion. It became teal, her second-favorite color. Off she went.

The bicycle was equipped with brakes on the handlebars and seven gears, which she shifted with her right hand. I talked about different pathways to her pull-free goal. She had already experimented with keeping her hands busy, using determination, physically sitting on her hands, experiencing her hands as too heavy to move, and feeling them floating up higher than her head. And now she could, when she felt an urge to pull come to visit, hop on her bike, allow her hands to comfortably grip the handlebars, apply the brakes anytime it was necessary, and freely change the gears to make it easier to pedal into a headwind, or harder to pedal but quicker to arrive at the ice cream joint.

If you have a solution-focused therapy background, you will have noticed that this hypnotic undertaking had the effect of transporting Katherine's hands into a future when she'd already gone a week without pulling. Of course, it's always easier to maintain a habit that's already established, so when Katherine returned to the present, she arrived with a multisensory, embodied grasp of how she had let go.

A week later, Katherine came to the session in a teal T-shirt with purple (her favorite color) lettering. Her sense of mischief was in full evidence.

> **KATHERINE:** Nothing much to report. {long pause, until she couldn't contain herself} I haven't pulled since Wednesday at noon [immediately after our last session], and it was easy peasy. I just don't want to do it anymore.

I asked Liz what she'd noticed.

> **LIZ:** The same thing. In fact, true to form, Katherine has even
> tested herself. I watched while she took a hair in her hand like
> she used to when she was preparing to pull it, and she didn't
> feel the urge. She hasn't had to use effort to stop because she no
> longer wants to pull. Everything is back to normal.

I complimented Katherine's commitment to creative learning. We
talked about her and her mother's plan for her to ride to the ice
cream store the next day at 4:00 p.m., and we decided together that
the time had come for her to fire me, at least for now.

The next evening, Liz sent me a picture of Katherine enjoying
her cone, and she touched base a couple of times over the next few
weeks to let me know that her daughter was doing well. Katherine had started going outside without a hat, unconcerned about her
appearance.

Two and a half months later, Liz scheduled an appointment after
discovering that Katherine had started pulling again a few days
earlier, when she was sick at home from camp with a sore throat.
Katherine considered the appointment unnecessary because, she
said, although she wasn't happy about it, the pulling wasn't that
bad. I commended Liz for taking action so quickly, as it is so much
easier to take care of urges to pull when they're not a big deal.

I asked Katherine what it would sound like if the urge were to
come and knock at the door of their house. She said its voice would
be high-pitched and annoying. I wondered if she remembered what
she did the last time to facilitate the loss of the urge to pull. She
didn't, so I reminded her of how she'd put her hands on the handlebars of her bicycle and that losing the urge had been easy cheesy.

> **K:** It's "easy peasy."
> **DOUGLAS:** "Easy cheesy?"
> **K:** No, not "easy *cheesy*": "easy *peasy*."
> **D:** "Easy cheesy" is the vegetarian version of the expression.
> **K:** {looks unimpressed}
> **L:** "Easy peasy" is the vegan version.

D: What? Was that cheesy for me to say?

K: {slowly looks down and shakes her head; adopts a disappointed tone} Oh, Douglas.

I know I'm doing something right when my clients—even young ones—feel comfortable and playful enough to tease me. During our repartee, in her effort to correct me, Katherine underscored more than once, with humor and commitment, that "it is easy peasy." Yep, unknotting problems can be easy peasy.

Once Katherine recovered from my punning, we explored how she could get her hands back on those handlebars. After failing "843 times" to pull off a back walkover in gymnastics, she had recently mastered it, so we decided she could put her hands on the pedals and arch backward to get her feet on the handlebars. As we were talking, a song came into Katherine's head, and after a while she was tapping the tune out with her feet. This offered an opportunity for avolitional emulation:

D: Isn't it cool how a song can start in your head and end up in your feet? It's just like how an idea or an image or a feeling— about letting go of pulling—can start in your head and end up in your hands.

I floated the possibility of sending a message to the urge-to-pull, thanking it for trying to help her in some way, but then reassuring it that she was no longer in need of it. Committed to the notion that hypnotherapy is best practiced as a nonconfrontational, boundary-dissolving enterprise, I underscored the importance of delivering the message with kindness rather than rudeness. What better way to give voice to a polite "no, thanks" than to articulate it with an English accent? Katherine experimented with several different voices from the Harry Potter films, and I joined in with British, Scottish, and Irish variations. We laughed, we played, we chatted with the urge-to-pull over high tea.

A week later, Liz caught me up on recent developments. Katherine hadn't pulled any hair since the appointment. Liz said that Katherine had come away from the session with two big takeaways:

L: First, that just because she hears that little urge to pull, she doesn't have to do it. The other thing that really helped her was getting a lot more playful with the little voice. She actually started having fun with it, and I think that made a really big difference.

An unbidden urge or other avolitional symptom can feel decidedly intimidating, which is why people so often try to mount a counter-offensive: They hate feeling victimized by the unpredictability and strength of it. Katherine had discovered a much more effective and less taxing alternative: playful, resourceful responsiveness.

Three months later I contacted Liz for a final follow-up.

L: Katherine's hair has grown back beautifully, and she's chosen to keep it cut short. She loves the freedom that it gives her. She doesn't feel self-conscious about it at all.

She then mentioned that several weeks earlier, Katherine had pulled some eyebrow hair. But it was an isolated incident and she'd been "able to stop on her own." Liz reflected on what she considered Katherine's biggest change:

L: She is able to separate out the urge from the action. She doesn't get the urge very often anymore, but if she does get it, she doesn't feel compelled to act on it. That's given her tremendous peace of mind, because she's not worried about the urge returning. She knows that she can handle it if it does.

Everything that unfolds within a hypnotherapy session happens within a context of connection—between you and your clients and between them and their experience, particularly their experience of their problem. As I mentioned in Chapter 1, the separations that then occur—the avolitional dissociative processes characteristic of hypnotic phenomena—are *associated* dissociations, made possible by the connections that contextualize them. It is within this associative network that boundaries can dissolve and a problem can thus be altered. Losing the urge to pull hair is an associated dissociation, as is being able to recognize the call to pull but not feeling compelled to act on it. Both changes have an unraveled, loss-of-significance quality to them.

I've talked throughout the book about various ways to dissolve the boundaries of the circumscribed self. Individually, it can be accomplished through meditation and involvement in other flow activities. Interpersonally, it happens through empathic communication and, of course, through hypnotic entrainment and utilization. With hypnotherapy, you turn your attention to bridging the divide between the clients' circumscribed self and the affliction they're struggling with, facilitating the dissolution of the defining boundaries of each.

When a hypnotherapy session ends, the client's circumscribed self recollects itself, as regular self-conscious awareness returns. But if the session has gone well, if you and your client have reconstituted something of the problem's defining pattern and/or have reconfigured something of the client's relation to it, then this re-collection of the self will reflect a shift in orientation. No longer having to mount a defense against the problem as the only means of staying safe, the client can let go of countering strategies, and the qualities or playing out of the affliction can change or even disintegrate as it relaxes its grip on the client's life.

One way to alter a problematic pattern of experience is to invite clients to purposefully match or replicate it. This is what I did with Brian, a high-powered trial lawyer plagued with sleep-preventing earworms.[*] Most earworms are catchy melodies. Brian would get these sometimes, but more commonly he'd hear a 10-second loop of a charged conversation from earlier in the day, an exchange from a recent trial, or an anticipated cross-examination.

INVITING VOLITIONAL MATCHING OF AVOLITIONAL SYMPTOMS

"You might assume," Brian said to me at the beginning of his first session, "given my profession, that I'd be a type A personality. But

---

[*] I first wrote about this case in Chapter 2 of *Relational Suicide Assessment* (Flemons & Gralnik, 2013).

you'd be wrong." His eyes narrowed. "I'm type AA." Was he intense? Let's just say I wouldn't have wanted to face him in a courtroom. Or in any setting, for that matter. I'd have been no match for him. But then he was no match for his insomnia. He'd tried many different interventions, from warm milk and sleep meds to relaxation and hypnosis tapes. Nothing had helped. He said he got five to six hours on a good night, and two to three, or none at all, on a bad one. For the past few years, most nights had been bad.

Brian was used to applying his laser focus to whatever challenge lay in front of him and then working quickly and relentlessly to accomplish his goals. But this skill, which worked so well when preparing for trial, backfired when he implemented it at bedtime. When he'd lie down to go to sleep, a loop would form in his head, and it would torture him for hours. After tossing and turning in frustration for way too long, he'd leave his bedroom and roam the house, looking for some magic location that might afford some relief. He'd never find it. He couldn't *make* himself fall asleep and he couldn't successfully *will* the loop in his head to stop—not because he wasn't trying hard enough, but because, given the way negation and awareness works (see Chapter 1), he was trying too hard. I helped him reverse the direction of his intentionality, which, in turn, allowed relief and sleep to develop avolitionally.

I didn't ask Brian to exercise extra patience or tolerance toward what had been driving him nuts and robbing him of sleep. That would have been a teeth-gritting challenge for someone as driven as him. Instead, I asked him, as he sat there in my office, to find a way to conjure up a loop—to do his best to initiate what he spent every night trying to eliminate.* He looked at me somewhat askance but was willing, he said, to give it a shot. Within a few minutes, he had an earworm going full tilt in his head.

DOUGLAS: While the loop continues, repeating over and over, you can listen to it with the back of your mind and to me with

---

* Unlike some of my brief-therapy colleagues, I don't consider the paradoxical nature of such a request to be the deciding factor in its therapeutic efficacy. I return to the issue of paradox at the end of the chapter.

the front of your mind. . . . Or you can follow the loop with the front of your mind while the back of your mind monitors where I'm headed. It doesn't really matter. You might even find them switching back and forth {pause}.

I first established a distinction between the front and back of Brian's mind, and I then crossed back and forth across the difference, suggesting that each area of the mind could interchangeably carry out the functions of the other. This process of indifferentiation foreshadowed the structure of what I was going to ask next. But first I told a story that foreshadowed something of the process of the experiment I had in mind.

D: This morning at breakfast, I told my 6-year-old daughter to quit dawdling, as we needed to leave soon to drop her at school. "Finish up your cereal, Honey," I said.

She looked at me with a twinkle in her eye and said, matching my tone of voice, {said in falsetto} "Finish up your cereal, Honey."

{said in regular voice} "Hey, what are you trying to pull?"
{said in falsetto}"Hey, what are you trying to pull?"

I complimented her on how well she was able to imitate not only my words but also the quality of my voice. She smiled at this, so I asked whether she could repeat what I was saying *while I was saying it.* She looked intently at my mouth and managed to form each of the consonants and vowels of the words just a fraction of a second behind my articulating them. I said, {shifting back and forth on each syllable between regular and falsetto voices} " I I ho ho pe pe you you ha ha ve ve a a goo goo d d day day a a t t schoo schoo l l, Swe Swe eet eet heart heart."

I found myself s l o w i n g   w a y   d o w n as she spoke almost in unison with me, and at the end of the sentence, we both burst out laughing. And then she got up and got ready to leave.

Note the plotline of the story:

My daughter needed to get going but was overstaying her welcome. When the effort to get her to hurry up backfired, the two sides of the tug-of-war (I versus my daughter) synced up, speaking almost in unison. Our voices became almost indistinguishable—indifferentiated. As a result of the indifferentiation, the situation lightened up (we laughed) and my daughter got up to leave.

Now read the plot synopsis again and substitute "Brian's earworm" for "my daughter" and "Brian" for "I":

Brian's earworm needed to get going but was overstaying its welcome. When the effort to get it to leave backfired, the two sides of the tug-of-war (Brian versus the earworm) synced up, speaking almost in unison, which allowed them to become almost indistinguishable—indifferentiated. As a result of the indifferentiation, the situation lightened up (Brian could laugh) and Brian's earworm was able to leave.

The substitutions help illuminate the associational way the story established a metaphoric correspondence for what I was soon going to more directly invite to happen. But first, I made anecdotal note of an instance of boundary dissolution.

> D: A funny thing happens when you have two or more people voicing the same thing at the same time. If you're in a choir, holding a certain note, and everyone around you is singing the same note, then the boundary separating you and them dissolves, and your experience of yourself melts a little. You and the other singers kind of blend together, somehow.

And now I was ready to introduce my suggested experiment:

> D: I wonder what would happen if the front of your mind were to pull [my daughter's stunt] and start imitating, in unison, that back-of-your-mind loop? Instead of trying to stop it, it could create an exact replica, so you'd have two loops going, the automatic one that you can't get to stop, and an on-purpose one, giving you a stereo experience. Go ahead and try that and let's see what happens. Match the voice or voices in speed, {pause} articulation, {pause} accent, {pause} volume, {pause} and tone.

When both are in unison, you may not be able to tell if the on-purpose loop in the front of your mind is following the automatic one in the back of your mind, or if the automatic one has synced up with the on-purpose one. Both can move together, in unison, around and around, giving you that stereo experience.

I continued on like this for a while, and when I checked in with him, Brian told me that the loop had petered out—something that had never before happened. I immediately asked him to get a new one started, and we ran through the same process again, and then once again. Each time the pattern unraveled.

By inviting Brian to volitionally imitate and match an avolitional loop in real time, I facilitated a dissolving of the boundary between his circumscribed self and his symptom—a previously othered part of his experience. Late in the session, I taught Brian a self-hypnosis technique to use at night and suggested that he practice "singing in unison" with whatever loops appeared at bedtime. He came back two weeks later, having slept well almost every night, and he no longer felt "trapped" by the workings of his mind. He liked the irony, he said, of feeling empowered by *not doing anything* to the loops. We did some fine-tuning of his self-hypnosis, and he left, able to sleep and no longer at war with himself.

Another, more common, way to facilitate change in a symptom is to play with its avolitional presentation, inviting it to develop and change as you would any hypnotic phenomenon.

INVITING AVOLITIONAL DEVELOPMENT OF AND CHANGE IN SYMPTOMS

I saw Denise and her husband five times over six weeks.[*] In their mid-20s, they were smart and happily married college graduates, thinking about going back to school but needing to first work for a while. Except that Denise couldn't. She'd lost a job six months earlier

---

[*] A slightly expanded description of my hypnotic work with Denise can be found in an article I wrote for *Family Therapy Magazine* (Flemons, 2008).

due to stomach problems, and since then, panic attacks, cramps, and diarrhea had kept her at home, feeling anxious, depressed, and desperate, scared to drive and unable to go to interviews or enjoy restaurants with her husband. Anytime Denise had attempted to go back to work, the anxiety would hit and her stomach would start hurting, which in turn would intensify the anxiety. If her discomfort escalated to diarrhea, a common occurrence, she could look forward to an unremitting four or five days of misery. The diarrhea could also be triggered by certain kinds of food, so she felt the need to be exceedingly careful about where, what, and when she ate.

Denise said that her stomach problems, anxiety, and depression had started a few years earlier, after Stuart had endured a string of medical problems and surgeries. It was at the tail end of these difficulties that the anxiety and stomach problems cropped up. All in all, Denise had consulted five GI docs, and the consensus was that she was suffering from irritable bowel syndrome (IBS), a condition exacerbated by emotional distress. Before all the medical involvement, she had led an active and normal life, able to eat whatever she wanted and to engage in any and all activities that interested her.

A psychiatrist had prescribed antidepressant and antianxiety medications for the sadness and hopelessness she felt at not being able to live the life she had prior to getting swallowed up by her symptoms. The therapist who referred her to me had helped her better deal with her predicament, and Stuart provided patient support and understanding, but she was still grappling with significant pain and panic.

Partway into our second session, with Stuart at her side, I invited Denise into hypnosis and asked her to tell me what she was noticing in her body. She said that she could feel some fluttering in her upper abdomen, a sensation that often presaged the impending development of more severe stomach distress. I asked her if it was okay if that continued for a bit. In saying yes, she was allowing for a turn toward the sensation and the worrying about it, rather than scrambling to distance from it. This in itself changed her relationship to it. She was also accepting that I'd put some time constraints in place: She was allowing for the possibility of the sensation to continue for "a bit."

I asked Denise to follow the fluttering and notice any changes that might occur, perhaps a change in the location (after all, I said, butterflies are able to flutter about, able to go higher and higher or explore new territory) or some other subtle shift in the sensation itself—perhaps in its intensity or in the quality of the feeling. I continued on in this manner for a few minutes, and when I checked in with her again, Denise said that the sensation had "kind of stopped." I asked her to see if it could start up again. It was able to do so, and this time, as I talked, it transformed into "a white brightness."

Instead of trying to constrain or control the fluttering as she had in the past, Denise was willing and able to follow it and, when it stopped, to actually commit to its starting again—a 180-degree shift in orientation. Connecting with a symptom in this way—not just allowing for but *encouraging* its expression—facilitates the indifferentiation of the difference between awareness and sensation. With the boundary defining it at least somewhat dissipated, the sensation is freed up to transform in any number of ways. I floated the possibility that the lightness of the sensation could shed its light all through her, then ended both the hypnosis and the session with a suggestion that Denise experiment in "trusting her gut" and that she and Stuart both notice any interesting differences in the usual state of affairs during the week.

At the beginning of the third session, the couple described getting into a fight a day or two after our previous appointment. In the past when they would argue, Denise's anxiety would get the best of her, and Stuart would end up feeling guilty for upsetting her and undermining her digestive tract. Not this time. Instead of becoming anxious, Denise became appropriately angry, holding her own with confidence and strength. And on two other occasions—once when their dog got sick and another when she and Stuart were late for a dinner with her parents—she surprised herself by being able to effortlessly remain calm. She'd had no panic attacks, but she had experienced some cramping and subsequent diarrhea after eating something she wouldn't have expected to cause a problem.

Noting that Denise's body seemed to be doing an excellent job now of automatically differentiating times when it was appropriate to be anxious from those when it was appropriate to be upset, I asked her if she was able, yet, to distinguish cramps from anxious feelings. She said that menstrual cramps were recognizably unique, but she couldn't tell the difference between regular "get-ready-for-diarrhea" stomachaches and sensations of anxiety, particularly since a cramp was understandably a source for much anxiety. She was always on edge, knowing that once a stomachache started, it could too easily get out of hand. Back when she was working, Denise dealt with the unpredictability of her digestive system by limiting her food intake, often not eating until she got home in the evening.

I invited Denise back into hypnosis and asked her once again to tune in to what was happening in her body. She noticed butterflies and a light feeling in her hands, so I suggested that the two feelings, in two different locations, could perhaps find themselves communicating in some way, sharing information and sensations.

DOUGLAS: The fluttering might become {pause} lighter {pause} or the lightness . . . might begin {pause} fluttering {pause} or some other interesting development might begin, such as the comfortable {pause} warming that so often accompanies sun {pause} light, . . . or the comfortable {pause} cooling that accompanies a fluttering breeze.

Over the next several minutes, the sensations in Denise's hands moved up to her upper arms and the fluttering mostly fluttered away from her stomach. When I commented on how helpful it can be for her whole body to collaborate in giving her stomach a break, the sensations in her stomach gradually dissipated and the ones in her arms continued. By the end of the session, she felt some tingling throughout her hands and arms and nothing in her stomach, and she was comfortable with the possibility that other parts of her body could lightly hold on to the ability to feel the tingle of anticipation.

At the fourth session, Denise and Stuart noted a continued improvement in Denise's symptoms. They'd had another couple of fights, during which, they happily reported, Denise was again able to feel angry, rather than anxious, and she'd stayed calm upon hearing distressing news about a relative's health. However, her stomach had been a mess, and, in fact, it was hurting now in the session, with lots of (non-menstrual) cramping and pressure. In the hypnosis that followed, I offered possibilities for how her heart and stomach could find themselves collaborating, her stomach learning to take heart and her heart gleaning ways to digest complex emotions. I also offered suggestions regarding a protective sheath that could line her digestive system, protecting it and helping it to heal. After reorienting Denise to the therapy room, I talked with her about the possibility of her experimenting with eating normally, rather than withholding food in an effort to prevent problems.

In the final session, Denise and Stuart reported a good week. She said her anxiety was gone, and although she'd had some minor cramping, she hadn't been "freaked out," it hadn't turned into a stomachache, and she'd had no diarrhea. Able now to distinguish between pain and anxiety, she'd felt free to drive, and the previous day she'd begun looking for a job. In the past when Denise started feeling better, she would be "afraid to jinx it," but now she was able to accept feeling normal without getting scared. Stuart said it had been a long time since he'd heard her talking in such a relaxed and confidently comfortable way, and he described several other notable differences in how things were going. Her stomach was no longer knotted up, and much of her anxiety had unraveled.

A few weeks after our last session, Denise called and left a message, saying that she wanted to thank me for "giving me back my life." She'd been to four job interviews, she was enjoying eating in restaurants again, and she was back to feeling like herself. Ten years later, she reached out to see if I could recommend a therapist for a friend who lived in another city. In passing, she mentioned how much she and Stuart were enjoying their jobs and their two young children.

INVITING AVOLITIONAL EMULATION AND OTHER CORRESPONDENCES

> *Now if you have phantom pain in a limb, you may also have*
> *phantom good feelings. And they are delightful.*
> —Milton Erickson (Erickson & Rossi, 2014a, p. 107)

In his late 70s, my father-in-law, Bill, a retired Air Force colonel, landed in the hospital with multiple blood clots threatening his heart and lungs. My wife, Shelley, had flown out to be with him and his wife, Judy, in the ICU. One afternoon, Shelley called to tell me about the hard day he'd been having. Seven different nurses had been in his room over the previous few hours, each trying and failing to find a vein in an arm or hand so they could get an IV started. Even the phlebotomy nurse had given up, blaming Bill's edema and low blood pressure for her inability to help.

Despite all the unproductive sticks and disgruntled nurses, Bill was maintaining his characteristic good spirits; however, he was exhausted and not a little frustrated himself. I asked Shelley if he was up to doing a little hypnosis with me. He said he was, so she cleared it with the staff nurse and cardiologist, who were amenable to pretty much anything, given that they'd run out of options themselves. Shelley put the phone on speaker.

> DOUGLAS: Helluva day.
> BILL: It's good to have your bride here. And Judy, of course.
> D: Maybe *they* should have a go at putting in the IV.
> B: {laughs} Couldn't hurt. Apparently, my veins are playing hide-and-go-seek.
> D: I thought perhaps I'd talk to your veins for a minute.

Sometimes Bill didn't know what to make of me, but he'd long embraced me and my quirks.

> B: You do your thing.
> D: I remember once when I was on a fly-fishing trip with my dad.

Bill and my father had met at our wedding, 20 years earlier, and Bill fondly asked after him whenever we spoke.

> D: He was upstream a bit. I'd found this nice secluded spot where the stream widened and slowed, and I was casting, lightly dropping the fly onto the almost still surface of the water. And then at some point I cast my eyes down, and I see below the surface of the stream a twig that had somehow gotten wedged in the rocks. I prod it lightly with the tip of my rod, and it

comes *loose* and *floats to the surface*, freed *up* to do its thing. Isn't it so interesting that a submerged twig, when released, just naturally, easily *floats up* to the surface and now, *freed up* and *buoyant*, can be carried along by the current?

I continued in this vein (sorry) until Shelley spoke up, telling me that while I was talking, one of the nurses had returned and effortlessly slipped a needle in. I said my goodbyes and hung up. Five minutes later, Shelley called back and asked which I wanted first, the good or the bad news. I chose the bad. It turns out that the nurse in her excitement had forgotten to secure the IV needle in place, so as soon as she left the room, it slipped out again. Fortunately, there was also good news. While Judy tracked down the nurse and brought her back, Shelley continued talking to her dad in the same way I had. Once again, the needle went in without a hitch, and this time, with some well-placed tape, it stayed put.

As I explained in Chapter 5, hypnotic suggestions are often structured to invite an avolitional response through some kind of presented correspondence. This can be done *implicitly*, as I did in the anecdote I told Bill, via an unlabeled metaphor—

$$X = Y$$
A twig *is* a vein.

—or *explicitly*, in the form of a simile or an articulated correspondence:

$$X \sim Y$$
A vein *is like* a twig.
or
Just as X, so too, Y.
Just as a submerged twig can float to the surface of a stream, so too a submerged vein can float to the surface of your hand or arm.

Both forms of analogical connection—metaphor and simile— invite, as the poet Naomi Shihab Nye puts it, a process of *thinking in poems*:

You are living in a poem. . . . When you're in a very quiet place, when you're remembering, when you're savoring an image, when you're allowing your mind calmly to leap from one thought to another—that's a poem. That's what a poem does. (Tippett, 2021)

Thinking in poems is a form of engagement—a form, which I introduced in Chapter 1, of connected knowing:

You're not battered by thought in a poem, but you are sort of . . . riding the wave of thought, as if you're allowing thought to enter. You're shifting, you're changing, you're looking—you are in a sensibility that allows you that sort of mental, emotional, spiritual interaction with everything around you. (Tippett, 2021)

Nye was once in Japan teaching this poetic sensibility to schoolchildren. After the class was over, one of the girls wrote to her and said:

Well, here in Japan, we have a concept called *yutori,* and it is spaciousness. It's a kind of living with spaciousness. For example, it's leaving early enough to get somewhere so that you know you're going to arrive early, so when you get there, you have time to look around. . . . And after you read a poem, just knowing you can hold it. You can be in that space of the poem, and it can hold you in its space, and you don't have to explain it. You don't have to paraphrase it. You just hold it, and it allows you to see differently. (Tippett, 2021)

This is the promise of hypnotherapy. Communicating with your clients analogically, you create the spaciousness necessary for "thinking in poems" to be a vehicle for inventing therapeutic change.

This may sound, oh, I don't know, too *poetic* for your taste. After all, who knows if it was the imagery I was offering to my father-in-law that made the difference in his vein availability? Perhaps if I'd used the same relaxed tone of voice while telling him of recent exploits of his grandchildren, it would have produced the same result. Short of conducting a controlled study, there's no way to know.

Except for this: I would argue that the tendency for some kinds of symptoms to intensify and ramify (e.g., those having something to do with anxiety and depression) is also often the result of people thinking in poems—of their thinking associationally, analogically. Not spacious poems, to be sure. Oxygen-deprived poems maybe, but poems, nevertheless. Metaphor matters. And if metaphor matters, then metaphors matter: The specifics matter. I'll give you a for-instance.

Take a woman who has a car accident on a wet road, say in Miami. Even if she isn't physically harmed, the experience shakes her up. For weeks after the crash, she can't keep herself from tensing up whenever and wherever she drives. Every street is suggestive of the one where the accident occurred. Then one day, during a South Florida rainstorm, she drives her light car through a deep puddle and starts hydroplaning, momentarily losing the ability to steer. She doesn't crash, but the experience vividly and terrifyingly rhymes with the accident—water, loss of control, potential for serious injury or death. Rattled, she is now white-knuckling it wherever she goes, particularly if the road is at all wet. She—her body—is driving in a poem, a poem that metaphorically links two isolated incidents and, electrified by anticipation, imagines future lines, future incidents to be brought in and rhymed. At some level of automatic experience, the hydroplane site *is* the crash site, and this wet street now being driven, this street is wet, this wet street *is* the hydroplane site, and the next street around the corner, that street too will be wet, that wet street *is* this wet street *is* the hydroplane site *is* the crash site. Every location, every moment in this driving poem—whether current, remembered, or anticipated—is dangerous.

You can approach hypnotherapy as a writing lab for reworking—playing with and rewriting—painful, frightening, or otherwise disconcerting poem-thinking or poem-experiencing. You create a safe, expansive context for old connections to be forgotten, for old poems to lose their vivid imagery and rhyme scheme, and for new connections to be made, connections that feel safe and resource-ful and that, carried outside your office, make for more satisfying everyday poem-living.

Some years back, one of my graduate students, Renata, volun-teered for a hypnotherapy demonstration in my doctoral hypnosis and meditation course. She was the woman I just described, who'd had a car accident in Miami and was now finding it difficult to drive back and forth to school and work every day. The fear had, as she put it, "become part of me," and it was getting worse.

> RENATA: I'm noticing when I drive when it's raining, I'll get sweaty palms, . . . my heart will start beating super hard in my chest, and I'll get really tensed up.

But she was contending with something else, too. Two months before the car accident, seated on a plane on the tarmac for a return flight home from California, her heart had started racing and she'd started sweating and hyperventilating. The physical symptoms were so intense that the airline staff escorted her off the plane, tell-ing her that they couldn't risk having "someone who was freaking out like that" at 30,000 feet. Ashamed and embarrassed, she'd had to spend an extra night in a hotel and fly home the next day, assisted by "some help," which, I assumed by the smile on her face, was of the liquid and/or chemical variety. Nevertheless, she'd booked another flight to the West Coast three months hence. She mur-mured agreement when I commented that making the reservation had taken courage.

We agreed that we would focus on altering her experience driv-ing, given that it was a more immediate concern. However, because her symptoms in both contexts were almost identical, differing only in severity, I proceeded with the assumption that a shift in her body in response to either circumstance could be helpful for responding to the other. A success in one area could prompt avolitional emula-tion in the other.

I asked what she would be noticing when she was more comfort-able driving.

R: Not freaking out about the fact that there's water on the ground. It rains in Miami all the time. Just being okay with it again like I remember, I mean I—I used to drive up and down the whole state of Florida, Miami to Tallahassee, and it would be raining, and I would drive normally, like nothing was a problem.

After inviting Renata into hypnosis and checking in with her a few times, I started telling her a story about a woman who, a few years earlier, had signed up for my yearly seven-day hypnosis intensive in Fort Lauderdale. At the end of the second day of training, the woman had approached me to say she wasn't sure whether she could continue coming the rest of the week, given her recently developed intense fear of driving.

DOUGLAS: Interestingly enough, she was in a very similar situation. She'd had an accident on wet roads in Miami and there was a lot of rain that year, so driving to my workshop from Miami was a challenge. So, she just wanted to let me know that if she didn't come back, it wasn't because she wasn't enjoying it, it was just that she didn't think she'd be capable of coming.

Before relaying to Renata the story of this woman's experience, I made an analogical connection between the two of them in the form of a simile:

$$X \sim Y$$

[The woman in the story] was in a very similar situation [to yours].

The explicit analogy structured an extended opportunity for avolitional emulation—an opportunity for Renata to empathically entertain the possibility of experiencing a similar change in her fear. Normally the stories I tell clients are more metaphorically structured: I don't label the association between the client and the protagonist as I did here, and the story does not so directly evoke the client's struggle. After all, dissimilarity is what gives metaphor such boundary-crossing sizzle: It defies the conventions of logic and rationality, privileging *relationality* instead. I could have told her a story, for example, of a construction worker I'd worked with who'd become afraid of heights, or a musician who'd developed stage fright.* In presenting a story with a protagonist and scenario so closely aligned with Renata's identity and circumstances, I perhaps risked her more easily discounting or dismissing it. Fortunately, she did neither.

> D: I asked [the woman] if it would be possible, if the next day it was raining, for her to find a way of coming [back to the workshop] anyway, and we would use the opportunity to do a demonstration. The next day, it actually did rain, and she did make it in, and so we did a demonstration. And she discovered a way of feeling safe.

Learning to feel safe is a different goal from, say, exorcising anxiety, as it entails no negation. I told Renata that I'd asked the woman how she'd recognize later that what we were about to do in the demonstration had made a difference. I was shifting the focus from anticipating anxiety to anticipating change.

> D: She said, well, she'd be able to continue coming to the workshop, but the real test would be when she missed her exit off the turnpike, 'cause she used to love driving so much, she would drive a lot, and she loved listening to loud music. Since the accident, she was only driving carefully and of necessity. And no music, no potential distractions. She wasn't enjoying it at all; she was just doing it in order to get it done, and . . . she certainly wasn't driving to her favorite soundtrack.

I talked for a bit to Renata about how hypnotic change can be incremental, which it had been, I said, for the woman in the workshop. This allowed me to create for Renata an expectancy for small, almost unnoticeable shifts in experience.

---

* The stories I tell clients are always true. I never describe changes that didn't happen or enhance or exaggerate the details. If I'm recounting something experienced by one of my other current or former clients, I make sure to alter identifiers to ensure the person's confidentiality.

D: She made it to the rest of the workshop. . . [and] by the end, . . . her stomach wasn't in knots. She still wasn't enjoying driving, but her stomach wasn't in knots. And her hands were relaxed on the wheel [as she made her way] {said in time with Renata's breathing} back {pause} and forth, {pause} back {pause} and forth to Miami.

I'd perhaps lulled Renata into thinking that this was it—she could perhaps expect a gradual, even boring, improvement. Not uncommonly, hypnotherapeutic change displays this escape-your-notice quality. Problems more often incrementally dissipate than suddenly vanish. But sometimes a change that has been developing under the surface comes into stark relief:

D: About a month after the workshop, . . . I got a voice mail from her, and the message said, "I just wanted you to know that I didn't miss my turnpike exit today. {pause} I missed 10! I ended up in Florida City!* Thanks a lot, Lady Gaga!"

Like a punch line in a joke, a surprise ending to a story recalibrates the listener's expectations, upending the initial understanding. The workshop participant's phone message set me up (and now I was using it to set Renata up) to believe that there had been a lack of meaningful change ("Once again today I drove only as far as needed, in a way that suggests I'm having no fun"). Only then was it revealed that the message was about delight and joy: She had her groove back—driving beyond necessity, and with a soundtrack! Laughter is an excellent way of initiating or marking a transformative reorientation to what has felt like an impossible problem. Getting there sometimes involves passing through uncertainty, even disorientation.

D: It's interesting how the body and unconscious mind can make adjustments, necessary adjustments to allow both for safety and for an expression of adventure, of exploration, of new territory.

---

* A good 20 miles south of where she lived.

And I don't know, and I'm sure your *conscious* mind doesn't know, how that transition will unfold.

Where I went next involved the invitation of avolitional communication and collaboration between different parts of Renata's embodied mind.

INVITING INVENTIVE SYNERGY

Conceiving of and practicing hypnotherapy as a collaborative process expands the range of possible avenues for inviting change. Rather than limiting yourself to preparing and delivering suggestions designed to be passively received by "susceptible" subjects, you're offering suggestions designed to be avolitionally realized by engaged participants. The goal is not some version of "reprogramming faulty subconscious code" but, rather, inviting synergistic cooperation, not only with you, but also between and among the various systems of the body (e.g., circulatory, respiratory, digestive, endocrine, immune, nervous, and/or other relevant systems), as well as the intrapersonal strands weaving—and knotting up—your clients' experience—their imagination, sensations, perceptions, thoughts, images, behaviors, emotions, and dreams.

Such an approach is grounded in the idea that body processes are integrated and mindfully capable of discernment, coordination, information sharing, and learning. I brought this sensibility into the next part of my demonstration with Renata, introducing the expectation that creative change in her body's response to driving and flying was possible.

> D: I would like to now invite your unconscious mind to be in conversation with the palms of your hands, with your heart, with your stomach, with your whole digestive system, with your *eyes*: to have a—I guess it's not quite accurate to call it a *brainstorming* session 'cause so much of your body is an intelligent contributor to that creative thinking. So, a *brain-and-body-storming* session perhaps?

Her panic no doubt felt storm-like in both mind and body, so this phrase reframed such tumult as an opportunity for generative integration, rather than spiraling panic.

> D: And the interesting thing about brain-and-body-storming is [that] every contribution is to be honored and digested, allowing for the essence of a possibility to be derived or for it to emerge, for it to be extracted, for it to click into place.

If every contribution is honored, no boundary need be erected between the circumscribed self and a body response that feels uncomfortable or scary.

> D: I'd like you to invite your hands to share with me a little bit of information. Allow one of the fingers on one of those hands to just automatically lift to let me know that the brain-and-body-storming is underway.
> R: {index finger lifts}
> D: Excellent, . . . {pause} exploring *all* of the facets and *all* the elements. And venturing safely into that fresh perspective, fresh understanding. Like the way the *air smells* after a nice rainfall.

For months, rain had been a sign of danger, an indicator of slippery roads and the potential for losing control. My suggestion introduced a different association—rain as a signifier of new growth, new developments—to occasion a shift in orientation. I continued using other water-based metaphors to indicate the emergence of positive changes.

> D: And in any kind of brain-and-body-storming, possibilities can just *bubble up* from anywhere. Get *floated*. Get entertained.

The campus of the university where I was conducting the demonstration is located a few miles from the Fort Lauderdale airport, directly in the flight path of low-flying jets. This presented an excellent opportunity for me to incorporate the pronounced roar of the planes in what I was saying. I didn't reference the sound directly, say as part of a specified correspondence (e.g., "Just as the planes make their way into the air, so too you can find your own way of taking flight"). Instead, I made implicit (metaphoric) allusions to them, choosing phrases that accorded with our aural landscape and that reframed these signifiers of Renata's fear of flying.

> **D:** {sound of plane flying} [Brain-and-body-storming] is really an *uplifting* experience. Of course, there is an uncertainty to it. So, you're *up in the air* for a while. Wondering and not yet knowing where you can venture. And [there's] something so *free floating* about [the] discovery [that's] available when you're just a participant in the wholeness of that. {sound of plane flying}

I offered the possibility that this experience could give rise to meaningful learning:

> **D:** Dream researchers have determined that one of the things that happens with *dreams* is a consolidation of learning. And a creative exploration of change. {sound of plane flying} You can *stay up in the air,* knowing all the ways that this experience can ripple all the way through your body. And why not just now have a dream, a mind-and-body-brainstorming dream. {pause}

Have you ever had a close friend who could finish your sentences? You know at such times that the other person is so closely tracking what you're saying, you're of one mind, co-constructing your shared understanding. Your thought becomes theirs. Something similar can happen in hypnosis.

> **D:** What is that expression? April {pause} showers bring May {pause}
> **R:** {whispers} flowers.

In completing the rhyme of the proverb, Renata, an active participant in our collaborative brain-and-body-storming, gave voice to this reframed orientation to rain.

> D: Flowers, yeah. I don't know the way the dream will flower. {pause} And the lovely thing about a dream is it, it has its own logic and so it can be delightfully surprising.

Up until now, uncertainty had been a driving force of panic. I was suggesting that the outside-of-conscious-control nature of a dream could now, in this and future settings, be surprisingly different.

> D: There can be whole series of dreams extending into future nights, into brain-and-body-storming discoveries that you might not even remember when you wake up. The nice thing is that there is no need to manage it consciously because that sensitive embodied intelligence can contribute so much, {sound of plane flying} it is like *floating on air.*

I was introducing the possibility of a safe consolidation of unconscious learning, derived from coordinated creative contributions from various parts of her mind and body, some of which I incorporated in body-based expressions:

> D: Each dream highlighting a contribution, highlighting your contribution from this finger or that palm or this part of your digestive system or this heartfelt shift. So much to contribute, each part of you freed up to float a possibility inside the safety of a dream, consolidating, instantiating. I don't know if it'll be your fingers that lead the way, if you'll discover you *have it in the palm of your hand*, or if there'll be a trajectory initiated in your *digestive intelligence* or your *heart's wisdom*. At which point you'll have a *taste of things to come.*

Although no planes were audible at this point, I made metaphoric reference to them in suggesting to Renata that she could begin reorienting to regular awareness.

> D: And take all the time you need to bring this to a comfortable landing. {long pause}

And then, before closing, I offered a post-hypnotic suggestion for continued dream-based brain-and-body-storming that could give rise to a reframed appreciation of the adrenaline surges that she would no doubt be experiencing in the future.

> D: And let all of you decide whether the first one to emerge . . . will be your hands, . . . {pause} your digestive system, . . . your eyes, or . . . your heart. Know that there can be a meeting of minds, or I guess a meeting of mind-and-body, {pause} . . . as you dream. The root of the word *conspiracy* is "to breathe together." Your brainstorming can be a conspiracy of discovery, and you can get back together again, night after night, dream after dream, finding that delicious doubleness of safety and adventure.

I followed up with Renata four months after we met, and then again three years after that. Her updates characterize well the nature of avolitional change. She found some of the changes surprising and difficult to describe, and a few times she noticed that she had let go of her high-alert focus or had seemingly forgotten to be nervous. She said that immediately after our demonstration, "it felt like anxiety while driving was completely gone." Then at some point, perhaps a year later, someone ran a red light and T-boned her. She wasn't physically hurt, but she had a panic attack and continued to feel anxiety "even being on the road when it was dry." However, over time, she "thought about it less and less, until it was no longer in focus." She subsequently had another accident, but this time her response was very different:

> R: I was able to [maintain] a sense of calmness that is hard for me to describe, as it came from deep within. In the past, this . . . would have sent me into a state of panic, where I wouldn't have been able to communicate effectively. Instead, I somehow balanced my awareness of the chaos with an awareness of my body and what I had to do in that moment.

I also asked about the flights Renata took to and from California a few months after our demo.

R: I think it was helpful that we got to the airport with plenty of time, but I was surprised to notice that I didn't really have a somatic reaction. It was almost like I forgot about it. However, with both flights, I did become very aware of [my reaction] when . . . stepping foot on the plane. I took a lot of deep breaths and my heart became calm fairly quickly. Once we were sitting in our seats, I suppose I just became distracted. Normally, I am very aware of every move the plane makes before takeoff, but for some reason, I didn't care or just didn't think of it. When the plane started to take off, I felt the same sort of heart spike, but I breathed through it. Once we were in the air I was completely fine. Usually, I am also . . . highly alert when landing, but I didn't even notice we were landing until the wheels touched the ground! As I experienced with driving in the rain, I'm not exactly sure how to explain how this happened, but I'm really happy it did.

After that trip, Renata and her boyfriend continued to fly, including to Europe:

R: Since then, I have barely felt physiological symptoms of anxiety when flying at all. Flights have even become enjoyable when I am so immersed in a book that I can read it cover to cover!

UTILIZING STRANDS OF THE PROBLEM

Utilization (Erickson, 2008a) involves accepting and bringing into therapeutic service any potential resource for, interruption to, or distraction from the flow of the experience or the therapeutic resolution of the problem.[*] When taken to its logical (or, better, analogical) conclusion, utilization involves repurposing the problem itself,

---

[*] You may recall my utilizing Taylor's artistic skills (described in Chapter 5) and Grace's math and teaching skills (described in Chapter 4) to help facilitate therapeutic changes. Also in Chapter 5, I demonstrated the utilization of barking dogs to reference how bodies issue warnings and call out with alert attention.

or at least certain strands of it, as an essential resource for its own resolution.

I mentioned in the last chapter that some of the best examples of utilization can be found outside the realm of psychotherapy—in meditation, in the writing of poetry, in improv theater. It can also turn up in a karate studio. Lisa Feldman Barrett (2020) tells the story of her 12-year-old daughter feeling nervous before testing for her black belt in karate. Her teacher, Grandmaster Joe Esposito, told her, "Get your butterflies flying in formation" (lesson 4, extended note 79: https://sevenandahalflessons.com/notes/Butterflies_flying_in_formation).

Utilization is also a defining feature of jazz, where players on a stage accommodate to and are inspired by what their fellow musicians are playing. A dramatic example of how encompassing this accepting attitude can be took place in 1963 between the legendary trumpeter Miles Davis and his young piano player, Herbie Hancock. Miles's quintet was on a European tour at the time. One night, during a performance in Stuttgart, Germany, in the middle of one of Miles's solos, Herbie played a "completely wrong" chord, a chord that "sounded like a big mistake" (SafaJah, 2014). The effect was so jarring that he jerked his hands up off the keyboard. What happened next taught Herbie "a very big lesson not only about music, but about life":

> Miles paused for a second. And then he played some notes that made my chord right. He made it correct. . . . I couldn't believe what I heard. . . . With . . . the choice of notes that he made, and the feeling that he had, . . . Miles was able to make something that was wrong into something that was right. What I realize now is that Miles didn't hear [my chord] as a mistake. He heard it as something that happened, just an event. And . . . he felt it was his responsibility to find something that fit. And he was able to do that, . . . turn[ing] poison into medicine. (SafaJah, 2014)

Like Miles, Milton Erickson turned poison into medicine. Gilligan (2017) said that Erickson's principle of utilization "was his most radical contribution to the practice of psychotherapy. The utilization principle states that under proper conditions, a problem can become a solution. . . . Creative acceptance of a problematic pattern allows you to turn it into a resource." Rather than conceiving of solutions as the absence of a problem, Erickson (2015) looked for ways to utilize elements of the problem itself to invite its amelioration:

> The patient comes to you and says, "Get rid of my headache for me; get rid of my broken arm for me; get rid of my cancer for me; remove all these distresses from me; I want freedom from my stomachache." . . . They . . . come in with the fundamental attitude that you are going to *abolish* certain things. You should *abolish* this severe headache, or this aching back, or the pain in that broken leg, when actually, what ought you to do? I tell a patient: "Now, you have rather a bad headache there. I think you ought to make some kind of use of it." (pp. 90–91)

Some years ago, I worked with a 40-year-old man, Alastair, who made his living translating religious books and legal documents back and forth between German and English. He was requesting help with what he described as ritualistic, compulsive masturbation, connected to a 25-year-long porn addiction. Alastair loved his wife and four kids, none of whom, he was certain, knew anything about his daily solo-sex practices. Despite his warm feelings for all of them, he wasn't emotionally expressive. His wife wanted him to tell her that he loved her, and she told him often that he should be saying it to the children, too. He thought the fact that he demonstrated his love should be enough; putting it into words felt too uncomfortable—he just couldn't do it.

Recently, Alastair had begun to lose his erection during sex with his wife, which unnerved both of them. He generally felt "numb" both emotionally and sexually, and he thought that if he could get his "compulsion and addiction" under control, he would be able to "stop disappointing" his wife. We did a few different hypnotic experiments during the course of our first four sessions, and they made a difference, but the most significant change occurred after our fifth and final appointment. Two years later, when Alastair reached out about another matter, he started the phone call by saying, almost accusatorily, "I don't know what you did the last time we met, but you turned my world upside-down {long pause}—in a good way. The sex addiction is gone. You changed my life. My relationship with my wife and my children has changed dramatically. So thank you—you and God changed my life."

What I didn't do, for reasons you know well by this point in the book, was to attempt to help him get his "compulsion and addiction under control." Just before embarking on the formal hypnosis portion of that fifth session, I told him I had a solution for his problems with his wife but he wouldn't like it. Once I'd invited him into hypnosis, I asked him to access the familiar urge to seek out porn and masturbate, to identify the physicality of it, the intensity of it, the way it could grab him and carry him away. He was able to do that. I then switched to talking about his skills as a translator, the way he could move back and forth so effortlessly, so fluidly, between German and English, between English and German. I noted that although there were fundamental differences between the two modes of expression, he knew how to bring the essence of one into the other. When he acknowledged this, I suggested that he automatically (and silently) translate everything I was saying into German so that he could, in a way, experience it twice, or in stereo. I joked that I appreciated his assistance in helping me feel "almost bilingual," able to articulate something in a new language, opening up a new mode of expression. Even though his professional work involved working methodically with texts, not on the fly with voices, Alastair was up to the task.

Switching back to his urges to see porn and to ritualistically masturbate, I suggested that Alastair automatically, effortlessly translate them into messages of love and desire for his wife, into verbal protestations of attraction and devotion. He might, I said, even experience it as a compulsive need to do so, a compulsive desire to tell his wife, "I love you," even though she would no doubt find it odd and out of character for him to say out loud what he had been holding in his heart. And then how weird would it be for his children if his daily need to tell his wife that he loved her were translated into a daily need to tell them of his love for them? They might mutter that there was something wrong with him, while secretly enjoying being told what they already knew.

When the translating was complete, it took Alastair a long time to reorient back to everyday awareness. Upon opening his eyes, he said that he remembered nothing of what had happened during the hypnosis. I didn't fill him in.

I put Alastair's skill as a translator to work as a means of transforming the essence of his problem—the compulsive need to look at porn and to masturbate—into the essence of its solution: the compulsive need to verbally express his love and desire for his wife. The problem morphed into its solution.

Most of us are attuned to and organized by the notion that there's some kind of existential gap between defined opposites—that there's an expanse of time between past and future, a range of middling temperatures between freezing and blazing, a world of difference between comfort and pain, or a conceptual chasm between weakness and strength, meanness and kindness, poison and medicine, problem and solution. The assumption of a temporal, physical, sensory, or ideational distance between opposites gives rise to unhelpful habits of thought. For example, both clients and clinicians can get organized by the idea that the absence of X is a necessary precondition for the presence of Y (that, say, anxiety must first be quelled before comfortable action can be undertaken), or that the presence of X is a necessary precondition for the absence of Y (that, say, motivation must be searched for and found before lethargy or reluctance can begin to be addressed).

Utilization can be thought of as a gap remover, a Taoist sewing kit for stitching together separated polarities as connected complementarities. Lao Tzu, the legendary (but probably not historical) founding philosopher of Taoism, articulated 2,500 years ago the mutually defining nature of seeming opposites:

Difficult and easy complement each other.
Long and short exhibit each other.

High and low set measure to each other.
Voice and sound harmonize each other.
Back and front follow each other.
(Wu, 1989, p. 5)

Brought into the realm of hypnotherapy, a Taoist sensibility can help you more easily question the assumption that problem resolutions necessarily reside out of arm's reach, way over *there* somewhere, achievable only through time and purposeful effort. From a Taoist perspective, the two sides of any distinction are in a dynamic, mutually defining and circular relationship, with the essential quality of one side locatable inside the other:

I'd like to offer you an experiential opportunity to get a tangible feel for this idea of entwined complements, undertaking a short experiment similar to those in Chapter 2. After that, we'll move into a case illustration. For the experiment, let's take the polarity *inward/ outward* and use the breath to explore what happens to the boundary between the two sides if they are explored as mutually defining binaries.

> *At the end of this paragraph, pause your reading, find your breath, and follow it in {pause} and out, and in again, {pause} and out, till your noticing isn't interfering too much with the process of breathing. When you're able to do that, able to appreciate the easy rhythm of your breathing without the breath feeling too self-conscious, come back to the page and continue reading.*
>
> . . . . .
>
> *Do you remember as a kid playing on a teeter-totter? You went up when your friend on the other end went down, and then when you were going down, the other kid was going up, perfectly in sync, but opposite. And before or after that stint on the teeter-totter, you were on the swing, and this time, the up-and-down movement was*

accompanied—entwined—with arcing forward, and then back, first in one direction, then in the other. Up and forward, down and back, back and up, forward and down, up and forward . . .

When you're on a swing, your forward momentum is aided by leaning back and thrusting your legs out in front of you. You make it to a certain threshold before gravity asserts itself, and then, on the trip down and back, you tuck your legs in and lean forward. You lean back as you go forward and lean forward as you go back, increasing the arc of that smooth easy swing.

Take a moment to recall the feeling of that, the wind-in-your-face freedom of that self-propelled curved trajectory.

. . . . .

Even as a child, you knew as you were heading up and forward on the swing that the reverse journey was in the cards, that it was ready and waiting inside your forward momentum. Your trip back, smoothly curving down and then back up behind you, was prearranged, as it were. Inevitable, actually, given gravity and the thresholds established by the length of the swing's chains.

So in a very demonstrable way, the going forward somehow includes or contains the going back. And the going back holds the seed of going back forward. You can bring this same easy recognition with you into your breathing. You breathe in effortlessly, you breathe out effortlessly, and the breathing in occasions the breathing out. It facilitates it. And, of course, the easiest way to take an effortless breath in is just to relax into breathing all the way out. The breathing out prepares you for, creates the conditions for, the next breath in. Go ahead and check that out for a moment.

. . . . .

In a curious way, your breathing out contains—embraces, embodies—your breathing in, and your breathing in contains, embraces, embodies your breathing out. You can actually get a feel for that, the completeness, the wholeness of that movement—the circularity of it. On your next inhale, you can imagine the potentiated exhale inside of it, and then on the exhale, tune in to its inner potentiated inhale.

. . . . .

If you'd like to vivify the sense of it, you may find it interesting to feel the sensation of your lungs filling as you're breathing out. And

*then of course you'll want to balance that out, so that as you're phys-
ically breathing in, you can, in your imagination, sense the satisfying
emptying of your lungs.*

. . . . .

*If you continue with this for a little bit, with your imagined breath-
ing just an easy full arc in front or behind your physical breathing,
at some point there's just the circularity of it, the wholeness of it. No
need to track in {pause} and then out {pause} when in is out and out
is in.*

. . . . .

*And then when you're ready, you can shift your imagined breath-
ing from syncopation to unison with your physical breath, so that
rather than on the off-beat, it is on the on-beat, and breathing in is
once again just breathing in, and breathing out is just breathing out.
At which point you can just swing back into regular awareness.*

. . . . .

The embodied experience of this experiment may help you get
a feel for how the resolution of a problem can sometimes emerge,
in some form or other, from within where clients already are or as
part of what they're already doing or experiencing. And although
they need to make the conscious decision and expend the effort to
reach out to you, and then persevere in working with you, the actual
therapeutic-change part of the hypnotic process has an effortless
quality to it. Lao Tzu had something to say about this, too:

> Do the Non-Ado
> Strive for the effortless. . . .
> Difficult things of the world
> Can only be tackled when they are easy.
> Big things of the world
> Can only be achieved by attending to their small beginnings.
> (Wu, 1989, p. 129)

The original Chinese phrase that Wu translated as "Do the Non-
Ado" is *Wei Wu Wei*, literally "to act (爲) without (無) acting (爲)."
An important concept in Taoism, it conveys the sense of flow-based

action, of acting without self-conscious contrivance or purpose-driven effort. With this as a guiding notion, you can shift yourself and your clients from working hard to get the problem away from them or themselves away from the problem. Resolution may be close at hand, perhaps through a slight shift in the composing elements of, or orientation to, the problem. Let's see how these ideas play out in an actual case.

Edgy and exhausted from continually failing to control his body's stress response, Azran—"Az"—was referred to me by a therapist who'd tried unsuccessfully to help him with hypnosis-infused relaxation training.* Anytime Az had to deal with someone he deemed an "authority figure"—a teacher, coach, supervisor, cop, doctor—he would become hyperalert and self-conscious, which was soon followed by intense anxiety. The same sensitivity would arise whenever he felt another person's eyes staring at him. Unfortunately, this was not an infrequent occurrence, as he had the face of a movie star and the powerful build of a professional athlete. An accomplished tennis player and gifted graduate student, he moved gracefully and spoke eloquently.

Az's shift to a heightened, reflexive focus was triggered by either the social status or lingering scrutiny of others, but it was jet-fueled by his anticipation and dread of what people would think of him once they noticed what typically happened next. Beads of sweat would form on his forehead, and then, when he failed to calm his pounding heart or contain his mounting panic, his thoughts would race and his whole body would heat up. He could, he said, "soak through a shirt in two minutes flat." His previous therapist had offered hypnotic imagery of cool locations and breezes to counteract this automatic response. When he could picture such conditions during their sessions, it helped him feel more comfortable, he said, but it didn't make a difference outside the office.

Az and his family had immigrated to the United States eight years earlier, when the political situation in his home country had become untenable. Eighteen months prior to their leaving, back when Az

---

* A slightly expanded description of this case first appeared as a chapter (Flemons, 2019) in Hoyt and Bobele's excellent *Creative Therapy in Challenging Situations.*

was 16, his older brother, driving alone, was detained at a military checkpoint. A search of his car was initiated. A scuffle ensued. A severe beating followed, and then imprisonment. Some months later, while still in custody, long before any trial, Az's brother died.

A few months after the funeral, Az was in a car with some friends when they were pulled over for speeding. As the policeman approached the driver-side window, Az, sitting in the back seat, started trembling. Somehow, he managed not to draw the officer's attention, but by the time his friend had offered a sufficient bribe and they'd been waved back into traffic, Az felt spent and his clothes were drenched.

Now, nine years later, Az, living in the States, wasn't sure he could continue pursuing his graduate studies. He believed his current struggles traced back to what had happened to his brother, but his symptoms involved more than the trembling and sweating he experienced that day in the back seat of his friend's car, and they could be set off by virtually anyone—authority figures, sure, but also family, friends, neighbors, fellow students, and both tennis opponents and tennis partners. The person didn't even have to be in his presence; he'd sometimes start having a panic attack and get tongue-tied while talking on the phone. He felt so impossibly caught and interpersonally shut down, he'd been thinking about suicide. His mother, recognizing his struggle and self-doubt, was afraid for him; his father was just disappointed and critical. He told Az that he needed to "get control" of himself.

The previous therapist's strategy of offering hypnosis-induced relaxation training was well-meaning and no doubt skillfully delivered. But the logic informing the approach was in keeping with what Az had already been frantically doing on his own—trying to tamp down or counteract his symptoms. Relaxation necessarily involves a softening, a letting go. But when it is raised as a shield to protect against frantic, visceral sensations, or when, Alexander the Great–style, it is raised as a sword to smite unrelenting anxious thoughts, it freezes into something hard and brittle, rendering it useless—nothing more than an experiential oxymoron.

Az and I met for three sessions, each 90 minutes long. Our time together was interlaced with hypnotic interactions, though I seldom labeled them as such. Az hadn't been demonstrably helped by his previous experience of hypnotherapy, so I wanted to mark what we were doing as somehow different. I thus offered no formal hypnotic invitations, and I never suggested that he close his eyes and relax. His finely tuned, avolitional mind-body connection was very much in evidence in his hair-trigger visceral responses to challenging circumstances. It only made sense, then, to utilize these easily evoked reactions as efficient segues into mini–hypnotherapeutic interactions. Az could never quite put his finger on what was happening to his body as we worked together, and he was never quite comfortable with the process, but he could tell that something significant was shifting—something he was unable, but also didn't need, to control.

Early on in the first session, I told Az a story of an initiate who went to Nepal to study with a Buddhist teacher. The monk literally lived in a cave in the mountains, so he recognized the urgent necessity of his new student's learning to use meditation to raise his body temperature. The young man would need to master the skill in order to survive the fast-approaching winter. "Isn't it interesting," I mused, "what you already know how to do automatically, the student had to travel all the way to Nepal to learn." He laughed nervously and said, "Let's go the other way. Let's cool me down."

Az's worried appeal for "going the other way" was prompted by the disjunctive idea that problems must be counteracted—confronted and summarily dismissed. However, utilization is predicated on the associative idea that problems are best *en*counteracted—embraced and assisted in unraveling. Over my three sessions with Az, I used anecdotes and experiments to invite shifts toward acceptance, inclusion, and Taoist circularity. The first experiment, designed for him to fail, helped him reconsider his and his father's assumption that what he needed was more control over his body.

DOUGLAS: Would you like to do an experiment?
AZRAN: Okay.
D: Okay, can you purposefully raise the temperature of your forehead right now? Not by imagining something, just by you consciously making it happen, by saying to your forehead, "Okay, temperature, up you go."

A: {after some time spent trying} No.

D: Try harder. Use more willpower. Demand it.

A: {after several seconds} I can't do it.

D: Gives you a sense of why that meditation student had to head to Nepal. Okay, can you purposefully speed up your heart?

A: {after several seconds} Can't do that either.

D: No. You've been thinking something was wrong because you can't, on cue, cool your forehead or slow your pulse. But you can't heat or speed up your body, either. Not on purpose. . . . You can't police your body.

A: As hard as I try.

D: Right! Your body isn't going to let anyone mess with it—not your dad, not even you.

Rather than try to protect Az from his symptoms by helping him arm himself against them, I invited his panicky thoughts and body reactions into our sessions, both directly and indirectly, so he could practice relating to them differently—resourcefully rather than fearfully. Az dated the beginning of his problem to the time the police officer was walking toward the car he was riding in as a teenager, and of course this followed the death of his brother at the hands of the military. With this in mind, I evoked the presence of such authorities through my metaphoric language choices ("You can't police your body"), and I made sure to sip my tea out of a cup that had the initials *FBI* prominently displayed on the side.[*] Near the end of the first session, I asked him, "So, is it okay for your conscious mind to take off the badge?" He said it was.

Hypnotherapy is most commonly a collaboration between a therapist and an individual client,[†] but as I've talked about in previous chapters, the context for the work and the resolution includes the client's relationships with significant others. I thus pay close attention to not only the intrapersonal but also the *inter*personal patterns

---

[*] A gift from Laurie Charlés when, as my dissertation student, she was conducting qualitative research with data she obtained from the FBI.

[†] Unless you're Camillo Loriedo, who often conducts clinical hypnosis sessions with couples and whole families (e.g., Loriedo & Torti, 2011).

of relationships composing the client's experience. I heard in Az's voice the anger and frustration he felt in response to his father's dismissive belief that his son wasn't strong or determined enough to get his symptoms under control.

> A: He thinks I should just buck up.
> D: He thinks if you only try harder, you'll be able to beat it.
> A: Yes.
> D: Your body understands that bucking up, fighting back, doesn't help—it actually makes it worse.
> A: My father doesn't.
> D: Your father doesn't understand that, no.

What better, more satisfying, way for a young man to come into his own, to find his confidence, his bearing, than in contradistinction to an overly critical father, a father who didn't, and probably could never, understand? What better way to launch into trusting, rather than fighting against, his body?

Having experientially discovered that he couldn't purposefully lower *or raise* his temperature or heart rate, Az was amenable to experimenting with a different approach.

> D: Like other elite athletes, you have a highly refined mind-body connection. When you're on the tennis court, your conscious mind doesn't issue orders to your feet and your shoulders and your arms and your grip. You rely on a virtually instantaneous, integrated coordination between different parts of your body—right hand and left foot, left eye and right hand, right hip and left shoulder—and between all of these parts and your awareness. When you're in the zone, it's all effortless.
> A: Yes. Very much.
> D: Being in the zone, being in sync with your mind-body coordination, is an excellent way to learn. Hypnosis is just a means for getting in the zone without having to be on a tennis court.
> A: Okay.

Anecdotes and stories allow ideas to be offered and considered analogically, rather than analytically. The fabric of them, the pattern organizing them, implicitly communicates a shift in orientation, a shift in relationship between the person and their experience. The following story, and the subsequent experiments that evolved out of it, offered to Azran the possibility of cooling down without having to fight against the heat spikes. As I did with the first story I told him about the meditation student headed to Nepal, I started by describing a problem having to do with being too cold.

D: I once directed a clinic that developed an air-conditioning problem. Actually, the AC in most of the building was just fine. But the largest room, the one where we met for staff meetings and group supervision, it got to where it was way too cold all the time. Anyone who was going to be in there for any length of time made sure to bring a sweater; otherwise, it was unbearable. Over the course of a year, we probably had the AC guy come out half a dozen times, and every time, he told us the same thing in the same irritated, authoritative voice: "Nothing is broken: the condenser checks out, the air handler is fine, and the thermostat isn't stuck." But my staff and I were still miserable, so I asked the office manager to call yet again. I guess the usual guy was away, or maybe he was sick of dealing with us. Anyway, a new technician comes out, and he does the usual equipment check, and then he does something the other guy didn't. He comes and stands with me in the cold room. Doesn't say anything, just stands there, feeling the temperature, looking around the room. And then he asks, "How long has that floor lamp been there in the corner, next to the thermostat?" I think for a while. "Oh, I don't know, I guess about the same amount of time that we've been freezing our asses off."

A: {laughs and continues looking at me}

D: The heat from the lamp was perpetually warming the air right next to the thermostat, so from the thermostat's perspective, the room was never cold enough to trigger it to send a signal turning off the AC. Once we moved the lamp, the AC would cool down the room and the thermostat, and when that

lower-level threshold on the thermostat was reached, it tripped
a switch and the AC would turn off, just like it was supposed
to. This would allow the room to start warming up, and
when the thermostat registered that the room had warmed
sufficiently, when the upper-level threshold had been reached,
it sent a signal that fired up the AC, and the room started
cooling down again. Just like it was designed to do. The room
had to cool down enough for the thermostat to know it was
time for it to trigger the warming process, and it had to warm
up to the necessary threshold before the thermostat could send
the signal to start the cooling process. For the thermostat, it's
all just a circle: you cool down so you can heat up, and you heat
up so you can cool down.

This put in place the Taoist conception of interdependent complementarities and established the foundation for avolitional change.
Rather than furiously trying to counter his body's heating response
to social discomfort, Az could allow the heating up to effortlessly
produce a cooling down. This is the essence of utilization—finding
the means of, or inspiration for, a therapeutic resolution by repurposing the problem and/or by applying discovered resources of the
person and/or the context.

> D: Let's facilitate your body remembering or learning, perhaps for
> the first time in a long time, how to heat up till you reach that
> threshold where your metabolism, your internal thermostat,
> triggers an automatic cooling down. Instead of trying to make it
> happen, you can just allow your body to activate the balance of
> that circular process.

As I spoke about in Chapter 5 and earlier in this chapter, stories
introduce the possibility for change through the medium of avolitional emulation. I was suggesting that Az could trust his body,
which uses checks and balances (i.e., thresholds and feedback processes) to maintain homeostatic stability, to work like the clinic thermostat in the story. This created a hypnotic correspondence: *Just as*,
when freed up to work properly (by relocating the floor lamp), the

thermostat for the AC was able to maintain a comfortable ambient temperature, *so too* Az's internal thermostat, when freed up to work properly, could determine a comfortable threshold at which internal warming could trigger automatic cooling. With the associative logic of this in place, we could begin experimenting.

A: Okay.

D: So you can just become aware of my eyes looking at you.

This was the sum total of my hypnosis invitation; nothing more was needed.

A: {nervously laughs} Oh, I just knew you were going to do something twisted.

D: {laughs} Is that okay? Are you okay registering the fact that I, in my twisted way, am looking at you?

This was the first of many times that I checked in with Az to confirm that he wasn't feeling steamrolled. Throughout the three sessions, he was both uncomfortable with *and* accepting of the process. Notice my use of the word *registering*, which I'd used when talking about the thermostat.

A: Yeah, it's okay.

D: You're comfortable with feeling uncomfortable?

A: {laughs} Yeah, well, no, but okay.

D: Great, so as you notice my eyes, even focusing on them, what else are you registering?

A: My heart is beating faster.

D: Yes! Excellent! What else?

A: I'm heating up . . .

D: Yes, your heart and your temperature can work together that way. Faster and hotter, hand in hand, heart and head, faster and hotter.

A: I can feel your eyes on me. That's what's killing me.

D: Good.

A: Oh boy, {laughing} this is rough. Ahhh.

D: What's happening?

A: Oh, it's still going.

D: Oh, it *is*.

This endorsement of his experience contributed to the framing of the context as hypnotic in nature.

A: Yeah, 'cause I can feel like your eyes on me and I can't stop it.

D: Terrific, so go ahead and look at me.

And this embrace of what was happening framed his response as hypnotherapeutically helpful. He was distinctly uncomfortable about his inability to control his body response, and I was warmly letting him know that was just what was needed.

A: {laughs} I don't want to look at you.

D: {smiles} I know you don't.

A: {laughs}

D: Just allow it to continue until the upper-level threshold is reached and your internal thermostat sends the signal to automatically initiate the cooling and the slowing process. Keep heating up till you reach that threshold. I don't know if the signal will first be from your heart, registering that it got fast enough to trigger the slowing down, . . . or whether your heart will get the message secondhand from your forehead, or from somewhere else in your body, that the upper-temperature threshold has been reached and the cooling-down process has been triggered, in which case the slowing of the heart can be fast on the heels of the cooling down.

Erickson referred to such offerings of options as *therapeutic double binds* (Erickson & Rossi, 2008c). I brought explicit focus to the uncertainty of exactly *how* the threshold being reached would be communicated so as to trigger the cooling response. What was common to all the options offered was the implicit certainty that the threshold would indeed be reached, that news of this would be communicated throughout the body, and that the cooling would begin. And that's just what happened.

A: That's crazy.
D: What's crazy?
A: I got cool.
D: Cool. So, what happened?
A: I felt your eyes on me, and I just started heating up.
D: Terrific. And what happened then?
A: I don't know, I just relaxed.
D: Ah-ha.
A: I don't know. I can't explain it.
D: You can't explain it consciously, but your body understands it.
A: It's happening again right now, but it's not as bad.
D: Great. Keep looking at me, then. Allow your body to recycle this learning again and again. With more practice, it just becomes second nature. Just like in tennis. It's one thing to understand this intellectually. Now you've shifted to knowing it in your body, viscerally. You've shifted to unconsciously employing it. A kind of tennis knowing. I don't know if your conscious mind will ever figure out what your body already knows.
A: Oh, it just happened again.

Az later said that in that first 90-minute session, he had a "double-digit number of panic attacks," that is, times when his heart and his temperature rocketed up. And each time, he'd reach an upper-limit threshold that triggered a slowing of his heart and a cooling of his body. It got so that by the end of the appointment, the cooling would start before he broke a sweat. He left gratified but also troubled. In the second session, he explained why.

A: I really didn't want to come here. But this is helping.
D: Talk to me about the not wanting to come.
A: I still don't understand it, but the attacks are so fast from hot to cold, it's awesome.
D: Yeah . . .

A: But double-edged.
D: What is double-edged about it?
A: I don't understand why it starts in the first place.
D: And if you understood it?
A: I'd stop it.

Az hated not knowing why he heated up, and he hated not understanding how his body was able to automatically cool down. We devoted much of the session to running more hypnotic experiments so that at least his body could "get the hang of it."

During the third and last appointment, we had the following conversation:

A: I don't know what you did to me {laughs}, but it's good.
D: Well, I don't know that I did anything *to* you. I think your body has figured out a different way of getting comfortable.
A: I'm amazed. But I'm not cured.
D: What does that mean?
A: I'll still feel the heat. But it goes away. So. And the fact that I have no voluntary control of stopping. I hate that.

I reiterated my view that striving for voluntary control isn't necessary or helpful.

A: {laughs} Yeah.
D: Last time you found it disconcerting that you couldn't understand how it was happening. So, can you be comfortable going into the future, saying, "That was some weird shit [we did]?"
A: {laughs} Yes, I can, I can.
D: All right. You're an academic, so of course you want an intellectual understanding. But you can forgo that?
A: Yes.
D: You're sure? You can be comfortable with your body figuring it out?
A: Yes, because it happens so fast. It's amazing.
D: Sounds like your body has discovered the wisdom of circles.

Az described his mother as "elated" at the changes she had seen. She was "glowing" at seeing his life back on track. His father, predictably, was not effusive. But Az could meet the gaze of other people, his words weren't getting tangled when talking to his professors or classmates, and his body reliably knew how to heat up to cool down.

Six months after our last appointment, I was leaving a store, walking to my car, when I heard someone calling my name. I turned and saw Azran, waving and then striding across the parking lot toward me. We shook hands. Smiling, he said, "I guess you can tell how well I'm doing by how dry my grip is."

You meet clients who are exhausted by the fight they've been losing against their problem, and you invite them into a relationship with you and their experience that facilitates a shift in orientation. Feeling victimized by an affliction they can't control, they have felt compelled to hide from or fight against it—to counter it. You make it safe and possible for them to turn toward and engage with it, instead—to *en*counter it. Your office is a studio or lab or workshop for synergistic play, avolitional discovery, and effortless learning. You invite your clients to think, feel, and act in poems that dissolve boundaries, that metaphorically imagine the seemingly paradoxical or ironic—but really just Taoist—truth that the strands of a knotted problem, once loosened and unraveled, can be rewoven into a braided resolution. This is the heart and mind of hypnotherapy.

REFERENCES

Bányai, É. (1991). Toward a social-psychobiological model of hypnosis. In S. J. Lynn & J. W. Rhue (Eds.), *Theories of hypnosis* (pp. 564–598). Guilford.

Barabasz, A. F., & Barabasz, M. (2017). Hypnotic phenomena and deepening techniques. In G. R. Elkins (Ed.), *Handbook of medical and psychological hypnosis: Foundations, applications, and professional issues* (pp. 69–76). Springer.

Barad, K. (2012, Summer). Intra-actions: Interview with Adam Kleinman. *Mousse Magazine, 34,* 76–81. https://mycourses.aalto.fi/pluginfile.php/1144177/mod_resource/content/1/Intra-actions_Interview_of_Karen_Barad.pdf

Barber, T. X. (1984). Changing "unchangeable" bodily processes by (hypnotic) suggestions. In A. A. Sheikh (Ed.), *Imagination and healing* (pp. 69–127). Baywood Publishing.

Barker, R. (2016, April 4). *Stage hypnotist Richard Barker on FOX 35 hypnotized crew* [Video]. YouTube. https://www.youtube.com/watch?v=6Yvih0Ni70k

Barrett, L. F. (2020). *Seven and a half lessons about the brain.* Houghton Mifflin Harcourt.

Bateson, G. (1991). *A sacred unity: Further steps to an ecology of mind* (R. Donaldson, Ed.). HarperCollins.

Bateson, G. (1997). Epistemology of organization. *Transactional Analysis Journal, 27*(2), 138–145. https://www.doi.org/10.1177/036215379702700210

Bateson, G. (2000). *Steps to an ecology of mind.* University of Chicago Press.

Bateson, G. (2002). *Mind and nature: A necessary unity.* Hampton Press.

Bateson, G., & Bateson, M. C. (2005). *Angels fear: Towards an epistemology of the sacred.* Hampton Press.

Bateson, G., Jackson, D. D., Haley, J., & Weakland, J. H. (1956). Toward a theory of schizophrenia. *Behavioral Science, 1*(4), 251–264.

Bateson, G., & Rogers, C. (1975). *Gregory Bateson–Carl Rogers dialogue.* Event sponsored by the Marin Association of Mental Health, held May 28, 1975, at the College of Marin, Kentfield, CA. Audio transcribed by K. N. Cissna, Z. Flowerree, & R. Anderson.

Bear, A., & Bloom, P. (2016). A simple task uncovers a postdictive illusion of choice. *Psychological Science, 27*(6), 914–922. https://www.doi.org/10.1177/0956797616641943

Beilock, S. (2015). *How the body knows its mind.* Atria Books.

Berman, M. (1989). *Coming to our senses.* Simon & Schuster.

Bohm, D. (1996). *On dialogue* (L. Nichol, Ed.). Routledge.

Boorstein, S. (2011). *Don't just do something, sit there.* HarperOne.

Bowers, P. (1979). Hypnosis and creativity: The search for the missing link. *Journal of Abnormal Psychology, 88*(5), 564–572.

Brach, T. (2003). *Radical acceptance: Embracing your life with the heart of a Buddha.* Bantam Books.

Buswell, R. E., & Lopez, D. S. (2014, June 26). Slow-motion satori. *Trike Daily.* https://tricycle.org/trikedaily/slow-motion-satori/

Cameron, D., Inzlicht, M., & Cunningham, W. A. (2015, July 12). Empathy is actually a choice. *New York Times.* https://www.nytimes.com/2015/07/12/opinion/sunday/empathy-is-actually-a-choice.html

Chödrön, P. (2013). *How to meditate.* Sounds True.

Chödrön, P. (2016). *When things fall apart.* Shambhala.

Christensen, C., & Gwozdziewycz, N. (2015). Revision of the APA Division 30 definition of hypnosis. *American Journal of Clinical Hypnosis, 57*, 448–451. https://www.doi.org/10.1080/00029157.2015.1011498

Cleese, J. (2020). *Creativity: A short and cheerful guide.* Crown.

Cohen, L. H. (2009, November 27). Alice Munro's object lessons. *New York Times.* https://www.nytimes.com/2009/11/29/books/review/Cohen-t.html

Collins, B. (1988). *The apple that astonished Paris.* University of Arkansas Press.

Collins, B. (2012, October 15). On poetry. *The Poetry Department . . . aka the Boynton Blog.* https://thepoetrydepartment.wordpress.com/tag/billy-collins/

Collins, B. (2019a). Lesson 4: Writing the poem. *MasterClass.* https://www.masterclass.com/classes/billy-collins-teaches-reading-and-writing-poetry

Collins, B. (2019b). Lesson 11: Turning a poem. *MasterClass.* https://www.masterclass.com/classes/billy-collins-teaches-reading-and-writing-poetry

Corbett, R. (2016). *You must change your life: The story of Rainer Maria Rilke and Auguste Rodin.* W. W. Norton.

Crichton, M. (2008). *Prey.* Harper.

Csikszentmihalyi, M. (1990). *Flow: The psychology of optimal experience.* Harper Perennial.

Csikszentmihalyi, M. (1996). *Creativity: Flow and the psychology of discovery and invention.* Harper Perennial.

Damasio, A. (2010). *Self comes to mind: Constructing the conscious brain.* Vintage Books.

Descartes, R. (1641/1911). Meditations on first philosophy. In *The philosophical works of Descartes* (E. S. Haldane, Trans.). Cambridge University Press.

de Shazer, S. (1985). *Keys to solution in brief therapy.* W. W. Norton.

Diamond, M. J. (1987). The interactional basis of hypnotic experience: On the relational dimensions of hypnosis. *The International Journal of Clinical and Experimental Hypnosis, 35*(2), 95–115.

Dickinson, E. (2019). *Hope is the thing with feathers: The complete poems of Emily Dickinson.* Gibbs Smith.

Doty, J. R. (2016). *Into the magic shop: A neurosurgeon's quest to discover the mysteries of the brain and the secrets of the heart.* Penguin Random House.

Douglas, S. (2019, June 27). To run your best, call yourself "you." *Runner's World.* https://www.runnersworld.com/training/a28198094/talking-to-yourself -better-performance/

Dowling, J. E. (2018). *Understanding the brain: From cells to behavior to cognition.* W. W. Norton.

Elkins, G. R., Barabasz, A. F., Council, J. R., & Spiegel, D. (2015). Advancing research and practice: The revised APA Division 30 definition of hypnosis. *International Journal of Clinical and Experimental Hypnosis, 63,* 1–9. https:// www.doi.org/10.1080/00207144.2014.961870

Elkins, G. R., & Olendzki, N. (2019). *Mindful hypnotherapy.* Springer.

Erickson, M. H. (2008a). Further clinical techniques of hypnosis: Utilization techniques. In E. L. Rossi, R. Erickson-Klein, & K. L. Rossi (Eds.), *The collected works of Milton H. Erickson: Vol. 1. The nature of therapeutic hypnosis.* (pp. 271–301). The Milton H. Erickson Foundation Press.

Erickson, M. H. (2008b). Hypnosis: Its renascence as a treatment modality. In E. L. Rossi, R. Erickson-Klein, & K. L. Rossi (Eds.), *The collected works of Milton H. Erickson: Vol. 2. Basic hypnotic induction and suggestion* (pp. 61–85). The Milton H. Erickson Foundation Press.

Erickson, M. H. (2014). An introduction to the study and application of hypnosis in pain control. In E. L. Rossi, R. Erickson-Klein, & K. L. Rossi (Eds.), *The collected works of Milton H. Erickson: Vol. 13. Healing in hypnosis* (pp. 217– 277). The Milton H. Erickson Foundation Press.

Erickson, M. H. (2015). Symptom-based approaches to mind-body problems. In E. L. Rossi, R. Erickson-Klein, & K. L. Rossi (Eds.), *The collected works of Milton H. Erickson: Vol. 15. Mind-body communication in hypnosis* (pp. 61– 175). The Milton H. Erickson Foundation Press.

Erickson, M. H., & Rossi, E. (2008a). Autohypnotic experiences of Milton H. Erickson. In E. L. Rossi, R. Erickson-Klein, & K. L. Rossi (Eds.), *The collected works of Milton H. Erickson: Vol. 1. The nature of therapeutic hypnosis.* (pp. 189–217). The Milton H. Erickson Foundation Press.

Erickson, M. H., & Rossi, E. (2008b). Indirect forms of suggestion. In E. L. Rossi, R. Erickson-Klein, & K. L. Rossi (Eds.), *The collected works of Milton H. Erickson, Vol. 2. Basic hypnotic induction and suggestion* (pp. 181–220). The Milton H. Erickson Foundation Press.

Erickson, M. H., & Rossi, E. (2008c). Varieties of double bind. In E. L. Rossi, R. Erickson-Klein, & K. L. Rossi (Eds.), *The collected works of Milton H. Erickson: Vol. 2. Basic hypnotic induction and suggestion* (pp. 161–180). The Milton H. Erickson Foundation Press.

Erickson, M. H., & Rossi, E. (2014a). *Hypnotherapy: An exploratory casebook.* Volume 11 in E. L. Rossi, R. Erickson-Klein, & K. L. Rossi (Eds.), *The collected works of Milton H. Erickson.* The Milton H. Erickson Foundation Press.

Erickson, M. H., & Rossi, E. (2014b). *Experiencing hypnosis: Therapeutic approaches to altered states.* Volume 12 in E. L. Rossi, R. Erickson-Klein, & K. L. Rossi (Eds.), *The collected works of Milton H. Erickson.* The Milton H. Erickson Foundation Press.

Erickson, M. H., & Zeig, J. (2008). Symptom prescription for expanding the psychotic's world view. In E. L. Rossi, R. Erickson-Klein, & K. L. Rossi (Eds.), *The collected works of Milton H. Erickson: Vol. 4. Advanced approaches to therapeutic hypnosis* (pp. 285–288). The Milton H. Erickson Foundation Press.

Fey, T. (2011). *Bossypants*. Little, Brown.

Feynman, R. (1998). *The meaning of it all: Thoughts of a citizen-scientist*. Perseus Books.

Fischer, N., & Moon, S. (2016). *What is Zen?* Shambhala.

Flemons, D. (1991). *Completing distinctions*. Shambhala.

Flemons, D. (2002). *Of one mind: The logic of hypnosis, the practice of therapy*. W. W. Norton.

Flemons, D. (2008, July/August). Hypnosis, indifferentiation, and therapeutic change. *Family Therapy Magazine, 7*(4), 14–23.

Flemons, D. (2019). Heating up to cool down: An encountering approach to Ericksonian hypnotherapy and brief therapy. In M. F. Hoyt & M. Bobele (Eds.), *Creative therapy in challenging situations: Unusual interventions to help clients* (pp. 70–79). Routledge.

Flemons, D. (2020). Toward a relational theory of hypnosis. *American Journal of Clinical Hypnosis, 64*(4), 344–363. https://www.doi.org/10.1080/00029157.2019.1666700

Flemons, D., & Gralnik, L. (2013). *Relational suicide assessment: Risks, resources, and possibilities for safety*. W. W. Norton.

Flemons, D., & Green, S. (2018). Therapeutic quickies: Brief relational therapy for sexual issues. In S. Green & D. Flemons (Eds.), *Quickies: The handbook of brief sex therapy* (3rd ed., pp. 9–45). W. W. Norton.

Fourie, D. P. (1991). The ecosystemic approach to hypnosis. In S. J. Lynn & J. W. Rhue (Eds.), *Theories of hypnosis* (pp. 466–481). Guilford.

Frischholz, E. J. (1997). Medicare procedure code 90880 (medical hypnotherapy): Use the code (not the word). *American Journal of Clinical Hypnosis, 40*(2), 85–88. https://www.doi.org/10.1080/00029157.1997.10403412

Gafner, G. (2006). *More hypnotic inductions*. W. W. Norton.

Gafner, G., & Benson, S. (2000). *Handbook of hypnotic inductions*. W. W. Norton.

Geary, B. B., & Zeig, J. (Eds.). (2001). *The handbook of Ericksonian psychotherapy*. The Milton H. Erickson Foundation Press.

Geary, J. (2011). *I is an other: The secret life of metaphor and how it shapes the way we see the world*. Harper.

Gibbons, D. E., & Lynn, S. J. (2010). Hypnotic inductions: A primer. In S. J. Lynn, J. W. Rhue, & I. Kirsch (Eds.), *Handbook of clinical hypnosis* (2nd ed., pp. 267–291). American Psychological Association.

Gilligan, S. G. (1987). *Therapeutic trances: The cooperation principle in Ericksonian hypnotherapy*. Brunner/Mazel.

Gilligan, S. (2017). Three minds and three levels of consciousness: A self relations framework for generative trance [Blog post]. https://www.stephengilligan

.com/new-blog/2017/3/16/three-minds-and-three-levels-of-consciousness-a
-self-relations-framework-for-generative-trance

Goldstein, J. (2016). *Mindfulness: A practical guide to awakening.* Sounds True.

Goldstein, J. (2020). Essential advice: 2. Dealing with distractions [Video interview with Dan Harris]. *Ten Percent Happier* [Mobile app].

Green, J., Barabasz, A. F., Barrett, D., & Montgomery, G. H. (2005). Forging ahead: The 2003 APA Division 30 definition of hypnosis. *International Journal of Clinical and Experimental Hypnosis, 53*(3), 259–264. https://www.doi.org/10.1080/00207140590961321

Green, J. P., Laurence, J. R., & Lynn, S. J. (2014). Hypnosis and psychotherapy: From Mesmer to mindfulness. *Psychology of Consciousness: Theory, Research, and Practice, 1*(2), 199–212.

Greenleaf, E. (2001). Transference/countertransference. In Geary, B. B., & Zeig, J. (Eds.), *The handbook of Ericksonian psychotherapy* (pp. 93–111). The Milton H. Erickson Foundation Press.

Gross, T. (1994). Interview with Sonny Rollins. *Fresh Air.* NPR. Replayed September 7, 2020. https://www.npr.org/2020/09/02/908838552/celebrating-sonny-rollins-octavia-spencer

Gross, T. (2010, March 3). Interview with Siri Hustvedt. *Fresh Air.* NPR. https://www.npr.org/programs/fresh-air/2010/03/03/124275191/

Gunaratana, B. H. (2011). *Mindfulness in plain English.* Wisdom Publications.

Hadhazy, A. (2010, February 12). Think twice: How the gut's "second brain" influences mood and well-being. *Scientific American.* https://www.scientificamerican.com/article/gut-second-brain/

Hagen, S. (1997). *Buddhism plain and simple.* Broadway Books.

Haley, J. (1968). An interactional explanation of hypnosis. In D. D. Jackson (Ed.), *Therapy, communication, and change: Human communication* (Vol. 2, pp. 74–96). Science and Behavior Books.

Haley, J. (1973). *Uncommon therapy.* W. W. Norton.

Haley, J. (1981). A quiz for young therapists. *In Reflections on therapy and other essays (pp. 237–243).* The Family Therapy Institute.

Hammond, D. C. (1990). *Handbook of hypnotic suggestions and metaphors.* W. W. Norton.

Harris, D. (2014). *Ten percent happier.* HarperCollins eBooks.

Harris, S. (2014). *Waking up.* Simon & Schuster.

Held, R., & Hein, A. (1963). Movement-produced stimulation in the development of visually guided behavior. *Journal of Comparative and Physiological Psychology, 56*(5), 872–876. https://marom.net.technion.ac.il/files/2016/07/Held-1963.pdf

Hilgard, E. R. (1965). *Hypnotic susceptibility.* Harcourt, Brace & World.

Hilgard, E. R. (1991). A neodissociation interpretation of hypnosis. In S. Lynn & J. Rhue (Eds.), *Theories of hypnosis: Current models and perspectives* (pp. 83–104). Guilford.

Hirshfield, J. (1997). *Nine gates: Entering the mind of poetry.* HarperCollins.

Hirshfield, J. (2015). *Ten windows: How great poems transform the world*. Alfred Knopf.

Hustvedt, S. (2008, February 4). Arms at rest. *Migraine: Perspectives on a Headache* [Blog]. *New York Times*. https://migraine.blogs.nytimes.com/author/siri-hustvedt/

Jensen, M. P. (2017). *The art and practice of hypnotic induction*. Denny Creek Press.

Kekecs, Z., Bowers, J., Johnson, A., Kendrick, C., & Elkins, G. (2016). The Elkins Hypnotizability Scale: Assessment of reliability and validity. *International Journal of Clinical and Experimental Hypnosis, 64*(3), 285–304. https://www.doi.org/10.1080/00207144.2016.1171089

Kirsch, I. (1985). Response expectancy as a determinant of experience and behavior. *American Psychologist, 40*, 1189–1202.

Kirsch, I. (1990). *Changing expectations*. Brooks/Cole.

Kirsch, I. (1994). Defining hypnosis for the public. *Contemporary Hypnosis, 11*, 142–143.

Kirsch, I. (2011). The altered state issue: Dead or alive? *International Journal of Clinical and Experimental Hypnosis, 59*(3), 350–362. https://www.doi.org/10.1080/00207144.2011.570681

Kirsch, I. (2017). Placebo effects and hypnosis. In G. R. Elkins (Ed.), *Handbook of medical and psychological hypnosis: Foundations, applications, and professional issues* (pp. 679–685). Springer.

Kohen, D. P., & Olness, K. (2011). *Hypnosis and hypnotherapy with children* (4th ed.). Routledge.

Krementz, J. (1996). *The writer's desk*. Random House.

Kroger, W. S. (2008). *Clinical and experimental hypnosis* (2nd ed.). Lippincott Williams & Wilkins.

Kubie, L. S. (1972). Illusion and reality in the study of sleep, hypnosis, psychosis, and arousal. *International Journal of Clinical and Experimental Hypnosis, 20*(4), 205–223.

Laing, R. D. (1970). *Knots*. Vintage.

Lakoff, G., & Johnson, M. (1999). *Philosophy in the flesh*. Basic Books.

Lang, A. (2013). The forty thieves. In D. L. Ashliman (Ed.), *Folklore and mythology electronic texts*. https://www.pitt.edu/~dash/alibaba.html

Lankton, S. (2004). Milton Erickson's contribution to therapy: Epistemology, not technology. In *Assembling Ericksonian therapy* (Vol. 1, pp. 25–38). Zeig, Tucker, & Theisen.

Loriedo, C., & Torti, C. (2011). Systemic hypnosis with depressed individuals and their families. In C. Loriedo, J. Zeig, & G. Nardone (Eds.), *TranceForming Ericksonian methods* (pp. 125–159). The Milton H. Erickson Foundation Press.

Loriedo, C., & Vella, G. (1992). *Paradox and the family system* (M. Olsen, Trans.). Brunner/Mazel.

LeGuin, U. K. (1996, September–October). Quit pro quotes. *Utne*. https://www.utne.com/mind-and-body/quit-pro-quotes-pracitce-of-quitting-visionaries

LeGuin, U. K. (2012). *The wave in the mind*. Shambhala.

Lynn, S. J., Kirsch, I., & Hallquist, M. N. (2008). Social cognitive theories of hypnosis. In M. R. Nash & A. J. Barnier (Eds.), *The Oxford handbook of hypnosis: Theory, research, and practice* (pp. 111–139). Oxford, UK: Oxford University Press.

Marchant, J. (2016). *Cure: A journey into the science of mind over body*. Crown.

Markovic, J., & Thompson, E. (2016). Hypnosis and meditation: A neurophenomenological comparison. In A. Raz & M. Lifshitz (Eds.), *Hypnosis and meditation: Towards an integrative science of conscious planes* (pp. 79–106). Oxford University Press.

Matthews, W. J. (1985). A cybernetic model of Ericksonian hypnotherapy: One hand draws the other. In S. R. Lankton (Ed.), *Elements and dimensions of an Ericksonian approach*, pp. 42–60. Brunner/Mazel.

McEwan, I. (2001). *Atonement*. Anchor.

McLuhan, M. (1967). *McLuhan: Hot & cool* (E. Stearn, Ed.). Signet.

McNeilly, R. (2013). *Utilisation in hypnosis: Building on an Ericksonian approach*. Amazon Kindle.

Mingyur Rinpoche, Y., & Tworkov, H. (2019). *In love with the world: A monk's journey through the bardos of living and dying*. Random House.

Moerman, D. E. (2002). *Meaning, medicine, and the "placebo effect."* Cambridge University Press.

Moyers, B. (1993). *Healing and the mind*. Doubleday.

Murphy, S. (2006). *Upside-down Zen*. Wisdom Publications.

Nachmanovitch, S. (1990). *Free play: Improvisation in life and art*. Tarcher/Putnam.

Nachmanovitch, S. (2019). *The art of is: Improvising as a way of life*. New World Library.

O'Hanlon, W. H., & Martin, M. (1992). *Solution-oriented hypnosis*. W. W. Norton.

Orne, M. T., Dinges, D. F., & Bloom, P. B. (1995). Hypnosis. In H. I. Kaplan and B. J. Sadock (Eds.), *Comprehensive textbook of psychiatry* (6th ed., pp. 1807–1821). Williams & Wilkins.

Paz, O. (1974). *Children of the mire: Modern poetry from Romanticism to the avant-garde* (R. Phillips, Trans.). Harvard University Press.

Percy, W. (1975). *The message in the bottle*. Farrar, Straus and Giroux.

Phelan, J. P. (1996). *Practicing with our breathing*. Chapel Hill Zen Center. http://www.chzc.org/Pat1.htm

Pintar, J. (2010). Il n'y a pas d'hypnotisme: A history of hypnosis in theory and practice. In S. J. Lynn, J. W. Rhue, & I. Kirsch (Eds.), *Handbook of clinical hypnosis* (2nd ed.). American Psychological Association.

Pintar, J., & Lynn, S. J. (2008). *Hypnosis: A brief history*. Wiley-Blackwell.

Plutarch. (1919). The life of Alexander. In *The Lives: Vol. 7. Demosthenes and Cicero. Alexander and Caesar* (Loeb Classical Library ed.). Harvard University Press.

Pound, E. (1957). *Selected poems of Ezra Pound*. New Directions.

Ramos, C. (2018). *Conversation analysis of relational hypnosis in the treatment of a phobia of blood and needles* [Unpublished doctoral dissertation]. Nova Southeastern University.

Remnick, D. (2017, November 24). Bruce Springsteen talks with David Remnick. *The New Yorker Radio Hour.* https://www.newyorker.com/podcast/the-new-yorker-radio-hour/bruce-springsteen-talks-with-david-remnick

Riess, H. (2017). The science of empathy. *Journal of Patient Experience, 4*(2), 74–77. https://www.doi.org/10.1177/2374373517699267

Rogers, C. R. (1957). The necessary and sufficient conditions of therapeutic personality change. *Journal of Consulting Psychology, 21*(2), 95–103.

Rogers, C. R. (1980). *A way of being.* Houghton Mifflin.

Rosen, S. (1994). One thousand induction techniques and their application to therapy and thinking. In J. K. Zeig (Ed.), *Ericksonian methods: The essence of the story.* Brunner/Mazel.

Rossi, E. L., Erickson-Klein, R., & Rossi, K. L. (2015). *Mind-body communication in hypnosis.* Volume 15 in *The collected works of Milton H. Erickson.* The Milton H. Erickson Foundation Press.

SafaJah. (2014, March 8). *Miles Davis according to Herbie Hancock* [Video]. https://www.youtube.com/watch?v=FL4LxrN-iyw&feature=emb_logo

Salzberg, S. (2011). *Real happiness: The power of meditation.* Workman Publishing.

Schaefer, J. (2007, September 19). Leo Kottke. *Sound check with John Schaefer.* https://www.newsounds.org/story/39959-leo-kottke/

Segal, L. (2001). *The dream of reality: Heinz von Foerster's constructivism* (2nd ed.). Springer.

Shor, R. E., & Orne, E. C. (1962). *The Harvard Group Scale of Hypnotic Susceptibility.* Consulting Psychologists Press.

Short, D. (2017). Resistance: Solving problems during hypnotic inductions. In G. R. Elkins (Ed.), *Handbook of medical and psychological hypnosis* (pp. 77–82). Springer.

Short, D., Erickson, B. A., & Erickson-Klein, R. (2005). *Hope & resiliency: Understanding the psychotherapeutic strategies of Milton H. Erickson, MD.* Crown House.

Siegel, D. J. (2010). *Mindsight: The new science of personal transformation.* Bantam.

Siegel, D. J. (2012). *The pocket guide to interpersonal neurobiology.* W. W. Norton.

Siegel, D. J. (2017). *Mind: A journey to the heart of being human.* W. W. Norton.

Slingerland, E. (2014). *Trying not to try: Ancient China, modern science, and the power of spontaneity.* Broadway Books.

Spiegel, H., & Spiegel, D. (2004). *Trance & treatment: Clinical uses of hypnosis* (2nd ed.). American Psychiatric Publishing.

Sutcher, H. (2008). A response to the commentaries on hypnosis, hypnotizability, and treatment. *American Journal of Clinical Hypnosis, 51*(2), 177–184.

Suzuki, S. (2006). *Zen mind, beginner's mind.* Shambhala.

Thatcher, C. (2009, Fall). Disconnect the dots. *Tricycle, 19*(1), 33–37.

Tippett, K. (Host). (2021, March 4). Naomi Shihab Nye: "Before you know kindness as the deepest thing inside." *On being with Krista Tippett.* https://

onbeing.org/programs/naomi-shihab-nye-before-you-know-kindness-as
-the-deepest-thing-inside/

Truax, C. B., & Lister, J. L. (1970). The effects of counselor accurate empathy
and non-possessive warmth upon client vocational rehabilitation progress.
Conseiller Canadien, 4(4), 229–232.

Vance, E. (2016). *Suggestible you: The curious science of your brain's ability to
deceive, transform, and heal.* National Geographic.

Varela, F. J. (1994). A cognitive view of the immune system. *World Futures: The
Journal of New Paradigm Research, 42*(1–2), 31–40. https://doi.org/10.1080/02
604027.1994.9972495

Varela, F., & Coutinho, A. (1991). Immuknowledge: The immune system as a
learning process of somatic individuation. In J. Brockman (Ed.), *Doing science: The reality club* (pp. 237–256). Prentice-Hall.

Waldman, K. (2021, March 26). The rise of therapy speak. *The New Yorker.*
https://www.newyorker.com/culture/cultural-comment/the-rise-of-therapy
-speak

Warren, J. (n.d.). Welcome to the party. *Ten Percent Happier* [Mobile app].

Watts, A. (1961). *Psychotherapy east and west.* Vintage.

Watzlawick, P., Bavelas, J. B., & Jackson, D. D. (1967). *Pragmatics of human communication.* W. W. Norton.

Watzlawick, P., Weakland, J. H., & Fisch, R. (1974). *Change: Principles of problem
formation and problem resolution.* W. W. Norton.

Weitzenhoffer, A. M. (1957). *General techniques of hypnotism.* Grune & Stratton.

Weitzenhoffer, A. M., & Hilgard, E. R. (1962). *Stanford Hypnotic Susceptibility
Scale, form C.* Consulting Psychologists Press.

Welty, E. (1980). *The collected stories of Eudora Welty.* Harcourt.

Whitehead, A. N. (1953). *Science and the modern world.* Free Press. (Original
work published 1925)

Wilk, J. (1985). Ericksonian therapeutic patterns: A pattern which connects.
In J. K. Zeig (Ed.), *Ericksonian psychotherapy: Vol. 2. Clinical applications* (pp.
210–233). Brunner/Mazel.

Wu, J. C. H. (Trans.). (1989). *Tao teh ching.* Shambhala.

Yapko, M. D. (2005/2006). Some comments regarding the Division 30 definition of hypnosis. *American Journal of Clinical Hypnosis, 48*(2/3), 107–110.

Yapko, M. D. (2011). *Mindfulness and hypnosis: The power of suggestion to transform experience.* W. W. Norton.

Yapko, M. D. (2014). The spirit of hypnosis: Doing hypnosis versus being hypnotic. *American Journal of Clinical Hypnosis, 56,* 234–248. https://www.doi
.org/10.1080/00029157.2013.815605

Yapko, M. D. (2019). *Trancework* (5th ed.). Routledge.

Zeig, J. K. (1985). *Experiencing Erickson: An introduction to the man and his work.*
Brunner/Mazel.

Zeig, J. K. (2014). *The induction of hypnosis: An Ericksonian elicitation approach.*
The Milton H. Erickson Foundation Press.

INDEX

ABOUT THE AUTHOR

Douglas Flemons, Ph.D., is Professor Emeritus of Family Therapy at Nova Southeastern University in Fort Lauderdale, FL, where, for over 30 years, he offered team-based live supervision of brief therapy and taught graduate courses on hypnosis and meditation, systems thinking, writing, suicide prevention, and sex therapy. A licensed MFT and an AAMFT Clinical Fellow and Approved Supervisor, Dr. Flemons is the author of *Of One Mind*, the coeditor of *Quickies: The Handbook of Brief Sex Therapy* (3rd ed.), and the coauthor of *Relational Suicide Assessment*. He presents nationally and internationally on hypnotherapy and meditation, empathy, brief therapy, sex therapy, and suicide prevention and assessment. In 2020, Flemons relocated with his wife to Asheville, NC. In 2021, the American Journal of Clinical Hypnosis presented him with the Milton H. Erickson Award for Scientific Excellence in Writing on Clinical Hypnosis for his article, "Toward a Relational Theory of Hypnosis," published in Volume *62*(4).